Salter S. (Salter Storrs) Clark

A Text-Book on Commercial Law

Salter S. (Salter Storrs) Clark

A Text-Book on Commercial Law

ISBN/EAN: 9783744667142

Printed in Europe, USA, Canada, Australia, Japan

Cover: Foto ©Suzi / pixelio.de

More available books at **www.hansebooks.com**

A

TEXT-BOOK

ON

COMMERCIAL LAW;

*A Manual of the Fundamental Principles Governing
Business Transactions.*

FOR THE USE OF

Commercial Colleges, High Schools and Academies.

BY SALTER S. CLARK,

Counsellor at Law,

REVISER OF YOUNG'S GOVERNMENT CLASS-BOOK.

———

NEW YORK:
CLARK & MAYNARD, PUBLISHERS,
734 BROADWAY.
1884.

PREFACE.

THE design of the author in this volume has been to present, simply and compactly, the principles of law affecting the ordinary transactions of commercial life, in the form of a class-book for schools and commercial colleges. Youths who are soon to take an active part in business matters should certainly know something of the responsibilities they are to assume, the legal consequences of their acts.

That heretofore this subject has formed but a small part of the ordinary educational system, is due partly, perhaps, to the idea that law is too weighty and intricate to be taught to the young. This would be so were it taught at all in detail, or technically. But, it is thought, a book confining itself to principles, stating them in the plainest language, and presenting them as a consistent and interdependent system, would be useful.

A knowledge of principles is often the only guide one has, and it must be useful because it indicates the general rule. Every man does govern his actions, in business and elsewhere, upon some principles gained or stumbled upon in the course of his experience. But it were much better to have these, and many others which could not be learned from experience, planted in the mind while it was plastic. Experience also gives its principles merely as isolated facts; a book does, or should, give them in their proper relations, and show how, as is very often the case, what appears to be an exception to some rule is but the application of one more important. Again the study of its principles must impress one with the fact that law is in the main only common sense and common morality, a conviction which is in itself a good guide, and sometimes in practical life the only guide one has.

The plan of the book is as follows:

After a short introduction upon the relations of National and State law, and of constitutional, statute, and common law, it is divided into two parts. Part I. treats of principles applicable to all kinds of business, in three divisions treating respectively of Contracts, Agency and Partnership, with a fourth division embracing the subject of Corporations and a few others general in their nature. Part II. takes up in order the most prominent kinds of business transactions, paying chief attention to the subjects, Sale of Goods, and Commercial Paper, and is to a large extent an application of the principles contained in the preceding part.

A few chapters on real estate are added, as likely to be useful, though the subject is not strictly within the title of the book.

The chief aim has been throughout to make it a book practically useful, and one easily taught, understood, and remembered. As subserving those purposes attention may be called to the following features among others: the use of schemes in graded type, which summarizing a subject impress it upon the mind through the eye; the summaries of leading rules at different points; a table of definitions; the forms of business papers most frequently met with; and the frequent use of illustrations and cross-references.

It is submitted with the hope that it may not be found unsuited to its design.

SALTER S. CLARK.

New York, 1882.

CONTENTS.

ANALYSIS.

INTRODUCTION.

A GENERAL CONSIDERATION OF LAW AND ITS SOURCES.

PART I.

GENERAL PRINCIPLES APPLICABLE TO ALL CASES.

DIVISION I.

GENERAL PRINCIPLES OF CONTRACTS.

DIVISION II.

AGENCY.

PART II.

PRINCIPLES OF PARTICULAR CASES.

DIVISION I.

SALE OF GOODS.

DIVISION II.

COMMERCIAL PAPER.

DIVISION III.

MISCELLANEOUS CASES.

ADDED CHAPTERS ON REAL ESTATE.

SHORT INDEX.

A
TEXT-BOOK
ON
COMMERCIAL LAW.

INTRODUCTION.

A GENERAL CONSIDERATION OF LAW, AND OF THE SOURCES
OF LAW IN THE UNITED STATES.

1. Existence of Law.—Law is a direction from the governing power of a country to its inhabitants, telling them what they must or must not do. It is, thus, a rule laid down by a higher power, limiting the absolute freedom of the individual. Every civilized nation has its system of written law. Even half-civilized nations and barbarous tribes have some law, sometimes written, and sometimes consisting merely of the will of a king or chieftain. Thus among human beings there is a higher authority than physical force. But animals are without law. Each one is absolutely free. Among them the strongest do as they please, and the weak ones suffer and have no remedy.

2. Its Necessity.—No country has a perfect system of law: human law cannot deal out perfect justice. But no nation could exist and be civilized without a system of some sort. Law in some form will be necessary, as long as people remain less than perfectly just and perfectly wise.

Note to Teacher.—In a book of this character there is no room to do more than suggest the ideas of these two sections. There are many ways in which they may be easily and profitably amplified and explained in teaching.

3. Each Nation has its own laws. Those laws are supreme within its own boundaries, and cannot be affected by the laws of any other nation, but on the other hand they have no force outside of those boundaries. Thus the laws of England govern all persons and all property within English territory: the laws of France govern those in France. And though the systems of the different nations upon commercial law have many similarities, because the principles of justice are always the same, yet in many particulars they widely differ.

But the laws of a country do affect all who are there, whether they are citizens of that country or of some other. Even when merely travelling we must obey the laws of the country where we are. So also if a citizen of one country has property in another, in respect to that property he is governed by the law of the place where it is situated.

4. The States of our Union are, in regard to most law which affects the private actions and relations of men, entirely separate and independent communities. In that respect they are like independent nations. Each has its own laws, which have no force beyond its own boundaries. Those laws affect not only the citizens of that State but all people who happen to be in it, and they affect all property within that State, no matter where its owner is.

5. Sources of Law.—If now, considering any particular State, we inquire what are the sources of its law, i.e., what documents and books shall we examine to find out all the law in force within its boundaries, we find that in each State there are five sources of law; viz., the United States Constitution, the laws of Congress, the State constitution, the statutes of the State, and what is called the common law. Let us consider first the State constitution.

6. State Constitutions.—Each State in the Union has its own constitution. This is a written instrument adopted

by the people of the State. It is the foundation of all
State law. The legislature cannot change any rule established by it, nor pass any law except such as the constitution allows. But constitutions treat in general only of
fundamental matters, such as how elections shall be held,
what officers the government shall consist of, freedom of
speech, etc. The regulation of commercial law directly is
left almost entirely in the power of the legislature.

7. Statutes and Common Law.—These are the two chief
sources of commercial law in any State, and of these the
common law supplies the greater part. *Statutes* are written
laws passed at different times by the legislature. The *common law* consists of a great body of unwritten rules or laws,
not enacted one by one by legislative authority, but established long ago in England by long usage, and adopted by
the particular State as a body of law. The statutes are of
the higher authority, and very often statutes are passed to
change some rule of the common law.

8. National Law.—The last two sections have treated
only of State law. But we have in this country, besides
each State with its own government and system of law,
another government, higher than all. That is called the
National Government and is founded on the United States
Constitution, which is the supreme law of the land throughout all the States. That constitution establishes a National
legislature (Congress), to which it gives power to pass laws
upon certain subjects enumerated in it. The laws of Congress have full force throughout all the States, and are of
higher authority than any State constitution or law.

Thus we see that there are in each State two systems of
law, the State and the National. Whenever they conflict
the former must give way. But they do not conflict, at
least in theory, for Congress has no power to pass any laws
except upon the subjects named in the United States Con-

stitution, and the power of the States to legislate upon those subjects ceases as soon as Congress has exercised its authority. In general the ordinary subjects of commercial law do not come within the power of Congress, but remain within the jurisdiction of the separate States. We shall therefore have occasion but seldom to refer to National law.

9. Uniformity.—One would suppose that since each State has its own system of law, these systems would differ greatly. But this is not so. In the main principles, such as this book treats of, they are uniform. The differences are in minor matters. One reason for this uniformity is that all the law has the same historical origin; viz., the common law of England.*

10. Ignorance of Law.—It is a universal principle that IGNORANCE OF THE LAW EXCUSES NO ONE. Every one is presumed to know all the law. Though he does something which he would not have done if he had known what the law was, yet he must bear all the consequences just as if he had done it knowingly. The only reason for this rule is the present impossibility of having any other. But practically a person must often act without exact knowledge of the law. His only feasible course in such cases is to act according to what his common sense teaches him is just and moral, for in the main law is only common justice and morality.

11. Contents of Book.—The purpose of this book is to state the chief principles of law in the United States governing the ordinary transactions of commercial life. Part I. will contain general principles applicable to all kinds of commercial transactions; viz., the general principles of contracts, of partnership, of agency, and some others. Part II. will take up in order the ordinary kinds of transactions,

---

* Except with regard to Louisiana. whose original law was Spanish.

such as sales, notes, drafts, transportation, insurance, etc.; will show how the general principles stated in Part I. apply to each case; and will also state some additional principles applicable to each. We shall consider first the *law of contracts,* for it is the foundation of all commercial law.

Sources of Law

in every State, arranged in the order of their relative authority.

I. THE UNITED STATES CONSTITUTION;
II. THE LAWS OF CONGRESS,
  upon subjects named in the U. S. Constitution;
III. THE PARTICULAR STATE CONSTITUTION;
IV. THE STATUTES OF THE STATE;
V. THE COMMON LAW.

[In the above scheme each one is of higher authority than all below it: where they conflict the former must prevail.]

PART I.

GENERAL PRINCIPLES APPLICABLE TO ALL CASES.

DIVISION I.

GENERAL PRINCIPLES OF CONTRACTS.

CHAPTER I.

DESCRIPTION OF CONTRACTS: THEIR BINDING FORCE.

1. **A Contract is** an agreement made between two or more parties. It may also be defined as a promise made by one and accepted by another; but the words *contract* and *agreement* are rather broader than *promise*.* Generally a commercial transaction between two parties consists of more than one promise, each party promising something, but the idea of a contract is best obtained if we think of each promise as a separate contract. Thus where one agrees to do certain work, and the other agrees to pay for

---

* *Contract* and *agreement* may relate to either the *present or future:* *promise* means only an agreement to do or not to do a particular thing at some *future* time. E.g., a sale of goods by me to you, which is an agreement that they shall immediately cease to be mine and become yours, is a contract, but cannot be called a promise, because there is nothing to be done in the future. It executes itself. Another distinction is that one person may make a promise: it takes two or more to make a contract or agreement. In other words, a promise is not a contract until the one to whom it is made accepts or assents to it.

it, we have two contracts, (1) the agreement that one shall
work, and (2) the agreement that the other shall pay; and
each party agrees to both agreements. But in common
language where all the separate agreements make part of
the same transaction, or are embodied in a single paper, we
speak of it as one contract.

2. The Importance of the Subject of contracts is very
great. As we shall see throughout the book, every kind of
business is a system of contracts, and its law is in great
part only the law governing all contracts. Nearly every
act in mercantile life is either the making or fulfilling of
some agreement. Thus every sale of goods, and every note,
draft, or indorsement, is a contract: every act done by a
clerk, or other agent, in his business, is but the carrying out
of the contract originally made with his employer: every
act of a partner is only a fulfilling of the contract made
between the partners when the firm was formed.

3. Freedom to Contract.—One great principle of our law
is that EVERY ONE IS FREE TO MAKE ANY CONTRACT HE
CHOOSES TO MAKE, except such as are forbidden by law.*
It is the theory of our system of government to allow everything except what is forbidden; not to forbid everything
except what is allowed. The latter might be the theory of
a parental or despotic government. Consequently if we
wish to know whether a thing is lawful or not we examine
the law to see whether it is forbidden, and if it is not forbidden it is lawful. The kinds of contracts forbidden by
law are very few, but on the other hand lawful contracts
are very numerous and of every conceivable kind.

4. The Fundamental Rule of law in regard to contracts
is that EVERY ONE MUST FULFILL EVERY AGREEMENT HE
MAKES, unless some new agreement has changed or abro-

---

* See chapter on " Illegal Contracts," p. 24.

gated it; i.e., a person must keep his promises.* While studying the many and important exceptions to this (Chap. III.), we must not forget that still it is the general rule. So important is this rule considered that the U. S. Constitution forbids any State to pass any law which shall release any person from the obligation to perform any contract he has made. Its justice is evident; for if one was at liberty to refuse to do exactly what he had promised, no reliance could be placed on any promise. Thus no one would work or do any act for another, because the other could refuse to pay for it, and no one would pay in advance because the other could then refuse to do the act.

5. Kinds of Contracts.—Contracts are either *written* or *oral.* Written contracts are those put on paper, by writing or printing: oral contracts are those made by word of mouth. Written contracts are express: oral contracts are either *express* or *implied.* An express contract is one definitely expressed in words: an implied contract is one implied from all the circumstances of the transaction.

6. Implied Contracts are quite common, and we shall meet them frequently.† They arise in those cases where, though there are no words of agreement by either party, such as "I agree," or "I will," or "I promise," yet something is said or done which in reality amounts to an agreement. Thus if I buy goods in a shop I am compelled to pay for them, though nothing is said about paying or the price, for my being there, asking for the goods and taking them away, are equivalent to my saying "I will pay for them." My acts say what my tongue does not. One is

---

* If A and B make an agreement to day, and to-morrow make another modifying the first, the first as modified by the second must be kept. This is in effect keeping both.

† See p. 20, sec. 7; p. 61, sec. 4; p. 62, sec. 7; p. 63, sec. 11; p. 91, sec. 12; p. 95, sec. 6 and 7; p. 156, sec. 2.

always considered as having agreed to whatever he knowingly leads another to believe he has agreed to.

7. Gratuitous Services GIVE NO CLAIM TO COMPENSATION. There is no implied contract, because the services were not requested. Were this not so any one might force upon us, and force us to pay for, what we did not want. But if the benefit of anything gratuitously done is retained when it could be refused, there arises an implied contract to pay.

CHAPTER II.

REQUISITES OF A BINDING CONTRACT.

1. Seven Requisites.—We have heretofore stated that the rule that every contract is binding has important exceptions. There are six things always necessary, and one more necessary in certain kinds of contracts. This makes seven requisites; and if any one of these necessary elements is absent from the contract, that contract is not binding.

Of these requisites the first two relate to its nature, and the remainder relate to other circumstances connected with it. They are: (1) it must be possible; (2) it must be legal; (3) it must be made by proper parties; (4) it must be assented to by each party; (5) it must have a consideration; (6) it must be made without fraud; and (7) in certain cases it must be in writing and signed.

a. *Relating to the Nature of the Contract.*

2. Possibility.—A CONTRACT TO DO A THING IMPOSSIBLE IN ITS NATURE IS VOID. Naturally any one is very foolish to rely on such a promise, and the law cannot attempt to guard one against his own folly. There are three kinds of impossibility: (1) that 'arising from the nature of the thing, as a contract to cross the ocean in a day; (2) that depending upon certain outside circumstances, which might have been foreseen, as where the fulfillment of a contract to transport goods by canal is prevented by the freezing of the canal, or an accident to it; and (3) that depending upon the personal disability of the person contracting, as where one agrees to do certain work and finds that he has not the skill.

It is only in the first case that the promise is not binding, for in the other two the thing is not impossible *in its nature.* In other words, it is the duty of one who makes an agreement to foresee and provide against all the circumstances which might prevent performance. The other party has the right to rely upon his doing so. Hence sickness does not excuse one, nor inability to find an article that one has agreed to furnish. Even death does not annul a contract, for, unless it involves some personal skill, the executor must carry it out.

3. Legality.—A CONTRACT THE LAW FORBIDS IS VOID. Such would be an agreement to smuggle goods,* or to pay a higher rate of interest than that allowed by law. The class of illegal contracts is not large, and the great majority of commercial agreements are legal. A later chapter will treat this subject more fully (Chap. III.).

b. Relating to Outside Circumstances.

4. Proper Parties.—A CONTRACT MADE BY A MINOR,† A LUNATIC, OR AN IDIOT IS NOT BINDING UPON HIM.‡ These persons are said to be *not able to contract;* i.e.,

---

* *Smuggling* is bringing goods from a foreign country, without paying the government the tax laid upon them, called the *duty.*

† A person under twenty-one years of age.

‡ Formerly married women were not able to contract, but they now are under some circumstances (p. 29).

they cannot make a binding contract. All other persons are able to contract. Those who cannot contract themselves cannot do it by agents. The subject of parties will be treated in a later chapter (Chap. IV.).

5. Assent.—A PROPOSITION NOT ASSENTED TO BY BOTH PARTIES IS NOT BINDING. A promise not accepted is void. Assent is implied in the word agreement, for it takes two to agree. Thus an offer is not a contract until it has been accepted. The ways in which assent may be given will be more fully treated in Chapter V.

6. Consideration.—A PROMISE WITHOUT CONSIDERATION IS NOT BINDING. The consideration of a promise is the thing given, done, or promised by the other party, as a reason for which the promise or contract is made. Thus the money paid or the note given on a sale of goods is the consideration for the sale, and the goods sold are the consideration for the promise to pay for them. But where there is a promise on one side, but nothing given, done, or promised on the other, as an agreement to make a present, it is not binding. This subject will be more fully treated in Chapter VI.

7. Fraud.—A CONTRACT WHICH ONE IS INDUCED TO MAKE THROUGH FRAUD OR DECEIT IS NOT BINDING UPON HIM. We have seen that assent is necessary, but there can be no true assent unless there is perfect freedom and full knowledge of the facts, or at least the chance to learn (Chap. VII.).

8. In Writing and Signed.—Some contracts are not binding upon a person unless they are in writing and signed by him. The classes which require this will form the subject of Chapter VIII. Not all contracts need to be written. The majority, perhaps, in commercial life may be oral. The reason for requiring a writing in any case is to avoid any uncertainty, and the contracts requiring it belong to one of these classes: (1) where the effect of any mistake would be particularly serious, because of the amount involved, and (2) where mistake or fraud might be easily committed.

9. Performance by One.—But even though a contract has all the requisites, it is not binding on one party if the other neglects to perform his part. ONE HAS NO RIGHT TO SUE ON A CONTRACT UNLESS HE HAS PERFORMED OR OFFERED TO PERFORM HIS PART. Thus if I hire you to work for me, you must do all you agreed to before you have any claim on me. We will find illustrations of this principle in all parts of the book.

REQUISITES OF A BINDING AGREEMENT.

I. **THOSE RELATING TO ITS NATURE:**
　　1. It must be POSSIBLE,
　　2. It must be LEGAL.

II. **THOSE RELATING TO OUTSIDE CIRCUMSTANCES:**
　　1. It must be made by one ABLE TO CONTRACT;
　　2. It must be ASSENTED to;
　　3. It must have a CONSIDERATION;
　　4. There must be NO FRAUD;　.
　　5. In certain cases it must be WRITTEN AND SIGNED.

CHAPTER III.

ILLEGAL CONTRACTS.

1. By Illegal Contract we here mean one which, on account of its nature, the law forbids any one to make. Such a contract is wholly void. Any agreement to commit any illegal act is itself illegal. ANY CONTRACT WHICH HAS FOR ITS PURPOSE THE FURTHERANCE OF ANY OBJECT CONTRARY TO JUSTICE OR COMMON MORALITY IS VOID. Thus any betting, gambling, or bribery agreement is void. It would be impossible to give a complete list of illegal contracts, and therefore we will merely state in the following sections some of those which are more commonly met with in commercial life.

2. Why Void.—The reason for the other six requisites of a binding agreement is private, (i.e. concerns only the particular parties to the contract,) viz., to save the other party from unjust loss; but with regard to the remaining requisite, legality, the reason is public, (i.e. concerns the public,) viz., because illegal contracts are considered as hurtful to the whole public. This will be seen as we examine each case. For this reason neither of the parties can enforce an illegal contract. The law considers it wholly vicious, and will help neither party, even though he has performed his part, or paid money.

3. Usury.—In most of the States it is illegal to agree to pay or take more than a certain rate of interest, and in those States no such agreement can be enforced; i.e., a borrower cannot be compelled to pay more than a certain rate, even though he promises it.* This rate is different

---

* Usury is that part of the interest agreed to be paid for a loan of money which exceeds the rate allowed by law. Thus if the highest

in different States. The theory with regard to usury has been that it injured the community as a whole. We shall examine this subject more fully in Chapter XXXIV.

4. Against the Revenue Laws.—Revenue laws are laws laying taxes and duties to raise money for the support of the government. Manufacturers of certain articles are required to pay the government a certain amount for all they make; importers are required to pay also when they import certain articles. It is illegal to make or import these taxed articles without paying the duties. Therefore any agreement the object of which is to violate the revenue laws is void. Such are agreements to smuggle, or to make or sell any dutiable articles without paying the duty, or any agreements aiding in such a purpose. If duties are not paid it is a loss to the country as a whole. Contracts made in this country to violate the revenue laws of a foreign country are not illegal.

5. Giving up a Trade.—An agreement not to carry on anywhere a certain trade, business, or profession is illegal and void. The reason stated is that it is not considered best for the community that any one should wholly give up his trade. But this rule applies only to a *general* surrender; i.e., an agreement not to carry it on anywhere. An agreement by which one agrees not to exercise his calling within certain limits, as when one sells his business to another and agrees not to pursue the same business within a mile of that place, or within the same city, is not illegal.

6. Made on Sunday.—In many of the States a contract made on Sunday, or an agreement to do anything on Sunday, except such as relate to works of necessity and mercy, is illegal and void. But the rule on this subject differs in

rate allowed is ten per cent, and one agrees to give twelve, two per cent is usury.

the different States.   The object is, for the good of all, to
preserve the religious character of the day.

7. War.—Usually contracts made with foreigners are as
binding as any others.   But when two nations are at war
all commercial intercourse between them is prohibited. A
contract made between a citizen of one nation and a citizen
of another with which it is at war, is illegal and void.   But
each can trade with a neutral nation.   Thus if England
and the United States were at war, we could not trade
with Englishmen; but if England and France were at war,
we could trade with either.

8. Others.—Each State makes such contracts illegal as it
thinks best, and in every State there are some which have
not been mentioned here.   They are so many and so various
in the different States that it is impossible to do more
than refer to them here.

9. Illegal Consideration.—A contract, the consideration
of which is a forbidden act or promise, is illegal and void.
An illegal consideration is no consideration.   Thus a
promise to pay a bribe, or a note given in consideration for a
person's promising not to prosecute an offender for a crime
that has been committed,* or a promise to pay one creditor
more than the rest if he will consent to a debtor's discharge,
are wholly illegal and void.   Both sides of a contract must
be legal, or it is all void.

---

* To make such a promise is itself a crime, called *compounding a
felony.* Merchants sometimes do this; promising not to prosecute
thieves if they will return stolen property.   Such a promise is altogether illegal, either as a contract or as consideration, besides being
punishable as a crime.

CHAPTER IV.

PERSONS NOT ABLE TO CONTRACT.

1. General Rule.—This has been stated to be that all natural persons may make any contract, except minors, lunatics and idiots. Corporations, which are artificial persons, may make such contracts as their charters or the law expressly gives them power to make (p. 72, sec. 6).

2. Minors.—A person ceases to be a minor and is of age the day before his twenty-first birthday.* In a few States a female becomes of age earlier; in some at eighteen, in others when she marries. The reason that prior to that day minors can make no binding agreement is that as a rule they have not obtained sufficient knowledge or experience to enable them to understand what agreements will be to their advantage and what will not. The law in this way protects them against those who would take advantage of them. Thus it will be seen that it is dangerous to make any bargain with a minor, for he may at any time refuse to carry it out.

3. Minor may Enforce it.—But if the minor chooses to enforce the contract and do his part, he may, and then the other party will be bound to perform his part; i.e., A MINOR HAS HIS CHOICE, WHICH THE OTHER PARTY MUST ABIDE BY, TO CONSIDER THE CONTRACT BINDING OR VOID. Were this not so he would be unable to enforce an advantageous contract, and might be defrauded in that way.

4. Necessaries.—There is one exception to a minor's inability to contract. It is this: WHERE A MINOR BUYS

---

* For convenience we use throughout the book only the words denoting the masculine gender, but the law must be understood as applying to the feminine as well.

THINGS NECESSARY OR APPROPRIATE FOR HIM IN HIS WAY OF LIFE, WHEN THEY ARE NOT SUPPLIED BY A PARENT, THE MINOR IS BOUND TO PAY FOR THEM. *Necessaries* include, (1) food, (2) clothing, (3) lodging, (4) medicine, and (5) education. The reason for this rule is the protection of the minor, for if a parent did not supply these things, and he could not contract for them himself, he might not be able to obtain them at all, even though he had property. But even in buying necessaries the minor is not bound to pay what he agrees to, but only what the articles are worth.

5. Ratification.—IF AFTER BECOMING OF AGE THE MINOR RATIFIES A CONTRACT MADE BEFORE, IT IS BINDING. It is the same as if it were made then. A ratification may be made in two ways: (1) by an express agreement to carry it out, or (2) in many cases by neglecting to disaffirm the contract after he becomes of age, and retaining all the benefit of it. This last rule applies especially to cases where a minor has bought property during his minority; if he retains it, or performs any act of ownership over it after reaching full age, it will be a ratification, and he must pay for it.

6. Lunatics and Idiots.—A *lunatic* is one who has lost his reason, an *idiot* one who never had any. THE CONTRACTS OF A LUNATIC OR AN IDIOT CANNOT BE ENFORCED AGAINST HIM; but the other party to the contract must fulfill it if the lunatic chooses to maintain it. Like the minor, he has his choice. To agree is an act of the mind, and therefore those deficient in mind cannot in reality agree. But the real and practical reason why a lunatic or idiot cannot contract, is the same as in the minor's case; viz., to protect him against designing persons. A person wholly intoxicated has lost the use of his mind for the time, and therefore the same rule applies to him. But all may make binding contracts for necessaries.

7. Married Women.—A woman having no husband, whether unmarried or a widow, can make contracts as freely as a man. But with regard to married women the rule used to be that they could make no contracts whatever. Now, however, in most States a married woman may, (1) carry on a business apart from her husband, and bind herself by any contract connected with it, or (2) make any contract connected with property which she owns separately. In most States still she is unable to contract except in connection with her business or her separate property. There is too much diversity to consider the subject further.

8. Agency.—If a contract cannot be made by any one personally, it cannot be made for him, i.e., by an agent. Thus a minor cannot make a binding contract through an adult who is acting for him. But both minors and married women may act as agents for others, even in making contracts. Thus if a wife buys articles necessary for herself or her household, she may not be sued for payment, but her husband may be, for she has an implied authority to act as his agent in making such contracts. So minors and married women employed as clerks, bind their employers by their acts.

CHAPTER V.

ASSENT TO A CONTRACT.

1. Meaning of Assent.—A promise, an offer, a proposition, a discussion, none of them amount to a contract until all parties have finally *assented* to the same thing. If we analyze any agreement we find it consists of two elements, (1) an offer on one side, and (2) an acceptance on the other.

For, instance, when a seller of goods tells their price to a buyer, it is an offer to sell them at that price, and the bargain is complete when the buyer says " I will take them." Now we may consider three ways in which this offer and acceptance may be made, (1) orally, where both parties are present, (2) by letter, where the parties are separate, and (3) by a formal written document signed and delivered.

2. First Case : Orally.—In this case it is perhaps seldom that any formal offer or acceptance is made. It makes no difference which does the talking, or even that there is none, provided an agreement is reached. If anything is said or done which indicates that both parties assent or agree to the same proposition, the contract is complete. That assent may be by words, written or oral, or acts, or sometimes (but not generally) even by silence. An offer made may be withdrawn at any moment, and if the parties separate, it continues no longer as an offer, unless there is an agreement that it shall. After withdrawal it cannot be accepted unless there is a renewal of it.

> *Note to Teacher.*—It would be a useful exercise to compose a number of hypothetical conversations, such as occur every day, and have the scholar state whether or not agreements had been reached in them, and why.

3. Second Case : By Letter.—An offer made by letter and accepted by letter is a contract. But here the offer remains open for several days unless withdrawn. The contract is complete the instant the letter of acceptance is put into the mail, if properly directed. It makes no difference whether the letter of acceptance ever reaches the first party or not, nor that the latter has meanwhile withdrawn his offer. The offer may be withdrawn at any time before it is accepted, but notice of the withdrawal must reach the other party before he has accepted, i.e., before he has mailed his acceptance.* If goods are ordered of a merchant by letter, it is an offer to buy, and his sending them is an acceptance of that offer.

> *Note to Teacher.*—Vary the dates in the example given below and have the scholar state in each case whether a contract has been made or not. It is sometimes a matter of minutes only. Practical suggestions could also be made of ways to guard against mistakes, as, for instance, asking for replies, or using the telegraph.

4. Acceptance with Modification.—But very often when one party makes an offer the other says (or writes) that he will accept with certain changes or on certain conditions. Such an acceptance is no acceptance, but is in effect a refusal and a new offer, which the first party may accept or not, and the contract is not made until he does accept. All the foregoing rules apply to such new offer and acceptance. In other words, an acceptance, to make a contract, must be unconditional.

5. Third Case: Formal Written Contract.—A written paper, signed by only one party, no matter how formal, is not a contract until it has been communicated to the other party and accepted by him. Until then it is merely an offer. This acceptance usually is made by keeping the paper, and consequently we may say that delivery is necessary to a written contract. If both sign, the signature of each indicates his acceptance. Usually the parties agree orally first, and a written agreement is then drawn up ; in such case the written agreement entirely supersedes the oral one.

6. Effect of Mistake.—It may be thought, where one

---

* Thus if A, in New York City, on January 2d, wrote a letter to B, in San Francisco, offering to sell certain goods at a certain price, and B received it on the 9th, and mailed an answer accepting the offer on the 11th, the contract would then be complete, even though B's letter should never reach A, and even though A had written a second letter on the 7th withdrawing the offer, unless the letter of withdrawal reached B before he mailed his letter.

makes a contract under some mistake, as for instance a miscalculation, or ignorance of the meaning of some word, that he really gives no assent.   But the law does not allow for any mistake of which the other party is ignorant. Every one must know at his peril the language used, its meaning, and its legal effect.   Thus if I, meaning to order 50 pieces of goods, carelessly say or write 500, I must take the 500 if the seller insists upon it.

7. Effect of Custom.—If any universal custom has grown up in a certain business, or in a certain class of transactions. it forms an implied part of every contract.   This is so whether the particular parties know of it or not.   In particular trades common words will often acquire by custom peculiar meanings, and such meanings are binding.   Thus, by a universal custom, a note is not due until three days after it purports to be   (p. 107, sec. 5).   But a custom to be binding must be universal in the trade.   If it is only a custom of the particular party, it is not binding on the other unless he knows of it.

CHAPTER VI.

CONSIDERATION.

1. The Rule, we have seen, is that a promise without consideration is not binding.*   Consideration is something either

---

* We shall consider here only promises.   But other contracts also require a consideration.   Thus a sale, which is not a promise, but an agreement executing itself, must have a consideration, viz., a price. But a promise once executed is binding.   It is then no longer a promise, but an act.   Thus a promise to make a present is not binding, but when made it cannot be recalled.

(1) given, (2) done, or (3) promised to be given or done by the person to whom the promise is made. Thus suppose A makes a promise to pay B a sum of money : A need not fulfill that promise unless B on account of it either (1) gives something (which is a case of sale), or (2) does something (such as services rendered to A), or (3) promises to give or do something in the future. Thus we see that even where both sides of the agreement are promises, relating to the future, each forms a good consideration for the other.

2. Its Reason.—Honor and morality often require one to keep his promises, though they are gratuitous, but the law cannot go so far. THE OBJECT OF THE LAW IS TO PREVENT INJURY, not to make people faithful ; and a person is not considered as injured by the breaking of a promise made to him, unless he has given, done, or promised something to balance it.

3. For Whose Benefit.—It is important to remember that a consideration is sufficient, whether it acts to the benefit of the person promising or not. If he requests it, it is presumed to be for his benefit. It is sufficient if it is given or done *for* him, whether it is given or done *to* him or not. Thus if A says to B, "If you will furnish C with books, I will pay for them," A makes the promise to B, but C receives the benefit, yet A must pay. This rule applies especially to the case of guaranty (p. 76, sec. 1). The reason for it is that any one who acts on the faith of a promise made to him would be injured if the promise was not carried out. B would lose his books if A did not pay for them. We may state the rule thus : ANY CONSIDERATION IS SUFFICIENT WHICH IS EITHER OF BENEFIT TO THE PARTY PROMISING, OR OF LOSS TO THE OTHER.

4. Adequacy.—THE VALUE OF THE CONSIDERATION IS UNIMPORTANT. Every one is left to judge for himself whether he is getting enough for his agreement. Thus if I sell for $50 what is worth $100, nevertheless I must abide by my bargain, unless I have been purposely deceived.

5. An Illegal Consideration, we have seen, is no consideration (p. 26). This means that when the thing given, done or promised by one party is an unlawful act, the other party is not bound by his part of the contract. The law will not help wrongdoers.

6. Exception.—There is one very important exception to the rule that a contract must have a consideration. It is the case of notes, drafts and other negotiable paper, transferred before they become due, to a party who has paid for them, and who does not know that they had no consideration in the beginning.*

7. Sealed Instruments.—There is no difference between written and oral contracts as to the necessity for a consideration. In some States, however, if a seal is affixed to a written contract, it requires no consideration.

CHAPTER VII.

FRAUD AND DECEIT.

1. Two Kinds.—Fraud may enter into a contract in two ways; (1) it may be fraud practiced by one party upon the other to induce him to make the contract, or (2) the contract may be a fraudulent device between the two to cheat some third party.

---

* This may not be understood at this point. It will be fully explained later. Reference should be made to the following sections Chap. XXII., sec. 7–12, and Chap. XXIII., sec. 15.

a. *Fraud Between the Parties.*

2. What it is.—As we have seen, ONE DEFRAUDED IN THE MAKING OF A CONTRACT NEED NOT CARRY IT OUT. Fraud, as we here use it, is deceit. It may be practiced in two ways, (1) by stating facts known to be false, and (2) by concealing facts known to be true, and which ought to be revealed. The former is the more frequent case. Thus, if one buys goods, representing that he is able to pay for them, while he is not, the seller may treat the sale as void and keep or recover the goods ; in insurance, any concealment of a material fact would make the contract void (p. 178). It is impossible to define fraud exactly.

3. The Effect.—THE DISHONEST PARTY MUST CARRY OUT HIS CONTRACT, IF THE OTHER PARTY WISHES TO TREAT IT AS VALID. In other words, like the case of a minor, (p. 27), the defrauded party has his choice to consider it all valid or all void. Thus, in a sale through fraud, the seller may at his option consider it void and recover the goods, or he may consider it valid and claim the price. Any different rule from this would allow a dishonest person to take advantage of his own dishonesty in a case where he had made some mistake as to its advantage to himself.

b. *Fraud on Third Party.*

4. By Illegal Means.—An agreement between two parties to cheat a third is an illegal agreement and wholly void, besides being often a criminal offense.

5. By Legal Means.—But an act entirely legal in itself may often work as a fraud upon other parties. The most common example of this is where a failing debtor transfers his remaining property so that his creditors shall not get it, but in such a way that he retains the benefit of it himself, as where he gives it to his wife. It is a legal act in itself, fraudulent only as to creditors, and as to them, only when he does not retain sufficient property to pay his debts. The rule therefore is this: such a transfer is binding upon the two parties, but, if done to defraud creditors, any creditor may sue to have it declared void.

CHAPTER VIII.

WRITTEN CONTRACTS.

1. When Necessary.—Any agreement may be put in a written form, and this is always prudent, for it saves all uncertainty as to what the agreement was. When written, no other evidence of what the party agreed to can be given. But, as before stated, some contracts to be binding must be in writing and signed. The chief classes, having reference to commercial transactions, are three in number, (1) agreements for the sale of personal property * over a certain amount in value, (2) agreements of guaranty, and (3) agreements not to be performed within a year.

a. Classes requiring writing.

2. Sale.—A SALE OF PERSONAL PROPERTY, OR AN AGREE-MENT TO BUY OR SELL, IF OVER A CERTAIN AMOUNT IN PRICE, MUST BE IN WRITING AND SIGNED, unless some part has been delivered or paid for. The amount under which the contract may be oral, is not the same in all the States,

---

* *Real estate* means land and buildings· *Personal property* means all other kinds of property, and hence includes all merchandise. All contracts for the sale of real estate must also be in writing, but we will not consider them, because they hardly fall within the scope of a book on commercial law.

varying from $30 to $200. ·Thus, if I orally order $300 worth of goods from you, I may refuse to take them when you send them. But oral orders of that kind are continually acted upon in business, and are binding contracts. The reason is that they are made effectual by either delivery of the goods or payment. These we will now consider.

3. **Delivery.**—IF ANY PART OF THE GOODS ARE DELIVERED TO THE PURCHASER AND ACCEPTED BY HIM THE WHOLE CONTRACT IS BINDING, though not written, i.e., the seller must deliver all, and the buyer must pay for all. Thus, in the last example, if I orally order goods, I need not receive them, but if I do receive them, or any part of them, I must pay the agreed price and take them all.

4. **Payment.**—IF ANY PART OF THE PRICE IS PAID AND RECEIVED, THE WHOLE CONTRACT IS BINDING, though it was not written, nor any part of the goods delivered. We may express the rules contained in these last three sections thus: over a certain amount a sale or an agreement to buy or sell to be binding must have one of these three elements: (1) a written contract, or (2) delivery of whole or part of the property, or (3) payment of the whole or part of the price. But if the goods are under that amount in price, then no one of these things is necessary (Chap. XVIII.).

5. **A Guaranty** MUST BE IN WRITING. A *guaranty* is an agreement by one with another that a third person shall duly fulfill some engagement. Thus, where A agrees to pay the debt of B, A is said to guarantee the debt. So where one agrees to indemnify an employer for any loss he may suffer through a certain clerk, he is said to guarantee the faithfulness of the clerk (Chap. XVI.).

6. **A Contract which cannot be performed within a year** MUST BE IN WRITING. This means a year from the time it is made. Thus an agreement to do any act eighteen months from the time it is made, or to do a thing which it is known

will take more than a year, must be written. If on April 6th I hire you orally to work for me a year, commencing May 1st, the agreement is not binding, but yet, as we shall see, if you do work I must pay (sec. 8).

b. What writing sufficient.

7. The Form of the writing is immaterial. It may be full and formal, or simply a note or memorandum embodying its substance. It may be in ink or pencil. It must be signed, but a signing with initials is sufficient. The fact that there is an authenticated written paper is the important thing, not the form of it.

8. If only one party signs he is bound by the contract, but the other one is not. Thus, if A signs a written contract to buy $500 worth of grain from B, but B does not sign it, B has his choice to complete the sale or to refuse. But where an agreement has been performed entirely on one side, and nothing remains to be done but for the other side to pay, payment may be enforced, though the one to make the payment did not sign, or even though none of the contract was in writing. If this were not so fraud might easily be perpetrated, for it is quite common where one party merely agrees to pay, for him not to sign.

9. Signature by Agent.—It is of course of no importance who writes the body of the contract. Nor is it always necessary that the party himself should sign it. Any one whom he authorizes to make the contract for him, as his agent, may sign it for him, and may sign either his own name or that of his principal.* The authority to sign may be given to the agent orally. The case of a sale by a broker illustrates the principles of this section. (See p. 99, footnote, also forms on p. 287.) The broker signs for both the

---

* See p. 48, for definition of principal and agent.

seller and the purchaser, and signs his own name, but that is sufficient to make a written contract.

10. Letters.—We have seen that the writing need not be formal. Where a letter is sent containing an offer, and it is accepted by another letter, the contract is written, and consists of the two letters taken together. If an order for goods is sent by mail, and acted upon, it is a written contract, so far as the writer is concerned, but not as to the other party. A telegram, in the same way, may be a written contract.

Note to Teacher.—The reason for any rule of law is important, as showing its substantial justice, and thus impressing it upon the mind. The whole subject of the requisites of binding agreements might be usefully reviewed by preparing a number of contracts illustrating the different points, combining two or more points in one case perhaps, and asking the scholar for the appropriate rule and its reason in each case.

COMMERCIAL AGREEMENTS

TO BE BINDING MUST BE

I. **POSSIBLE** in their nature;

       Those impossible because of
             { 1. unforeseen circumstances, or
             { 2. personal disability,
       still are possible *in their nature.*

II. **LEGAL;** the following agreements are illegal:

       1. To give or take USURY (in many States),
       2. Against the REVENUE LAWS,
       3. Giving up a TRADE generally,
       4. Made on SUNDAY (in many States),
       5. Between ENEMIES in war,
       6. Having an ILLEGAL CONSIDERATION,
       7. Some others in different States.

III. MADE BY ONE **ABLE TO CONTRACT;** that is, not

       1. A MINOR,
       2. A LUNATIC or IDIOT, or
       3. A MARRIED WOMAN,
           except in connection with
                 { 1. her separate business, or
                 { 2. her separate property.

IV. **ASSENTED TO;** by

       { 1. Appropriate words, written or oral, or
       { 2. Acts signifying assent, and communicated to
          the other party.

V. MADE FOR SOME **CONSIDERATION;** which must be something

       { 1. GIVEN,
       { 2. DONE, or } by the other party.
       { 3. PROMISED

VI. MADE WITHOUT **FRAUD OR DECEIT;**

VII. IN **WRITING AND SIGNED,** when they are either

       1. A SALE of goods over a certain amount, unless
               { 1. Part have been delivered, or
               { 2. Part of price has been paid.
       2. A GUARANTY, or
       3. Not to be performed in a YEAR.

CHAPTER IX.

1. Right: Remedy.—One has the right to have all contracts made with him fulfilled. But a right is almost useless without some means of enforcing it. Those means are called *remedies*. It is for this purpose, *i.e.* to apply the appropriate remedies to particular cases, that courts are established.

2. Kinds of Remedy.—When one does an illegal act, an act forbidden any one to do, such as to steal, he offends against the State, and the State punishes him, by imprisonment or fine. This is a *criminal* remedy. A *civil* remedy is one given to a party to whom a wrong has been done, to compensate him. We shall treat here only of civil remedies, for to break a contract is not a criminal offense. Civil remedies are of two kinds, *compensatory* and *preventive*.

3. Compensatory.—This consists of an award by the court of money (called *damages*), to be paid to the injured party by the other. The amount is to be sufficient to compensate him for his loss. In mercantile contracts this loss is generally easily calculated. Thus the loss to a seller of goods is the price the buyer agreed to pay, or to the holder of an unpaid note, the amount of the note. But quite often, the loss is more difficult to compute, as where one agrees to go into partnership with another, but afterward refuses to. Yet in every case the award of the court (called a *judgment*) must be for the loss occasioned.

4. Execution.—If the debtor fails to pay the judgment, the court may issue what is called an *execution*, and under it his property may be taken away from him and applied to pay the judgment. In some cases, involving fraud and dishonesty, the party may be imprisoned for a time, or until he pays the judgment.

5. Preventive.—But there are cases in which the allowance of damages for the injury already done would be only a partial remedy. This would be the case in all continuing contracts, such as an agreement never to carry on a particular business at a certain place. The most complete remedy is to compel the party to carry out his contract, and this remedy is sometimes allowed. Thus, in the last example, the court, besides granting damages, will order the person not to carry on the business. That remedy is called an *injunction.* So sometimes, where the agreement is affirmative, the court affirmatively orders the thing to be done.

6. When Allowed.—The compensatory remedy applies to all cases. When a contract is broken, the injured party may always sue for damages. The preventive remedy applies to but few cases in commercial law. In the ordinary contracts, such as notes, drafts, sales, etc., damages only can be obtained.

7. Insufficiency of Remedy.—Both these remedies are often insufficient to repair the loss. But the law can go no further. If a judgment for damages is obtained, yet the debtor may have no property, and it cannot be collected. Where an injunction or other order is obtained the party may perhaps refuse to obey it. He will then be punished and imprisoned, but perhaps he will still refuse. Thus, we see, law and remedy cannot fully protect one, yet they do far more than many think. Without them there would be practically little reason for any one to respect the rights of any other. It must be remembered that the vast majority of contracts are kept, not broken, and if we ask the reason why, the existence of law and remedy is at least a large part of the answer. They hinder many breaches that they could not repair.

SUMMARY OF LEADING RULES OF CONTRACTS.

I. THE FUNDAMENTAL RULE.

Every one must fulfill EVERY AGREEMENT he makes.

II. EXCEPTIONS TO IT.

1. A contract to do a thing IMPOSSIBLE in its nature is void.

2. A contract the LAW FORBIDS is void.

3. A contract made by a MINOR, a lunatic, or an idiot is not binding upon him.

4. A proposition NOT ASSENTED TO by both parties is not binding.

5. A promise WITHOUT CONSIDERATION is not binding.

6. A contract which one is induced to make through FRAUD or deceit is not binding upon him.

7. Some contracts must be WRITTEN.

8. One has no right to sue on a contract unless he has PERFORMED or offered to perform his part.

III. ILLEGAL CONTRACTS.

Any contract which has for its purpose the furtherance of any object CONTRARY TO JUSTICE or common morality is void.

IV. Persons not able to contract.

1. A minor has HIS CHOICE, which the other party must abide by, to consider the contract binding or void.

2. Where a minor buys things NECESSARY or appropriate for him in his way of life, when they are not supplied by a parent, the minor is bound to pay for them.

3. If after becoming of age the minor RATIFIES a contract made before, it is binding.

4. The contracts of a LUNATIC or an idiot cannot be enforced against him.

V. Consideration.

1. The object of the law is to PREVENT INJURY.

2. Any consideration is sufficient which is either of BENEFIT to the party promising, OR of LOSS to the other.

3. The VALUE of the consideration is unimportant.

VI. Fraud and Deceit.

1. ONE DEFRAUDED in the making of a contract need not carry it out.

2. The DISHONEST PARTY must carry out his contract, if the other party wishes to treat it as valid.

VII. Written Contracts.

1. A SALE OF PERSONAL PROPERTY or an agreement to buy or sell, if over a certain amount in price, must be in writing and signed.

2. If any part of the goods are DELIVERED to the pur-

chaser and accepted by him the whole contract is binding without writing.

3. If any part of the price is PAID and received the whole contract is binding without writing.

4. A GUARANTY must be in writing.

5. A contract which cannot be performed within a YEAR must be in writing.

REVIEW QUESTIONS.

Introduction.

1. What is law? Why is it necessary? Do all nations have laws?
2. Do the laws of one country have any effect in another? Upon whom? Do they have any effect upon foreigners who are traveling in that country? What force have the laws of one State in another?
3. Name the five sources of law in any State, and their relative authority. By which one of these are ordinary commercial transactions mostly governed?
4. Is commercial law uniform throughout the U. S.? Why?
5. What effect has ignorance of the law in any case? Why?
6. State the several parts and divisions into which the book is divided, and the general subject of each.

General Principles of Contracts.

7. What is a contract? The differences between a contract and a promise?
8. Explain why the law of contracts is important.
9. Explain the difference between forbidding everything except what is allowed, and allowing everything except what is forbidden. Upon which theory is our law based? What principle flows from that theory, as to contracts?
10. What is the fundamental rule of contracts? Its reason? Are there exceptions to it?

11. Define and distinguish written, oral, express, and implied contracts.
12. When must gratuitous services be paid for, and when not? Why?
13. Name the seven requisites of a binding contract. Into what two classes are they divided?
14. Name the three kinds of impossibility. In which is the contract binding, and in which not? Why, in each case?
15. Of the different kinds of commercial agreements, are the greater part legal or illegal?
16. Which party to an illegal contract may claim that it is void? Why?
17. Name some kinds of illegal contracts. State the reason in each case.
18. Who are persons "not able to contract"? Who are minors?
19. Is a minor's contract binding? Why? Is a promise made to a minor binding? Why? Is a contract with a minor illegal?
20. What is the rule as to "necessaries"? What are "necessaries"?
21. What is the effect of ratification? When must it be made? State the two ways in which it may be made.
22. State the effect of a lunatic's contract.
23. What contracts can an unmarried woman make? A widow? A married woman?
24. If an adult makes a contract as the agent of a minor, is the minor bound by it? If a minor makes a contract as the agent of an adult, is the adult bound by it?
25. What will change an offer into a contract?
26. In what ways may assent be given?
27. When may an offer be withdrawn? Can it be accepted after withdrawal? Can it be withdrawn after being accepted? If made and accepted by letter at what moment is the contract complete?
28. State the effect of an unconditional acceptance. Of a conditional.
29. If an agreement is signed by one party is anything more necessary to make the contract complete? If signed by both parties?
30. Is a contract binding upon one, which he made in mistake?
31. What effect do customs in trade have upon contracts? Why?
32. What is consideration? Why necessary? State the difference between what the law demands and what morality demands in this respect.

33. Must the consideration be of benefit to the party promising?
34. Is an inadequate consideration sufficient? Why?
35. Is an illegal promise a good consideration for a legal promise? Why?
36. What commercial contracts require no consideration, and when?
37. Does a written contract require a consideration?
38. State the two ways in which a contract may be fraudulent?
39. What is the effect of a contract by two parties, where one practices fraud upon the other? What may the defrauded party do? State the two ways of practicing fraud.
40. If a man transfers his property to his wife to keep it out of the hands of his creditors, may the creditors claim that it is still his, and that the transfer is void? If they do not, may any one else? If they do not, to whom will the property belong, to the wife or the husband?
41. Why does the law require some contracts to be in writing? State two reasons.
42. Name the three kinds which must be written.
43. State the three cases in which an oral sale of goods is binding.
44. Is an unsigned paper a written contract? Is it, when signed in pencil? With initials only? When signed by an agent?
45. When only one party signs a contract, which must be written, is he bound to fulfill it? Is the other party?
46. State how a letter may become a written contract.
47. When one party fails to perform his part of a contract is the other released?
48. What is a remedy? A civil remedy? A criminal remedy? Name and describe the two kinds of civil remedy. What are damages?
49. How is payment of a judgment for money enforced?
50. What is an injunction?
51. What kind of remedy is usually the only one applicable to breaches of commercial contracts?

DIVISION II.

AGENCY.

CHAPTER X.

AGENCY IN GENERAL.

1. Definition.—An *agent* is a person authorized to act for another with third parties. The *principal* is the one for whom he acts. The principal is in law the one who does the act; the agent is only the instrument or means by which he does it. The greatest importance here of the law of agency is in its relation to the making of contracts through agents. Thus, every sale made by a clerk in a store is a contract made by the proprietor.

2. Importance of Subject.—Agency is one of the most common and necessary relations of life, and it exists with regard to all kinds of subjects, commercial and otherwise. Nearly every one acts every day as the agent of some one else. Thus, every clerk in a store is the agent of the proprietor in everything that he does connected with the business. Almost all the business of brokers, commission merchants, lawyers, auctioneers, masters of ships, and many others, is some sort of agency. Corporations act wholly by means of agents; viz., their officers, clerks, etc. Therefore agency is one of the most important subjects in the law.

Note to Teacher.—A graphic picture could easily be drawn of the result to commerce and civilization were agency totally abolished, and every one did for himself all that he wished done.

3. Classification.—In every act done by an agent there are three persons involved: (1) the *principal*, (2) the *agent*, (3) the *third party*, i.e., the person with whom the agent acts, or who is affected by the act. Thus, where goods are sold in a store, the proprietor is the principal, the salesman the agent, and the buyer the third party. Therefore three classes of relations arise: the relations (1) of the principal and the agent to each other, (2) of the principal and the third party to each other, and (3) of the agent and the third party to each other. The first relation does not properly belong to the subject of agency, but is mentioned for the sake of fullness. Each one of these parties owes duties to each of the others, and therefore there arise six classes of duties. In the next chapter we shall treat of the duties of the principal and in the following one of the duties of the agent.

Note to Teacher.—Ask what the six classes are. At the end of the subject of agency, it might be presented in a different light by taking up each one of those six classes and summarizing the several duties falling under them respectively. Thus, the duties of the principal to the agent are to pay him and do all that he has agreed with the agent to do; of the principal to the third party, to assume the responsibility for all the agent's authorized acts, etc., etc.

4. Who May Be.—(1) *Who may be principal.* Any one may do any act by an agent which he may do personally, but no other. This is why a minor, lunatic, or idiot cannot make a contract through an agent. (2) *Who may be agent.* Any one having sufficient understanding to do as he is directed may be an agent. Therefore minors and married women may act as agents, though lunatics and idiots cannot (p. 29).

5. How Appointed.—In ordinary commercial matters agents may be appointed orally, and no particular form of words is necessary. Thus, if an employer tells his clerk to do a certain thing that makes the clerk his agent for that purpose. In important matters, the agent is often appointed by a written instrument, which is called a *power of attorney* (*form* 31).

6. Extent of Authority.—The employing of an agent is the act which gives him his authority. AN AGENT HAS AUTHORITY TO DO WHATEVER IS NECESSARY OR GENERALLY DONE IN CONNECTION WITH THE PURPOSES FOR WHICH HE IS EMPLOYED. Some employments give very wide powers, and leave very much to the discretion of the agent; others give a very limited authority. Thus, any act of the president or cashier of a bank in connection with the banking business binds the bank. On the other hand, a messenger would have authority simply to carry messages. So, also, if one is employed to do just one thing—as, for instance, to sign a particular paper—he has authority to do only that one thing.

7. Revocation of Authority.—THE AUTHORITY OF AN AGENT MAY BE TAKEN AWAY AT ANY TIME.* Here we must carefully distinguish between the right of a principal to revoke the agent's authority as to third parties and the right to break his agreement as to the agent. He has the former right, but if its exercise breaks his agreement with the agent, he is responsible to the agent for any injury. Thus if I hire you for a year to sell goods, and dismiss you, even without cause, before the end of the year, that ends the agency, and you can act for me no more, but you may sue me for any loss it causes you. The death or bankruptcy of the principal also ends the agency.

8. Sub-Agents.—An agent may himself act by an agent, the latter being called a *sub-agent*. All the rules of agency apply to the relation between the agent and the sub-agent;

---

* This is the general rule, but there are exceptions to it which we cannot notice here.

for as to each other they are principal and agent.* There are some cases in which an agent must act personally, but in most commercial transactions, where it is usual to employ sub-agents, they may be employed.

> *Note to Teacher.*—As an exercise in distinguishing between principal and agent something of this kind might be done: take a quantity of cotton as it grows, trace it through the different processes of cultivation, picking, transportation, manufacture, sale, etc., and have the scholar point out which ones of those concerned are principals and which agents, and for whom.

CHAPTER XI.

RESPONSIBILITY OF PRINCIPAL.†

a. Principal's Relation to Agent.

1. Duty to Agent.—As BETWEEN THE PRINCIPAL AND AGENT, AGENCY IS WHOLLY A MATTER OF AGREEMENT. Therefore the only duty each owes to the other is to carry

---

* Thus suppose A, a manufacturer, sends goods to B, a commission merchant, for sale, and B having a branch store in another place under the charge of C sends them to him, and they are there sold by D, a clerk, to E; the sale in reality is by A to E through the intermediate agents B, C, and D. D is the agent of C; C is the principal of D and the agent of B; B is the principal of C and the agent of A. If each principal has given to his agent the necessary authority, the sale is valid. In this way there may be any number of intermediate agents.

† *Responsibility* means the state of being answerable for an act, and being compelled to bear the consequences of it. *Liability* means about the same. Thus, when we say one is responsible for his agent, we mean that if the agent makes a contract for him he must carry it out; or, if the agent's negligence injures another, he (the principal) must pay for it.

out his agreement. In ordinary cases the chief part of this agreement on the principal's part is to pay for what is done. As to each other the parties are not really principal and agent. Their agreement is one for personal services and that subject will be treated in a later chapter (Chap. XXVIII.).

b. *Principal's Relation to Third Party.*

2. Responsibility to Third Party.—It is at this point that the most important rule of agency comes in. Ordinarily a person can only be made to answer for his own acts; but the theory of agency is that the act of the agent is the act of the principal. Therefore the rule is, that THE PRINCIPAL IS RESPONSIBLE FOR THE ACTS OF HIS AGENT. Thus if the agent makes a contract, the principal must fulfill it or pay damages. If the agent uses fraud or deceit, or acts negligently in a matter intrusted to him, the principal must bear the consequences of it. The principal is bound even though he was unknown at the time the act was done, for it was done for his benefit, and one who takes the benefit must also incur the responsibility. Thus if I buy goods of you, without saying that I am acting for any one else, you may sue the person for whom I am really acting.

3. Exceeding Authority. — But IF THE ACT IS NOT WITHIN THE AUTHORITY GIVEN, THE PRINCIPAL IS NOT RESPONSIBLE. The agent is not an agent except to do what he is directed or allowed to do: beyond that the act is his personal act. This rule is clear, though it is sometimes difficult to tell exactly what is authorized and what is not (p. 50, sec. 6).

4. Apparent Authority.—But sometimes a person appears to have authority which he has not. The question then simply is, who caused that appearance, for A PRINCIPAL IS RESPONSIBLE FOR ANY ACT DONE BY HIS AGENT

FOR WHICH HE HAS GIVEN AN APPARENT AUTHORITY. An agent's saying that he has authority does not give it to him. But if the principal himself has represented in any way that the agent has authority to do a thing, then he cannot repudiate it when done. This case often arises where one is employed to perform a general class of duties, but is privately instructed not to do certain things that otherwise would fall within his power. If the act falls within the general duties, or the general scope of the employment, the principal is bound by it. Thus if a salesman in a store is instructed not to sell certain of the goods, or not to sell to certain persons, but does, the sale will be binding unless the purchaser knew of the instructions, for making him a salesman is a representation to every one that he has power to sell anything in the store.*

5. **Ratification.**—If a person ratify an act done by one as his agent, after it has been done, he is bound by it whether he had given the agent any authority or not. SUBSEQUENT RATIFICATION IS EQUIVALENT TO PRIOR AUTHORITY. But if it is made under a mistake as to any of the circumstances, it is not binding. Thus suppose A pretends to be B's agent and buys something for him promising to pay $50 for it; if B, on hearing of it, ratifies the act, he is bound; but suppose that B is told he is to pay $45, his ratification under such a mistake is not binding. Ratification may be made in two ways: (1) by express words, and (2) by accepting the benefits of the act, as where one accepts the money or services or other consideration resulting from the act.

---

* Yet an agent has no right, as between himself and his employer, to disobey any instructions, for his contract is to obey. *Authority*, as used in agency, means power to bind principal. *Right* is another thing. An agent, having the right has also the power, but he often has the power and not the right (p. 54, sec. 2; p. 64, sec. 2).

CHAPTER XII.

RESPONSIBILITY OF AGENT.

a. *Agent's Relation to Principal.*

1. In General.—This, we have already seen, is merely a relation of contract, and therefore the agent's duty to his principal is simply to do what he has agreed (p. 51, and Chap. XXVIII.).

2. Implied Duties.—But we may notice here three implied portions of all such agreements: (1) that he will obey all instructions, (2) that he will act skillfully and carefully in every respect, and (3) that he will not place himself in such a position that his own interests are adverse to those of his principal. Thus, if by disobeying instructions he makes any loss, he is himself responsible for it, but if he makes any gain it all belongs to his principal. If one is employed to buy goods he must not buy of himself, for his own interest is adverse to his principal's.

b. *Agent's Relation to Third Party.*

3. Responsibility to Third Party.—The principal, we have seen, must bear the responsibility of his agent's acts, for they are in effect his acts. A corresponding fundamental rule is this: THE AGENT IS NOT HIMSELF RESPONSIBLE TO THE THIRD PARTY FOR ACTS HE PERFORMS AS AGENT.* The reason is that the third party acts as though he were

---

* Notice that we say "responsible *to the third party*." If any one does an illegal act (e.g., a crime) he is responsible *to the people*—i.e., he may be punished criminally for it, whether acting for himself or another. (See p. 41, sec. 2.)

dealing directly with the principal. Thus if I buy goods of you for some one else, I am not responsible for the price, because you trust only my principal. But this rule is subject to some important exceptions, which we will now consider.

4. Five Exceptions.—In the following five cases one acting for another is himself responsible for his acts and on his contracts: (1) where he exceeds both his real and apparent authority, (2) where he specially agrees at the time to make himself responsible, (3) where he professes at the time to be acting for himself though really acting for another, (4) where, though professing at the time to be acting for another, he does not disclose who that other is, and (5) where he acts fraudulently.

5. Exceeding Authority.—An AGENT WHO EXCEEDS HIS AUTHORITY IS HIMSELF RESPONSIBLE TO THE THIRD PARTY. The reason is that if he was not no one would be, for we have seen that in such case the principal is not bound (p. 52). This is so even though the agent acts innocently and believes he has the authority, for he has better means of knowing than the third party.

6. Special Agreement. — IF THE AGENT SPECIALLY AGREES AT THE TIME TO BECOME RESPONSIBLE TO THE THIRD PARTY, HE IS SO. This is merely the old rule that one must fulfill his contracts. Thus if A, as the agent of B, buys goods of C and makes himself responsible, both A and B are responsible; i.e., B must pay what he has agreed to through his agent A, and A must carry out his contract of guaranty if it becomes necessary.

7. Concealing Principal.—In the next two cases, where the agent pretends to be acting for himself, and where he does not disclose his principal, he is responsible because he is the one upon whose credit the third party acts. We may put these two cases together and say, AN AGENT CON-

CEALING HIS PRINCIPAL IS HIMSELF RESPONSIBLE TO THE THIRD PARTY. So far as the third party is concerned, he is the real principal, being the only one trusted. The real principal may be one whom the third party would not trust. But when the real principal is discovered, he is also responsible. Commission merchants often do business in this way (Chap. XX.).

8. Fraud.—AN AGENT ACTING FRAUDULENTLY OR DECEITFULLY IS HIMSELF RESPONSIBLE TO THE THIRD PARTY, for a person cannot relieve himself of responsibility for such acts. In this case, too, the principal must also bear the consequences of the fraud, for he obtains the benefit. Thus we see that in four cases of the five both agent and principal are bound. The third party may take his choice. But who shall finally bear the loss, the principal or the agent, is another question, wholly between them, and not one of agency.

9. Public Agents.—Officers under the National, State, City, or other government, are agents for the Nation, State, City, etc., respectively, and therefore are called *public agents.* Thus the mayor of a city acts not for himself but for the city. Their acts as agents are subject to all the foregoing rules of agency. But there is one exception, viz., that where a public agent exceeds his authority he is not himself personally bound. The reason for this is, that the agency being public, every one is presumed to know the extent of the authority.

c. *Responsibility of Third Party.*

10. This would logically form the subject of a new chapter, but as it is subject to no peculiar rules, and we have but a word to say, we consider it here. His duties are no different because he acts with an agent, but the same as if he was acting with the principal himself, viz., to carry out his contracts and act lawfully in every way. Whether he is responsible to the agent or to the principal is simply the question whether when he has done wrong the one or the other is the proper person to sue him, and that we do not propose to consider.

Summary of Leading Rules of Agency.

I. In General.

1. An agent HAS AUTHORITY to do whatever is necessary or generally done in connection with the purposes for which he is employed.

2. The authority of an agent may be TAKEN AWAY at any time.

II. Responsibility of Principal.

1. As between the principal and agent, agency is wholly a matter of AGREEMENT.

2. The principal IS RESPONSIBLE for the acts of his agent.

3. If the act is NOT WITHIN THE AUTHORITY given the principal is not responsible.

4. A principal is responsible for any act done by his agent for which he has given an APPARENT AUTHORITY.

5. Subsequent RATIFICATION is equivalent to prior authority.

III. Responsibility of Agent.

1. The agent is NOT RESPONSIBLE himself to the third party for acts he performs as agent.

2. An agent who EXCEEDS his authority is himself responsible to the third party.

3. If the agent SPECIALLY AGREES at the time to become responsible to the third party he is so.

4. An agent CONCEALING his principal is himself responsible to the third party.

5. An agent acting FRAUDULENTLY or deceitfully is himself responsible to the third party.

A PRINCIPAL IS RESPONSIBLE

I. To **AGENT,**
> For any violation of their agreement;

II. To **THIRD PARTY,**
> I. If agency was AVOWED;
>> For any act of agent in following cases:
>>> 1. Where REAL authority was given;
>>> 2. Where APPARENT authority was given; or
>>> 3. Where it was afterward RATIFIED,
>>>> 1. Expressly, or
>>>> 2. By retaining benefit.
>
> II. If agency was CONCEALED;
>> For any act of agent in following cases:
>>> 1. Where AUTHORITY was given, or
>>> 2. Where it was afterward RATIFIED,
>>>> 1. Expressly, or
>>>> 2. By retaining benefit.

AN AGENT IS RESPONSIBLE

I. To **PRINCIPAL,**
> For any violation of their agreement, or for
>> 1. DISOBEDIENCE to instructions,
>> 2. Want of SKILL or CARE, or
>> 3. Making his own interests ADVERSE.

II. To **THIRD PARTY,** in the following cases:
>> 1. Where he EXCEEDS the authority,
>> 2. Where he SPECIALLY AGREES to be,
>> 3. Where he CONCEALS principal, either by
>>> 1. Pretending to be principal, or
>>> 2. Not disclosing principal.
>> 4. Where he acts FRAUDULENTLY.

RESPONSIBILITY TO THIRD PARTY.

I.
> 1. Where agent acts as agent, but specially agrees to be responsible,
> 2. Where principal is concealed, by
>> 1. Agent's pretending to be principal, or
>> 2. Principal's name not being disclosed.
> 3. Where agent acts fraudulently.

Both agent and principal are responsible.

II. Where agent acts as agent, but exceeds his real and apparent authority.

Agent alone is responsible.

III. In all other cases.

Principal alone is responsible

DIVISION III.

PARTNERSHIP.

CHAPTER XIII.

RELATIONS OF THE PARTNERS TO EACH OTHER.

1. Definition.—*Partnership* is the relation established by an agreement between two or more persons to combine their money, property, labor, or skill in some lawful business, and share the profits in certain proportions. The partners collectively are in many respects considered as a single individual, and as such are often called a *house*, or *firm*, having partnership property, and a firm name, under which they do all their business. *Copartnership* means the same as partnership.

2. Sharing of Profits IS THE MOST IMPORTANT OF THE ELEMENTS GOING TO MAKE UP A PARTNERSHIP, and we may say that, in general, wherever profits are shared, the parties are partners. Thus, though one contributes all the money (called the *capital*), and the other does all the work, or if in a case where no capital is needed each contributes only his labor, still if they are to share the profits they are partners. But a clerk, who is paid by being given a share in the profits, even though he has no other salary, is not a partner.

3. Who May Be.—Any one who may do business alone— i.e., any one who may make contracts, may become a member of a partnership.* But no one can be made a partner against his will, for it is wholly a matter of contract. For the same reason no new member can be introduced into a firm without the consent of each one. This should be so, for the relation is so close, and the power of a partner so great (p. 63), that it would be dangerous to allow it to be exercised over one without his own consent. Thus if A and B are partners, and B could introduce a third he might bring in some one whom A would never have trusted as a partner.

4. **Formation.**—A PARTNERSHIP IS FORMED SIMPLY AND ONLY BY AGREEMENT. This agreement may be simply a contract in so many words to be partners, or it may be very full and minute in its details. The form on page 285 will give an idea of some of the common clauses. It may be oral or written: if written it is called *articles of copartnership.* The proportion of the profits each one is to have is usually specified. Parties may engage in business together without any definite agreement, but in such case also they are partners, for one is implied.

5. **Duration.**—The agreement may specify a time at which the partnership shall terminate (such as in two years), or, as is generally the case, nothing may be said. In the former case neither party has the right to dissolve it until the time expires, but if one partner commits some fraud, or otherwise misbehaves, or becomes insane, a court may end it. In the latter case, WHERE NO TIME IS SPECIFIED ANY PARTNER MAY DISSOLVE A PARTNERSHIP AT WILL. He may do it for any reason, and however small his interest. It may seem strange that so many partnerships should continue year after year, while it is in the power of any partner to dissolve them at any time without making him-

---

* Except, in a few States, married women.

self responsible to the others for any loss. The reason is that in such cases it is almost always to the best interests of each one to continue.

6. Transfer of Interest.—If the partnership is for no definite time, a partner may sell his interest in the common property to any one at any time. This is probably true also where it was formed for a definite period, though having contracted not to do so he would be responsible to his partners for having broken his contract. But the person to whom he sells does not thereby become a partner in his place, without the consent of the other partners (sec. 3).

7. Effect of Transfer.—The real effect of a transfer of interest is the dissolution of the firm. If the new person is received by all the others, that constitutes a new firm. In the same way, whenever an old member retires from the firm, it is the formation of a new one. This is so whether the name changes or not.

8. Death.—The death of any partner dissolves the whole firm. The legal representatives of the dead partner do not become partners themselves, but are simply entitled to his share of the partnership property; or, if it is sold, to his share of the proceeds. Thus we see that any change as to the members of a firm dissolves the old firm, and makes a new one. Such changes are continually occurring without any disturbance to the business.

9. Effect of Dissolution.—Upon a dissolution each partner is entitled to demand that there shall be an accounting of the affairs of the firm, that the common property be sold, and that he be paid his proportionate share of what remains after paying its debts. But to do this would not only take time, but in the case of a prosperous business it might cause much loss to all the partners, for the business itself, the trade, would be scattered and lost.

10. A Common Course.—Therefore it is quite common in such a case for the retiring partner to sell his interest as it is, for a given sum, to some of the old partners or to some one else whom they will receive as a new partner, and the business goes on as before. Such a transaction in legal effect, is simply a sale from the old firm to a new one of all the firm property and rights.

11. Rights and Duties.—Since a partnership is wholly a matter of contract, the partners have, *as to each other*, only such rights and duties as they agree upon. If any one acts contrary to that agreement, he breaks his contract, and is responsible to his partners for the injury. It is always an implied (if not expressed) part of the agreement, that each partner, who is to contribute his time or labor, shall exercise all skill, care, and diligence in the business, and without other compensation than his agreed share of the profits. (See sec. 1 of next chapter.)

CHAPTER XIV.

RELATIONS OF THE PARTNERS TO THIRD PARTIES.

1. Authority of Partner.—The most important rule connected with partnership is that EACH PARTNER HAS FULL AUTHORITY TO ACT FOR THE FIRM, in any matter connected with its appropriate business. Each is the agent for all, or in other words, for the firm. But as to matters outside of the business, he is not an agent, and if he attempts to bind the firm, it is the act of an agent without authority and only binds himself (p. 55). Thus in a house engaged in the cotton trade, each partner may buy and sell cotton or do any other acts necessary to carry on the business, but if one without authority from the rest should buy hardware, the firm would not be bound.

2. Authority: Right.—The authority of a partner does not depend upon the agreement but is a legal consequent of the relation, whatever the agreement provides. Hence a partner may have the *apparent authority* to do, what he has not the *right* to do as to his partners. This is the rule of agency, which we have before considered (p. 53, and note). Thus if several partners agree among themselves to attend each to a particular department of the business and no other, each binds the firm though he does an act outside of his department, but if any loss results to the firm from such act he is responsible to his partners.

3. Liability for Debts.—Every partner is liable for the whole indebtedness of the firm. This means that NOT ONLY THE COMMON PROPERTY BUT ALSO ALL THE PRIVATE-PROPERTY OF EACH PARTNER MAY BE TAKEN TO SATISFY THE DEBTS OF THE FIRM. This is so no matter what the arrangement between the parties is, and no matter how small an interest any one partner may have. This shows the danger of forming partnerships imprudently, and affords reason for the rule that no one can be made a partner against his will. A *secret* partner, i.e., a real partner but not known as such to the world, is responsible in the same way. He is an undisclosed principal (p. 52). He gets the profit : he must bear the loss.

4. Precedence of Claims.—A *failure* in business means inability to pay debts. When a firm fails the separate partners may perhaps have private debts also. In such case, if proper legal steps are taken, the private property of each partner may be reserved to pay his private debts, and the partnership property set apart to pay the partnership debts. When either class has been wholly paid, the surplus property is applied to the other class.*

5. Effect of Dissolution.—We have considered in the last chapter the effect of a dissolution of the firm as between the partners. Let us now consider its effect as to third parties ; (1) as to the debts owed by the firm, and (2) as to the authority of the partners.

6. As to Debts, a dissolution makes no change. All the old partners remain responsible for all the debts existing at the time. Thus when one partner retires and is bought out (as is said) by the rest, they may agree to assume all the responsibility themselves, but if they fail to pay the old debts he must do so. No debtor can rid himself of a debt unless the creditor consents.

7. As to Authority, dissolution makes a great change. The authority of each to act for the firm continues, but only for the purpose of winding up the affairs. He cannot bind the firm in any new transaction. Thus if it be a firm

---

* Thus, suppose the firm of A & B fails, owing $60,000, and having $30,000 partnership property ; suppose A alone owes besides $10,000, and has $5000, while B alone owes $5000 and has $10,000. The firm property is applied to the firm debts and pays half, leaving $30,000 unpaid. A's private property pays half his private debts leaving $5000 unpaid. B's $10,000 pays the whole of his private debts and $5000 is left to be applied to the remaining $30,000 firm debts. The net result would be that each would owe $25,000 of firm debts, and A would owe besides $5000. But suppose that instead of $10,000 B had had $50,000, all the rest being the same. This would first be applied to his private debts, leaving $45,000 to be applied to the remaining $30,000 of partnership debts, which it would entirely pay and still leave $15,000 his. The result would then be that A would owe $5000, but B would owe nothing and have $15,000 left.

Note to Teacher.—It would be useful to vary this example in different ways, and have the scholar calculate in each case the percentage paid.

of merchants each may sell the stock on hand but cannot buy new goods. Each has power to collect money due the firm, and pay its debts, but cannot incur new ones. This section, however, applies chiefly to a case where the business ceases and all the affairs of the firm are wound up ; if a new firm is formed and takes the whole business the partners of the old firm who do not remain have no authority.

8. Notice of Dissolution.—But, as we have seen, in many cases of dissolution a new firm takes the business, and immediately makes new contracts and incurs new debts. Such changes often occur without the knowledge of outsiders, who perhaps act upon the belief that the firm is the same. For this reason UPON A DISSOLUTION THE OLD PARTNERS ARE RESPONSIBLE FOR EVEN NEW DEBTS UNLESS THEY HAVE GIVEN NOTICE OF THE DISSOLUTION. This rule is especially important with regard to retiring partners. The notice required would be, as to those who usually dealt with the firm, some actual notice, but as to the rest of the world a publication in some newspaper would be sufficient.

9. Limited Partnerships.—The fact that when a person fails in business all his property may be taken, has somewhat hampered trade, and for this reason has led to laws in many States by which, if certain things are done, partnerships may be formed in which there may be some partners whose private property shall not be responsible for the firm debts. They are called *limited partnerships.* *General* partners are those liable as in the other kind; *special* partners are those putting in a certain amount of money at the beginning, and losing only that amount if a failure occurs. The things required in most States for the formation of limited partnerships are: (1) the arrangement must be in writing, signed and recorded in a certain public office, (2) there must be at least one general partner, (3) the special partners can take no active part in the business, and their names must not appear in the firm name, (4) the amount they contribute must be actually paid in as stated. If any one of these requirements is neglected, although accidentally, the partnership becomes one of the ordinary kind.

SUMMARY OF LEADING RULES OF PARTNERSHIP.

I. RELATIONS OF PARTNERS TO EACH OTHER.

1. Sharing of PROFITS is the most important of the elements going to make up a partnership.

2. A partnership is FORMED simply and only by agreement.

3. Where no time is specified, any partner may DISSOLVE a partnership at will.

4. The real effect of a TRANSFER of interest is the dissolution of the firm.

5. The DEATH of any partner dissolves the whole firm.

II. RELATIONS OF PARTNERS TO THIRD PARTIES.

1. Each partner has full AUTHORITY to act for the firm.

2. Not only the common property, but also all the PRIVATE PROPERTY of each partner, may be taken to satisfy the debts of the firm.

3. Upon a dissolution the old partners are responsible for even new debts, unless they have given NOTICE OF the DISSOLUTION.

A PARTNERSHIP

I. Is FORMED

I. By EXPRESS AGREEMENT,
    1. To contribute property, labor, or skill, and
    2. To share profits.
II. By IMPLIED AGREEMENT, implied from
    1. Contributing property, labor, or skill, and
    2. Sharing profits.

II. Is DISSOLVED

I. When formed for a definite time:
    1. By CONSENT of all parties,
    2. By EXPIRATION of time,
    3. By a COURT for good cause,
    4. By DEATH of a partner, or
    5. By TRANSFER of a partner's interest.
II. When no time is specified:
    1. By any partner AT WILL,
    2. By DEATH of a partner, or
    3. By TRANSFER of a partner's interest.

DIVISION IV.

CORPORATIONS: GUARANTY: TIME TO SUE.

CHAPTER XV.

BUSINESS CORPORATIONS.

1. A Corporation is a fictitious person.   It consists of a number of natural persons, treated under the law as a new and distinct individual.   These persons are, in business corporations, the stockholders.

A corporation (often called *company*) does not consist of the property it owns.   Thus "The New York and New Haven Railroad Company" would be one thing, and "The New York and New Haven Railroad" another.   The company may lose its railroad and yet exist.   Nor is a corporation a partnership.   In partnership the word "firm" is but a convenient name for all the partners taken collectively, just as the word "family" means the father, mother, brothers, etc., but a corporation is a different individual from its stockholders.   When a firm owns property each partner owns it jointly with the rest, but stockholders do not own the property of a corporation; the corporation owns it.

2. Subject to Laws.—Corporations are now very common, and are organized to carry on all kinds of business, such as railway transportation, insurance, banking, all kinds of manufacturing, mining, trading, etc.   All such companies are subject to all the laws, as other persons; must carry out their contracts; may sue and be sued in the courts; may own and transfer property, etc. In short, the rule is general that when the law says "person," it includes corporations as well as natural persons.

3. Formation.—CORPORATIONS ARE FORMED ONLY BY AN ACT OF THE LEGISLATURE. A number of persons cannot come together and make themselves a company, as they would a firm, by simply agreeing that they shall be. There are two ways in which they are formed: (1) by a special law (called a *charter*) enacting that certain persons (naming them) shall be a corporation, having a certain name and certain corporate powers, (2) by a general law providing that any body of men may organize a corporation of a certain character by doing certain things. Business corporations are more commonly organized in the latter way. The necessary acts are: (1) for the parties to make and sign, and file in some public office, a paper (often called *articles of association*) showing the name, location, and business of the proposed company, and (2) to subscribe a certain amount of money or property, which is to become the property of the corporation and to be used for its purposes, and (3) to elect officers and do certain other acts.

4. Stock.—The money or property so subscribed is called the company's *stock*, or *capital*, or *capital stock*. The persons subscribing (i.e., contributing) to the stock are called *stockholders*. The capital is divided into a number of shares, and each stockholder is given a certificate showing how many shares his interest amounts to. He is then said to own those shares.* He may sell them to any one

---

* Thus suppose they value the whole capital at $100,000, and divide it into 1000 shares. $100 is called the *par value* of a share. A. who has contributed $35,000 in money or property, receives a certificate showing that he owns 350 shares.

else, who thereupon becomes a stockholder in his place. Thus the members of a corporation may continually change, but the corporation remains the same all the time. (See p. 286 for form of certificate.)

5. How Managed.—A corporation acts by agents. The stockholders meet annually and elect from among their own number a body of men called *directors* or *trustees* (from 3 to 25), who have charge of the general management of the business. The directors also have regular meetings (monthly or otherwise) at which they decide upon the more important matters connected with the business of the company. Besides these, other officers, viz., a president, secretary, treasurer, etc., are elected by the stockholders, or sometimes by the directors, and they, with the other clerks and agents, carry on the ordinary every-day business of the corporation. If a stockholder thinks any of these officers have acted unlawfully and to the injury of the company, he may have the matter reviewed by a court.

6. Powers.—We have seen that a natural person may do anything not expressly forbidden by law (p. 18). With corporations—they being fictitious persons and having no natural rights—the rule is directly the opposite; viz., CORPORATIONS HAVE POWER TO DO ONLY THE ACTS EXPRESSLY ALLOWED BY THE LAW UNDER WHICH THEY ARE INCORPORATED. Therefore they cannot make all kinds of contracts, and it is important to study the special or general law under which a corporation was organized, when it is desired to ascertain exactly what it can do. The powers ordinarily granted them are all the powers usual or necessary in carrying on the business for which they were organized. Within its business a corporation may do all acts, and make all contracts, that a natural person could, but none outside of that business. Thus a corporation cannot buy more real estate than is necessary to its business.

7. Dissolution.—Though some corporations may and do last forever, others are formed for a limited time. The ordinary methods in which one is dissolved are: (1) if formed for a limited time, by its expiration, (2) by the voluntary surrender of its rights to the State, (3) in some cases by a law passed by the Legislature which created it, (4) by becoming insolvent, unable to pay its debts.

> *Note to Teacher.*—Interesting and useful historical references could here be made upon the subject of old corporations, to such as the Bank of England, the East India Company, Yale College, Harvard College, etc., etc.

8. Effect of Dissolution.—On dissolution all the remaining property of the corporation is placed in the hands of a responsible person, called a *receiver*, who sells it and distributes the proceeds among the creditors, in proportion to their debts, and if there is any left, distributes it among the stockholders.

9. Liability of Stockholders.—The debts are the debts of the corporation, not of the stockholders. A partner, we have seen (p. 64), is personally liable for all the debts of the firm, but it is at this point the strongest distinction lies between a partner and a stockholder. The rule at one time was that the stockholder was not responsible to any amount, and this is now the rule in the absence of some special provision. But this came to be used as a means of fraud, so that now stockholders of many business corporations are often made responsible to a limited amount. Thus, if one owns a certain amount of stock, he is often made responsible for an equal amount of the debts.

10. Purposes.—The chief purposes of corporations are three, the first being to the advantage of the public, and the other two to private advantage. (1) They are, at least a convenient if not a necessary, means for the carrying out of great business enterprises, such as the building of railroads, canals, etc. People would and could not come together in partnerships large enough or enduring enough for such purposes. (2) They allow of an easy transfer of ownership, while in partnership a transfer dissolves the firm. (3) The responsibility for debts is very much less.

Note to Teacher.—The first of these purposes should be illustrated by reference to real cases, showing why partnerships would be impracticable in cases of railroad enterprises, etc.

CHIEF DIFFERENCES BETWEEN A PARTNERSHIP AND A CORPORATION.

	PARTNERSHIP.	CORPORATION.
I. LEGAL CHARACTER:	A collection of natural persons.	A fictitious person.
II. FORMATION:	By agreement.	By the Legislature.
III. DEATH:	Of partner; dissolves partnership.	Of stockholder; those obtaining his stock become stockholders.
IV. TRANSFER OF INTEREST:	By partner; dissolves partnership.	By stockholder; new stockholder takes his place.
V. POWERS:	Has powers of the natural persons composing it.	Has only the powers especially conferred by law.
VI. DEBTS:	All partners liable for all debts.	In some, stockholders not liable; in others, liable to a limited amount.

CHAPTER XVI.

GUARANTY OR SURETYSHIP.

1. Definition.—A *guaranty* has been defined (p. 37). *Suretyship* is another word for the same relation.* A *guarantor* or *surety* is one who agrees that a certain thing shall be done by another. This relation is quite common in business life. Thus, it is often made the condition of a loan, or a sale, that payment shall be guaranteed by some one besides the debtor. Clerks in a bank and others in positions of trust, especially where employed to handle money, are often required beforehand to give *bonds of indemnity,* as they are called. Such a bond is a contract made by some friend of the person employed, agreeing to make good any loss caused by him (p. 286, for form). The indorser of a note is a surety (p. 133).

2. The Principal is the person for whom the guaranty is given; in other words, the *principal debtor.* A contract of guaranty implies the existence of some other contract made, or duty owed, by the principal. This may be called the *primary* contract, the guaranty being the *secondary* contract. Thus, in the case of a sale, the *primary* contract is the sale, and is between the seller and buyer; the *secondary* contract is between the seller and surety: in the case of the clerk, the *primary* contract is the employment, and is between the employer and clerk; the *secondary* contract is between the employer and surety.

3. Consideration.—A guaranty, being a contract, must have a consideration to be binding. If it is made at the

---

* In a popular, though not in a legal sense. We shall use them in the same sense here.

same time as the primary contract, the same consideration will support both. Thus if the loan or sale are made *on condition* that the guaranty be given, that is consideration (p. 33, sec. 3). But if the secondary contract is made after the primary, and not in pursuance of an agreement made with the primary, then there must be some new consideration. Thus, if the bond of indemnity was not required or given until after the hiring, it must have some additional consideration, as, for instance, something paid to the surety.*

4. Writing.—We have already seen that EVERY CONTRACT OF GUARANTY MUST BE IN WRITING AND SIGNED BY THE SURETY (p. 37).

5. Change of Primary Liability MAKES THE SECONDARY VOID. In other words, if I loan money to you on B's guaranty, and then afterwards release you, that also releases him. Any change in the primary contract makes the secondary invalid. Thus, if when a debt becomes due the time of payment is extended, as by taking a new note, this releases the surety unless done with his consent. But to merely delay suing the principal does not have this effect.

Note to Teacher.—This should be dwelt upon in connection with in- dorsed notes, as it is a common business operation to grant exten- sions, by taking new notes. If this is done without the consent of the indorsers, they are released.

6. Notice to Surety.—If the guaranteed debt is not paid when due, the creditor is under no obligation to the surety to sue the principal. He must, however, give notice to the surety as soon as he can. Thus, if the cashier of a bank steals its money, his bondsmen must be notified of it, or they are not bound. In the case of indorsers upon commercial paper the time within which this notice must be

---

* If, however, the bond itself says that there was a consideration, it cannot denied.

sent is fixed, being a day (p. 137). But in other cases of guaranty a longer time is allowed, though there is no fixed period. A week's delay might release the surety. The object of requiring this notice is that the surety may take such measures immediately as he sees fit, to secure himself against loss.

7. Surety's Right.—WHEN A SURETY HAS PAID THE DEBT, HE HAS A CLAIM FOR IT UPON THE PRINCIPAL DEBTOR. It is as if the creditor's claim were transferred to him. So, also, if the creditor holds any other security for the debt, such as stock, or bonds, these pass to the surety when he pays the debt. He stands, as we say, in the creditor's shoes.

8. Two or More Sureties.—If there is more than one surety upon any debt, all becoming sureties at the same time, each one is responsible for the whole, but if any one pays it, he may collect an equal share out of the others. Thus, suppose on the debt of B to A there are three sureties, C, D, and E. If B does not pay it A may claim it all from C, D, or E, but if D should pay it he might claim from C and E each one-third of what he paid. This section does not apply to indorsers, because usually they do not indorse at the same time. but successively (Chap. XXV., sec. 3, 6).

CHAPTER XVII.

LIMITATION OF TIME TO SUE.

1. Limitation.—In the chapter on Remedy we have seen that the remedy is obtained by applying to a court for it, i.e., suing. This the injured party may do as soon as the wrongful act has been committed, sometimes, as in cases of injunction, before it has been done, and when merely threatened. Thus in an ordinary contract to pay money, as a note, if it is not paid on the day when due, the contract is broken, and suit may be commenced the next day. But in every case and in every State the right to sue lasts only for a time, generally a few years. One may not reserve the right forever.

2. The Reason for this is two-fold: (1) old and stale claims are more likely to be ill-founded, for if the claim was just we may suppose some attempt would have been made to enforce it; (2) it is considered best that a person should not be troubled with an old claim, whether just or unjust, because he has been led to believe that it would not be pressed.

3. The Time within which suit must be commenced varies in different classes of cases from one to twenty years, and differs in different States. Each State fixes its own rule. FOR ORDINARY BUSINESS CONTRACTS THE TIME ALLOWED TO COMMENCE SUIT USUALLY IS FIVE OR SIX YEARS. Many States make six years the limit for oral contracts, but allow a longer time, ten to twenty years, on written contracts. The reason is that spoken words are more likely to be forgotten than written words. Other States allow the longer period only on contracts having a seal attached; because in former times a paper having a seal was considered a more formal and solemn instrument, and therefore there was less likelihood of mistake about it. After the time has expired the debt is popularly said to be *outlawed,* and cannot be enforced.

4. Change of Ownership in the claim does not affect the time. Thus if one buys a claim, on which the time is six years, five years after it is due, he has but one year to commence suit. The time occupied by the suit is of no importance. If commenced within the six years (or other period) after it could be, it is sufficient, though the suit itself should take years.

5. Part-Payment.—The period of limitation ordinarily begins to run on the day when the debt is due. But if at any time, either before or after that period has expired, there is any part-payment of the debt made, that renews the claim and the period begins to run on that day.*

6. Subsequent Promise.—So also if the debtor at any time after it is due makes a written promise to pay the debt, or a written acknowledgment of its existence in such form as to be equivalent to a promise, the claim is renewed and the period begins to run from that time. The reason why a part-payment, or subsequent promise, or acknowledgment thus extends the time is this: the object of the limitation is to prevent suits on uncertain claims, but any one of those three circumstances is clear evidence from the party himself that the claim is not uncertain. It amounts to a new promise (i.e., contract), and the creditor should have the full time to enforce the new contract.

7. Bank-Bills, issued and used as money, are an exception to the foregoing rules. They never became invalid from lapse of time.

---

* Thus suppose a note due on January 6, 1870, and not paid; the creditor may sue upon it any time between January 7, 1870, and January 7, 1876; suppose $10 paid upon it either as interest or principal (p.179), on April 24, 1875; the time would then expire April 24, 1881; if the payment was made after the time had expired, as for instance, March 5, 1877, it would revive the claim and the time would not expire again until March 5, 1883.

SUMMARY OF LEADING RULES.

I. CORPORATIONS.

1. Corporations are FORMED only by an act of the Legislature.

2. Corporations have POWER to do only the acts expressly allowed by the law under which they are incorporated.

II. GUARANTY.

1. Every contract of guaranty must be IN WRITING and signed by the surety.

2. CHANGE of primary liability renders the secondary void.

3. When a SURETY HAS PAID the debt he has a claim for it upon the principal debtor.

III. LIMITATION OF TIME.

1. For ordinary business contracts the time allowed to commence suit usually is FIVE OR SIX YEARS.

REVIEW QUESTIONS.

Agency.

1. What is meant by agency? Define principal. Define agent.
2. How many persons are concerned in an act of agency? State the different relations arising.
3. State the rule as to what contracts one may make through an agent. May minors act as agents?
4. How may agents be appointed? What is a power of attorney?
5. Where an agent is appointed or employed to do, a particular thing, has he authority to do anything else? What is his power, when employed for a general class of duties?
6. May the principal take away an agent's authority? When? What would be the effect of putting an end to an agency when by so doing the principal broke his contract with the agent? What is the effect of the death of the principal?
7. What is a sub-agent?
8. What is the principal's duty to his agent?
9. Is one party ever responsible for the acts of another?
10. What is the fundamental rule of agency? Explain the difference between a principal's duty to his agent and to the third party.
11. If one who is really acting as agent for some one else, causes or allows the third party to believe he is acting for himself, is the principal responsible for his acts? Why? State the rule as to the responsibility of an unknown principal.
12. What is the effect of an agent's doing an act which he was not authorized to do? Whose act is it?
13. Can an agent give himself authority? What effect has his saying that he has authority?
14. Give examples of an agent's appearing to have authority which he really has not. In such case is the principal bound by the act? Why? State the difference between the authority and the right of an agent to do an act.
15. What is ratification, in agency? Its effect? Its effect when made under a mistake as to the circumstances? How made?
16. What in general is the agent's duty to his principal? Name and illustrate the three implied duties.

17. If one buys goods as the agent of another is the agent responsible for payment? State the general rule of which that is an example. Its reason. Its five exceptions and the reason for each.
18. What are public agents? Are they personally responsible for contracts they had no authority to make?
19. What is the difference (if any) in the duties and responsibilities assumed by a person when he acts with the principal, and when he acts with the agent?
20. State the cases in which both agent and principal are responsible to the third party for an act of the agent. Those in which the agent alone is responsible. Those in which the principal alone is responsible.
21. Where both agent and principal are responsible, how do we determine which must finally bear the loss?

Partnership.

22. What is partnership? How is a firm formed? Will an agreement to share profits alone make a partnership?
23. Who may become partners? Can a majority of the partners introduce a new member without the consent of the rest? If there were ten partners, could nine do so? Why?
24. How long does a partnership last? If no time is specified may any partner dissolve it when he chooses?
25. What is the effect of a transfer by one partner of his interest in a firm to some one else? Does that person become a partner?
26. What is the effect of the death of a partner?
27. What becomes of the firm's property on dissolution? State a common way in which the business continues though a firm is dissolved.
28. What rights and duties have partners as to each other?
29. State the difference between the right and the authority of a partner.
30. How far does his authority extend?
31. State the rule as to the responsibility of a partner for the debts of the firm. Can a partner's private property be taken from him to pay the firm's debts?
32. What is a secret partner? Is he responsible for firm debts?
33. In a case of failure, where there are firm debts and firm property, and the separate partners also have separate debts and

private property, state the way in which the property is applied to pay the debts.

34. What is the effect of dissolution upon a partner's responsibility for the debts? In what cases, and for what purpose is a notice of dissolution necessary? How is it given?
35. What authority has each partner in winding up the business?
36. What is a limited partnership? How formed? What is a special partner?
37. Enumerate the different ways in which a partnership is dissolved.

Corporations.

38. What is a corporation? State the difference in character between a partnership and a corporation.
39. How formed? State two ways.
40. What is stock? A stockholder? May a stockholder sell his shares without the consent of the other stockholders? What is the effect of his so doing?
41. By whom are the every-day business affairs of a corporation conducted? By whom are the important affairs?
42. Have corporations all the powers to contract of a natural person? By what are their powers regulated? What in general are their powers?
43. When is a corporation dissolved? What becomes of its property on dissolution?
44. Are stockholders ever responsible for the debts of a corporation?
45. Why are corporations formed? State three reasons.
46. State the difference between a partnership and a corporation, as to, (1) legal character; (2) manner of formation; (3) death of partner or stockholder; (4) transfer of interest; (5) powers; and (6) debts.

Guaranty.

47. What is a guaranty? A principal? A surety?
48. Explain the primary and secondary contracts. Which of them is the guaranty? When is one consideration enough for both contracts?
49. Is an oral guaranty binding?
50. What is the effect upon the secondary contract of changing the primary?

51. State the rule as to notifying a surety.
52. What right has a surety who pays a guaranteed debt?
53. When there are two or more sureties what are their respective rights?

Time to Sue.

54. What is it to sue? Can one sue for a debt before it is due? What is the first day suit can be brought?
55. How long may one reserve the right to sue, in ordinary commercial cases? Why not forever?
56. What two circumstances will extend the time? How long will they extend it?
57. Name a kind of contract not subject to the rule of limitation.

PART II.

Principles of Particular Cases.

DIVISION I.

Sale of Goods.

CHAPTER XVIII.

REQUISITES OF A SALE.

1. A Sale is AN AGREEMENT TO EXCHANGE PROPERTY FOR MONEY. In other words it is an agreement by the owner of certain property with another that the property shall thereafter belong to the latter, and that he shall pay for it. It is a change of the ownership (often called the *title*) for money.

Possession is not the same as ownership. One may own what he has no right to possess, or he may have the right to possess what he does not own (p. 93. sec. 3). We also see that an agreement to sell at some future time is not a sale. Thus if A makes a sale to B, the property becomes B's instantly, and A is simply entitled to the price; but if A agrees to sell to B next month, it remains A's meanwhile, and if during that time he should make an actual sale of the same property to C, it would become C's, though A would have to answer to B for the breach of his contract.*

---

* A *sale* is an executed contract, an agreement as to the present, an agreement that the ownership *does* change: an *agreement to sell* is a promise, an agreement as to the future, an agreement that the ownership *shall* change.

2. When Sale is Complete.—The sale is complete as soon as the agreement is made. If there is a sale, the owner-ship changes immediately, and if there is an agreement that the ownership does change immediately there is a sale. This is so whether the goods are delivered or not, or whether the price is paid or not. Delivery and payment are not, in general, necessary to make the sale complete. In the ordinary case, when the parties come to an agreement but nothing is said about when the price shall be paid, or when the goods shall be delivered, the ownership changes immediately, though the seller has the right to keep them until he is paid.

3. Conditional Sale.—But the parties if they choose may agree that the goods shall not become the buyer's until certain things are done, as, for example, until they are paid for, or until they are delivered. So they may make any other condition. The result would be that such an agreement would not be a sale but only in the nature of an agreement to sell. The property would belong to the seller until the condition was performed.

4. The Importance of knowing the point of time when the ownership changes, i.e., of knowing whether an agreement is for a present or a future sale, is not very great if the whole agreement is carried out, the goods delivered and the price paid; but it is sometimes great if the agreement cannot be carried out. Thus suppose the property is meanwhile destroyed by fire. The owner at the time must bear the loss, no matter who possesses them. If it was a sale the buyer must nevertheless pay for them: if it was only an agreement for a future sale he need not pay, because the seller cannot carry out his part of the agreement.

5. The Requisites.—In defining a sale we have already really explained what is necessary to constitute one. But sales form so important a part of commerce that it will be well to state more fully what has been already implied. We may say that five things are necessary to every sale: (1) that the agreement should be binding, (2) that the property exist, (3) that it be owned by the seller, (4) that the agreement should be with regard to some particular property, or some particular property should be set apart as the property sold, and (5), that the consideration should be money. An agreement to sell only requires the first and the last, a sale all of the five.

6. A Binding Agreement.—In Chapter II. have been enumerated the seven requisites of a binding contract, and we need not dwell on them here. BEING A CONTRACT, A SALE MUST HAVE ALL THE REQUISITES OF A BINDING CONTRACT. Let us apply each one of those requisites in turn to the subject of a sale.

The sale of any kind of thing is possible in its nature, and we have seen that most commercial sales are legal (p. 21, and Chap. III.). Chapter IV. shows that all persons can sell or buy except minors, lunatics, idiots, and married women, and even they under certain circumstances. There must be assent; i.e., there can be no selling without a buying, no sale without a purchaser (Chap. V.). The consideration is the agreement made by the buyer to pay for what he buys (Chap. VI.; see also p. 91, sec. 12). Fraud in any part of the transaction gives the defrauded party his option to treat it as a sale or not as he sees fit (Chap. VII.). Finally, if the price be over a certain amount there must be either (1) a writing, or (2) a delivery and acceptance of part, or (3) part-payment (Chap. VIII.).

7. Existence.—PROPERTY TO BE SOLD MUST BE IN EXISTENCE. Thus, if A sells a horse to B, and, unknown to either, the horse had died before the sale, even though only a moment before, the whole contract would be null. If B had paid the price he must receive it back. But one may agree to buy or sell what is not now in existence, such as the fruit to grow on certain trees, or certain articles to be manufactured. Suppose an article to be manufactured should be paid for in advance, and then should be lost or destroyed before it was quite finished: the manufacturer would have to bear the loss, because it was still his, and the buyer would be entitled to another article or to receive back the money he had advanced.

8. Sale without Ownership.—If one attempts to sell what he does not own there is no sale; i.e., no one can claim a thing because he bought and paid for it, unless he bought it from the owner. THE TRUE OWNER OF PROPERTY CAN CLAIM IT AT ANY TIME, AND IN WHOSEVER HANDS HE FINDS IT. This rule becomes important when stolen or found property is sold in the market. It makes no difference that the article is delivered, or that both parties believe that the seller is the owner, or how many hands it has passed through since it left the real owner's possession. Buyers therefore must always take this risk, for it is unjust that the true owner should be deprived of his property without his fault or consent.*

9. Exception.—The rule of the preceding section applies to all kinds of property, with two very important exceptions, viz., *money* and *negotiable securities payable to bearer.†* WHOEVER OBTAINS MONEY OR NEGOTIABLE SECURITIES PAYABLE TO BEARER (1) BEFORE THEY BECOME DUE, AND (2) GIVES SOMETHING IN CONSIDERATION, AND

---

* But one may agree to sell what he does not own. A sale, payment to be made on delivery, is a conditional sale.

† For the kinds of *money* see p. 145. *Negotiable securities* include promissory notes, drafts, bills of exchange, checks, bonds of the National and State Governments, of cities, towns, etc., of railroads and other corporations, and some other securities. They only have the quality described in sec. 9 when made payable to the bearer. See also pp. 107–111 for meaning of *negotiable* and *payable to bearer.*

(3) HAS NO REASON TO SUSPECT THAT THE ONE FROM WHOM HE OBTAINS THEM HAS NOT THE FULL RIGHT TO TRANSFER THEM, OBTAINS THE SAME RIGHT TO THEM THAT HE WOULD IF THE OTHER PARTY WERE THE REAL OWNER. In other words, possession in this case is sufficient evidence of ownership. The buyer can buy from one not an owner. The reason for this exception is the benefit of trade. Money and commercial securities are passing daily from hand to hand, and are of great convenience. If, whenever any were offered to a person, he was obliged to stop and learn whether the party had the right to sell, it would greatly limit trade. But under any other conditions than the three stated the buyer does not deserve to be protected.

10. Illustrations.—If a thief steals a watch and sells it to a jeweler or pawns it to a pawnbroker, the true owner is entitled to it without reimbursing the jeweler or the pawnbroker, even though they were ignorant of the theft. But where a thief spends stolen money or sells a stolen bond payable to bearer, the one receiving them may keep them and the original owner must suffer the loss. If, however, a thief gave stolen money to a friend, the latter could not keep it. If a security were overdue, no one could deprive the true owner of it. If a banker buying such securities had reason to suspect they were stolen, the true owner could take them without reimbursing him. Thus, if a bond should be offered to him for $40 which he knew was worth $70 in the market, this would be so suspicious a circumstance that he would not be protected in buying it.

Note to Teacher.—These illustrations could profitably be multiplied to almost any extent. Cases, such as might arise, with differing circumstances, might be supposed and the scholar required to tell to whom the property should belong and upon whom the loss in each case must fall.

11. Particular Property.—A sale must refer to particular property (*that* house, or *those* goods), or it is only an agreement to sell or buy. Thus, if 1 order five pieces of cloth, the cloth does not become mine until the particular five pieces have been selected. THE SALE IS NOT COMPLETE UNLESS PARTICULAR PROPERTY IS REFERRED TO, OR SET APART. If no particular property is designated the contract is an agreement to sell.

12. **Price.**—AN AGREEMENT TO PAY MONEY IS A NECESSARY ELEMENT OF A SALE.* The exchange of certain property for other property is *barter*, and is not subject to the rules of a sale. But it is not necessary that a price should be agreed upon, for IN EVERY SALE WHERE THE PRICE IS NOT FIXED THERE IS AN IMPLIED AGREEMENT THAT THE BUYER SHALL PAY WHAT THE GOODS ARE REASONABLY WORTH. When nothing is said as to the time of payment, payment is due immediately. If the agreement is that it shall be paid for at some future time, the sale is said to be *on credit.*

13. **Sale of Debts.**—Like other property a claim upon a debtor may be sold by a creditor. Thus if A owes B $50, B may sell the debt to C. C should then give notice of the sale to A, for if A, before receiving such notice, should pay B and B should receive it, the debt would be discharged. A claim thus sold is subject to the same conditions in the hands of a purchaser as in the hands of the seller. Thus, if A owes B $50 for money borrowed, and B owes A $50 for services rendered, they could be set off against each other; and if C should buy one of the claims he would get nothing. But if the debt is represented by a note, draft, or other negotiable paper, it may sometimes be sold without being subject to the same conditions. This will be explained later (pp. 108–117 and p. 131).

---

* Though, as we have seen (sec. 2), the payment itself is not essential to make the goods the property of the buyer.

REQUISITES OF

I. A SALE;

I. That it be a BINDING CONTRACT; to this the following are necessary, viz.,
    I. If price is under a certain amount;
        a. The first six requisites of a binding contract. (See Chap. II.)
    II. If over that amount;
        a. The first six requisites of a binding contract, and
        b. The seventh requisite, viz., either
            1. A writing,
            2. Delivery and acceptance of part, or
            3. Part-payment.
II. That the property EXIST;
III. That it be OWNED BY SELLER;
    except in case of
    1. MONEY, and
    2. NEGOTIABLE SECURITIES PAYABLE TO BEARER.
IV. That it contemplate PARTICULAR PROPERTY;
V. That the consideration be MONEY.

II. AN AGREEMENT TO SELL;

I. That it be a BINDING CONTRACT; to this the following are necessary, viz.,
    I. If price is under a certain amount,
        a. The first six requisites.
    II. If over that amount;
        a. The first six requisites, and
        b. The seventh, viz., either
            1. A writing,
            2. Delivery and acceptance of part, or
            3. Part-payment.
II. That the consideration be MONEY.

CHAPTER XIX.

INCIDENTS OF A SALE.

1. Incidents. — We have considered in the preceding chapter the things essential to a sale, i.e., a change of ownership; we will now consider those incidental, i.e., those which usually or often accompany a sale of goods.

2. Delivery IS NOT ESSENTIAL TO A SALE, AS BETWEEN THE PARTIES, BUT IT IS AS TO THIRD PARTIES. In other words, the property becomes the buyer's, in general, whether it is delivered to him or not, but if on account of its not being delivered to him others are led to believe it still belongs to the seller it will be so considered. As to them the non-delivery is fraud. Thus suppose A should sell to **B**, but keep the goods, and then pretending they were his should sell them to C: if now B could claim them as his C would be defrauded. Therefore the first sale is void and the second one valid. A, however, must answer to B, if B is defrauded.

3. Seller's Lien. — In an ordinary sale, where there is nothing said as to when payment or delivery is to be made, the parties are supposed to contemplate that both shall be immediate. A BUYER HAS THE RIGHT TO TAKE THE GOODS WHEN HE PAYS FOR THEM BUT NOT UNTIL THEN. This right of the seller to keep the goods until paid is called his *lien* (pronounced lee'-en). But the right is lost as soon as he delivers them. When, however, the sale is on credit, there is no such right, for such a sale implies that the buyer is to have the goods immediately and be trusted for the price. Parties may make any agreement they choose, and it is very common for merchants to surrender this lien, by delivering the goods without payment. They can then only sue for the price.

4. What is Delivery.—As may be inferred from the last two sections, it is sometimes quite important to know just the point of time when an article can be considered delivered. It is delivered legally the moment it comes under the buyer's control, or the control of his agent, but not until then. Thus if a merchant sends his own carman after goods he has bought, delivery to the carman is delivery to the merchant. So if one orders goods from a distance, to be sent by railroad, he makes the railroad company his agent to receive them and delivery to it is delivery to him. Sometimes an act symbolical of delivery is enough, as where one delivers to another the key of a room where goods are stored, with the understanding that they shall be considered as delivered.*

5. Right of Stoppage.—We have seen that when a merchant has sent goods by railroad to a customer, they are delivered and he has lost his right to keep them until paid. If now the buyer should fail before they reached him still they would be his even although while they were on the way both parties knew he would be unable to pay for them. This seems a harsh rule and therefore there is this exception: IF BEFORE GOODS SOLD ON CREDIT REACH THE BUYER THE SELLER HEARS OF HIS FAILURE AND ORDERS THE CARRIER † NOT TO DELIVER THEM, THE SELLER MAY RETAKE THEM AND HOLD THEM UNTIL PAID. This is in effect an extension of the seller's lien.

---

* Throughout this chapter we use the word "deliver" in the legal sense of "give up the possession of." It sometimes has the popular meaning of sending to the house or store of the buyer. In this sense there is no obligation on the seller to deliver unless he agrees to. A buyer must take away his own property.

† See p. 159 for meaning of *carrier*.

6. Warranty of Ownership.—IN EVERY SALE OF PER-SONAL PROPERTY THERE IS AN IMPLIED WARRANTY OF OWNERSHIP. This means that if one sells as his own, what afterwards turns out to be another's, he impliedly agrees to reimburse the buyer if the real owner recovers his property. (See p. 89, sec. 8.) This is so whether anything is said upon the subject or not. Thus in the illustration on page 90, if the true owner of the watch recovers it from the jeweler, the latter has a claim upon the thief. If I, holding goods as a pledge, give them to a broker to sell, and he sells them to you as my own, and the true owner takes them from you, I must pay you your loss.

> *Note to Teacher.*—The relations of this rule to the one on p. 89, sec. 8, should be carefully marked. This applies to all kinds of personal property, negotiable or otherwise.

7. Warranty of Quality.—If on a sale the seller warrants (or *guarantees*) * that the article is of a certain quality or is suited to a certain purpose, and it turns out differently, he must suffer the loss, for it was his agreement. BUT IF THERE WAS NO EXPRESS AGREEMENT AS TO QUALITY OR FITNESS, THE BUYER MUST TAKE THE RISK, for none is implied. He must keep the goods, and suffer the loss if there is any. He has the opportunity to examine the article, and may refuse to buy unless the seller will expressly warrant.

But the rule does not apply where the buyer has no opportunity to inspect the articles before buying. Thus in a sale where he only sees a sample, or where the goods are to arrive by vessel, and are still at sea, there is always an implied warranty that they will be like the sample, or as represented. Nor does the rule apply so as to protect one from the consequences of his own fraud.

---

* *Guarantee* is perhaps more commonly used than *warrant* in this sense. But it should be distinguished from the sense of answering for *another* (p. 76). Here he answers for *himself*, or his own goods.

CHAPTER XX.

COMMISSION MERCHANTS.

1. Definition.—A *commission merchant* (also called a *factor*) is one employed to sell for another the goods sent him by the other for sale, and which are often manufactured or raised by the latter. Farmers and manufacturers who have large quantities of material to sell in the market, find it best to send it to the cities, to the commission merchants who sell it for them, and charge for the service a percentage on the price (called a *commission*). Therefore COMMISSION MERCHANTS ARE AGENTS TO SELL, and the owners of the goods are their principals. Their duties, powers and responsibilities are in general like those of any agents (Chaps. X., XI., XII.), and we will therefore only speak of a few rules which are peculiar to the relation.*

2. Duties.—As between a commission merchant and his principal, the whole matter is one entirely of contract, the contract being one for personal services (Chap. XXVIII.). His great duty is to sell the goods for the best price he can get, and pay over the money, when collected, deducting his commission. In doing this he must, like all agents, obey the instructions of his principal, conduct the business skillfully and carefully (e.g., not sell to one he knows cannot pay), render true accounts when called upon, and not make his own interests adverse to those of his principal (p. 54).

---

* Sometimes one acts as the agent of only one manufacturer, sometimes for a large number at the same time. Some also combine a commission business with a trade of their own, and sell some goods as principals and some as agents. We must always be careful to distinguish the character in which a person acts.

3. Powers.—These are also such as are agreed upon, but very often there is no special arrangement, and the commission merchant is left to conduct the business according to his own judgment, and in the way a commission business is usually conducted. In such case he has all the powers necessarily or usually exercised in the business. He may act according to the general custom of the trade, for any one employing him is presumed to know such custom (p. 32).

4. Responsibility to Principal.—He is responsible to his principal for any loss occasioned by his violating their agreement, or disobeying instructions, or acting negligently. If he was left to exercise his own judgment, as, for example, for what price, or when, or to whom he should sell, he is not responsible for any loss occasioned by his making a mistake, unless it was negligent or fraudulent. Thus if he has the right to sell on credit, and the buyer· fails to pay, the owner must lose, not the commission merchant.

5. His Commission.—A commission merchant is entitled to his commission when he has performed the service for which he was employed, i.e., in general when the sale has been made. If allowed to sell on credit he has performed *his* contract, though the buyer does not perform his, and *is* entitled to his commission, whether the buyer ever pays or not. But if he in any way breaks his contract, as by negligence or disobedience, he loses his claim to any commission on that transaction, no matter what he has done.

6. Guaranty Commission.—Sometimes it is made a part of the agreement between the commission merchant and the owner, that the former shall guarantee payment by the ones to whom he makes sales. In such case he is responsible to the owner, if the buyer does not pay. It is a contract of guaranty (Chap. XVI.). He has no different authority from that in the other case, but the commission charged is higher. That, however, is all a matter of agreement.

7. Advances.—It is quite common for the commission merchant to advance to the owner, before he has made any sale, some portion of what they think the goods are worth.* Then when the sale is made, these advances are deducted from the amount of the proceeds, and are retained by the commission merchant with his commission.

8. Lien.—Being an agent, his authority can be revoked at any time (p. 50, sec. 7), and then the owner will be entitled to take his goods away. But it can be seen that if the commission merchant has meanwhile incurred any expenses, or made any advances on the goods, the owner could, by taking the goods away, deprive him of his security ; therefore A COMMISSION MERCHANT HAS A RIGHT TO KEEP ANY GOODS OF HIS PRINCIPAL'S WHICH ARE IN HIS HANDS UNTIL HE HAS BEEN PAID ALL COMMISSIONS, ADVANCES, AND EXPENSES, DUE TO HIM FROM THE OWNER. This is called a *general* lien because he can keep any goods, whether the debt arose in connection with them or with others. Thus, if he earns a commission on one sale, and afterwards other goods are sent to him, he may retain them until paid the first commission.†

9. Relation to Buyer.—The relation and responsibility of a commission merchant to those purchasing from him, are the relation and responsibility of an agent to the third

---

* This is often done by draft (p. 117). The owner at the time he sends the goods to the commission merchant draws a draft on him, which the latter pays. This is called " drawing on the goods." It is in effect a way of lending money, and pledging the goods as security for the loan. It is not a sale to the commission merchant.

† This lien is a right existing only between him and the owner. If a sale is made, the buyer is of course entitled to the goods he buys.

party, which have been fully considered in Chapter XII. and need not be repeated here. Thus, if the owner is revealed to the buyer, the commission merchant assumes, in general, no responsibility himself; but if he says nothing about who owns the goods, or sells them as his own, acting as the principal, he assumes all the responsibilities of a principal.

CHAPTER XXI.

BROKERS.

1. Definition.—A *broker* is one employed by the owner of property in the negotiation of certain contracts with reference to it. A BROKER IS AN AGENT TO MAKE CONTRACTS. If the property is merchandise, and the contract he is employed to make is a sale, he is called a *merchandise broker.* This kind of a broker is much like a commission merchant, the difference being only that the former does not have possession of the property, while the latter does. A broker therefore has no lien on the property, for a lien is a right to *keep.**

2. Kinds.—Besides merchandise brokers there are many other kinds, and therefore the term "broker" is a broader and more indefinite term than "commission merchant." There are *bill and note brokers,* who buy and sell for others drafts, bills and notes; *real estate brokers,* who buy and sell real estate or mortgages on real estate, for others;

---

* When a merchandise broker sells goods, he makes out two papers, one for the seller and the other for the buyer, and delivers them to the respective parties. The two papers taken together make a written contract of sale (form 22).

stock brokers, who buy and sell for others the stock and bonds of States, railroads, etc.; *insurance brokers,* who act for the owners of property in obtaining insurance upon it, in settling losses, etc.; and several other kinds.

3. Responsibility to Principal.—The contract between the broker and the owner of the property for whom he acts is one of personal service, like all contracts of agency, and we need not here rehearse the general duties attending such a contract (p. 54). In order to understand all the duties assumed by a contract in brokerage, as well as in any kind of business, one must know all the general customs of that business, for unless the agreement makes particular specification of what is and is not to be done, those customs must be followed. They are in effect laws. This shows how necessary it is for any one to understand his business, for he may be assuming responsibilities that he has no idea of.

4. Relation to Third Party.—Here the rules of Chapter XII. are again applicable. Some kinds of brokers act wholly as agents and reveal the names of their principals, and therefore are not themselves responsible for any authorized and honest act : others do not mention their principals, and therefore are, so far as third parties are concerned, the real principals themselves. So also many combine a brokerage business with an individual business, but these rules only apply to them as brokers.

SUMMARY OF LEADING RULES OF SALE OF GOODS.

I. REQUISITES OF A SALE.

1. A SALE IS an agreement to exchange property for money.

2. Being a contract, a sale must have all the requisites of a BINDING CONTRACT.

3. Property, to be sold, must be IN EXISTENCE.

4. It must BELONG to the seller: the true owner of property can claim it at any time and in whosoever hands he finds it.

5. Except MONEY AND NEGOTIABLE SECURITIES payable to bearer: whoever obtains them (1) before they become due, and (2) gives something in consideration, and (3) has no reason to suspect that the one from whom he obtains them has not the full right to transfer them, obtains the same right to them that he would if the other party were the real owner.

6. A sale is not complete unless PARTICULAR PROPERTY is referred to or set apart.

7. An agreement to pay MONEY is a necessary element of a sale.

8. In every sale where the price is not fixed there is an IMPLIED AGREEMENT that the buyer shall pay what the goods are reasonably worth.

II. INCIDENTS OF A SALE.

1. DELIVERY is not essential to a sale as between the parties, but it is as to third parties.

2. A buyer has the RIGHT TO TAKE the goods when he pays for them, but not until then.

3. If, before the goods sold on credit reach the buyer, the seller hears of his FAILURE and orders the carrier not to deliver them, the seller may retake them and hold them until paid.

4. In every sale of personal property there is an implied WARRANTY OF OWNERSHIP.

5. If there was no express agreement as to QUALITY OR FITNESS the buyer must take the risk.

III. COMMISSION MERCHANTS.

1. Commission merchants are AGENTS TO SELL goods.

2. A commission merchant has a RIGHT TO KEEP any goods of his principal's which are in his hands, until he has been paid all commissions, advances, and expenses, due to him from the owner.

IV. BROKERS.

A broker is an AGENT TO MAKE CONTRACTS.

REVIEW QUESTIONS.

Sale of Goods.

1. What is a sale? Is it a contract? State the difference between a sale and an agreement to sell. What is title? Do possession and ownership always go together ? Is a sale complete until the goods are delivered? Or until paid for? At what moment is it complete? What is a conditional sale? Show when and why it is important to know the moment a sale is complete.
2. State the five things necessary in every sale. Take in order the seven requisites of a binding contract, and show how each one applies to the case of sales.
3. May one agree to buy a thing which does not now exist, but is to grow, or to be made?
4. If one sells property which he does not own, or which he has no right to sell, will the purchaser or the real owner be entitled to keep the property? Can one be deprived of his property without his consent? State the rule in this respect, as to negotiable securities. What are negotiable securities?
5. If something is ordered, but no particular article of the kind is designated, is there a sale? If something is ordered and a particular article is afterwards set apart in accordance with the order, but is destroyed before being delivered, whose is the loss?
6. Must a particular price be mentioned to make a sale?
7. What is the difference between sale and barter?
8. What is the sale of a debt?
9. What is the difference between a requisite and an incident of a sale?
10. Does property sold ever become the buyer's before it is delivered to him?
11. In what case (if any) is delivery necessary to make the property the buyer's? Why?
12. When has the seller a right to keep the property? How long may he? What is the right called? Has he this right when he sells on credit?

13. What is delivery in law?　Is there any obligation upon a merchant to send goods to the buyer when he does not agree to ?
14. Describe the right of stoppage.
15. What is warranty of ownership?　When does it exist?
16. What is warranty of quality?　When does it exist?
17. What is the implied warranty in a sale by sample?
18. What is a commission merchant?　Who is his principal?　Who owns the goods, the commission merchant or the principal?
19. State the general duties of a commission merchant to his principal.
20. What powers, in general, has he?
21. Where the custom of the trade and his special instructions differ, which must he follow?
22. When is a commission merchant personally responsible to his principal for what the goods are sold for?
23. How is a commission merchant paid for his services?　If he has sold the goods, but the buyer fails to pay, is he entitled to his commission?
24. What are "advances," made by a commission merchant?
25. When may a commission merchant keep the goods from one who has bought them of him?　May he ever keep them from his principal if the latter demands them?
26. What is his " lien"?　To what property of the principal's does it extend ?　What does it secure?
27. What is the position of a commission merchant who does not reveal his principal?
28. Define broker.　Name the different kinds.　What is the difference between a commission merchant and a merchandise broker?

DIVISION II.

COMMERCIAL PAPER.

CHAPTER XXII.

NOTES.

a.—Description of Notes.

1. Commercial Paper consists chiefly of three kinds, notes, drafts and checks. It is so called because it is so extensively used for the purposes of business; commerce meaning in one sense all kinds of traffic, on land as well as by sea. Many of the rules stated in this chapter, especially those which relate to negotiability (sec. 8 to 27) are common to all kinds of commercial paper.

2. A Note IS A WRITTEN PROMISE, SIGNED BY THE PERSON PROMISING, TO PAY A CERTAIN SUM OF MONEY, AT A CERTAIN TIME, TO A PERSON NAMED, OR TO HIS ORDER, OR TO THE BEARER.* It is thus a written contract. The following is a common form:

$200.   New York, Sept. 2, 1881.

Two months after date we promise to pay to the order of James S. Fay Two Hundred Dollars.

Value received.

Archibald Brothers.

---

* The word *note*, as we use it in this book, means the same as *promissory note*.

The person promising is called the *maker*, and the person named in the body of the note is called the *payee*. Thus in the above, the firm of Archibald Brothers are the makers, and Fay is the payee. The words *value received* are not generally necessary.

3. Use.—Notes are of very common use, and of great utility in business. Their use is, as clear and certain evidence of debt. In modern times a large part of trade is carried on on credit, i.e., a tradesman, instead of paying for his stock when he buys, promises to pay at a certain future time. Now that debt, that promise, whether oral or written, is itself property, and may be transferred from one to another, but in order for that, there must be distinct and unmistakable evidence of its existence, such as any one could rely upon. A note, being the written and unconditional admission of the debtor himself, is such evidence. Thus notes facilitate the use of credit, which has been a mighty factor in the extension of commerce.

4. Two Kinds.—At pp. 275-277 will be found the most common forms of notes. The most important particular in which they differ in kind is with regard to the payee named, and in this respect there are four kinds : those payable, (*a*) to a particular person or his order, (*b*) to the maker himself or his order,* (*c*) to a particular person or bearer, and (*d*) to the bearer. (*a*) and (*b*) are substantially the same, for when the maker makes a note in the form of (*b*) he at the same time indorses it and thus makes it payable either to a particular person or to the bearer as he chooses (sec. 23). (*c*) and (*d*) are also the same, for in each case the promise is to pay any one who may "bear," i.e.,

---

* "To the order of A" means exactly the same as "to A or order," and both mean that the maker will pay it to whomsoever A orders him to pay it.

own or hold the note when it is presented for payment. The name of the person in (c) has no effect whatever. Therefore, THERE ARE TWO KINDS OF NOTES, THOSE PAY- ABLE (1) TO ORDER, AND (2) TO BEARER. So also, there are the same two kinds of drafts or checks.

5. **When Due.**—The day of payment is often called the day of *maturity.* A NOTE PAYABLE AT A FUTURE TIME IS NOT DUE UNTIL THE THIRD DAY AFTER ITS SPECIFIED DAY OF PAYMENT. That is, an old and universal custom, ex- tends the time three days. These are called *days of grace.* If payable a number of months from date it becomes due the third day after the corresponding day in the proper month. Thus a note, dated Jan. 1 and payable ten days from date, is due Jan. 14 ; the note in sec. 2 (p. 105) is due Nov. 5. Whenever the last day of grace falls upon a Sun- day or a legal holiday,* the note is due the day before. A note payable on demand is due immediately and has no days of grace. One specifying no time of payment is due on demand.†

> *Note to Teacher.*—It is important to know the exact day a note is due. Draw up different forms, and ask the scholar when they become due.

b.—Negotiability.

6. **Maker's Responsibility.**—Notes are very frequently transferred by the payees to others. Many are made to be transferred.‡ There are therefore two classes of persons to whom a maker may become responsible, (1) the person originally receiving the note, and (2) the persons to whom

---

* The legal holidays are in general Jan. 1, Feb. 22, July 4, Dec. 25, and Thanksgiving Day, with some others in different States.

† But parties may exclude days of grace by adding to the note the words "without grace."

‡ See p. 110, sec. 11.

it is subsequently transferred.   These often stand in different positions with regard to the note, and therefore the
maker may sometimes be responsible to one party when he
would not be to another.   When it is transferred, those
transferring it themselves also often assume responsibility
to pay it.   The contracts of subsequent parties will be
treated in a later chapter (Chap. XXV.).   This chapter
relates simply to the maker's contract.

7. Not Transferred.—If a note remains the property of
the payee, or in a bearer note of the person to whom it is
originally given, until it becomes due, those two, the maker
and himself, are the only ones concerned in the whole transaction, and each has full knowledge of it.   Therefore there
is no reason why the contract should not follow the rules
of other contracts, and it does.   IN THE HANDS OF THE
ORIGINAL HOLDER OF A NOTE IT IS A BINDING CONTRACT
PROVIDED IT HAS ALL THE REQUISITES OF A BINDING CON-
TRACT, BUT NOT OTHERWISE.   It is peculiar in no respect.
Thus in forms 1–6, if Fay, receiving the note from Archibald Brothers, should retain it until maturity, he could
enforce it only if it represented a real, existing debt, such
as a loan, or sale, and was not illegal, fictitious or fraudulent in any way.   As between the original parties the note
is but a memorandum or evidence of the debt.

8. But when Transferred to a third party, this person
may not know all the details of the original transaction.   He
sees only the note, but does not know whether it represents
a legal, real, and honest debt or not.   It may be paid for
aught he knows.   Therefore the law, in order to protect
him, and thus allow notes to be readily transferred, changes
its character in his hands, as it were, by giving him the
right to enforce it in any event.   It becomes in his hands
more than evidence; it becomes property.   And it keeps
this character in the hands of all to whom it is successively

transferred thereafter. Each successive owner holds it in his own right and free from its defects in the hands of all prior owners. Thus it is that it is given currency, and may be bought without risk.

9. Definition of Negotiability.—And this character we call negotiability, which may be defined thus: NEGOTIABILITY, IN COMMERCIAL PAPER, IS THE QUALITY OF BEING ENFORCEABLE BY ONE RECEIVING IT, THOUGH NOT ENFORCEABLE BY THE ONE FROM WHOM IT IS RECEIVED.* It has no effect on contracts originally valid, nor on invalid contracts, when retained by the person originally receiving them. It only makes invalid ones valid when transferred. Notes which have this quality are called *negotiable notes.* There are other instruments which also have it, drafts, checks, bonds, etc. (p. 89, note). The transfer of negotiable paper is the transfer of the debt represented by it, but it differs from the transfer of other debts in this respect: that it carries rights which the person transferring did not have (p. 91). The effect of negotiability in different cases will be illustrated in the sections following.

10. Its General Effect.—This is, as implied in its definition, to make of no consequence certain circumstances which, if the note had not been transferred, would have made it void or not collectible. The next step is to examine what those circumstances are, for there are those which will render it void in the hands of any one. Thus, if the defect appears upon the note itself, as for instance in many States a usurious note, it cannot become valid. So also negotiability will not make the note of a minor enforceable. THE CIRCUMSTANCES WHICH, THOUGH RENDERING NEGOTIABLE PAPER VOID IN THE HANDS OF ONE PARTY, YET

---

* The word *negotiability* has had, and now has, several different meanings, but this is its common legal sense at present.

DO NOT AFFECT THE RIGHTS OF OTHERS RECEIVING IT THROUGH HIM, ARE, IN GENERAL, THOSE WHICH DO NOT APPEAR ON THE INSTRUMENT ITSELF. Outside agreements and circumstances do not affect it. This rule is common to all negotiable securities. It would be impossible to enumerate all such circumstances, but we may note four of the most common cases.

11. First: Accommodation Notes.—These are notes which represent no real existing debt, but are made as a means of borrowing money. Thus A, willing to lend money to B, but not having it at hand, may make his note payable to B, which B may sell to a bank or to any one. In B's hands the note is without consideration, and therefore void, but this absence of consideration does not affect the liability of A to the bank, whether it is known to be accommodation paper or not. So, also, if the note is fraudulent or illegal in its origin, nevertheless, one who receives it in ignorance of the fraud or illegality, may enforce it. These defects do not appear on the note itself.*

12. Second: Payment.—If paid or discharged before maturity the person to whom it is paid can make no second claim upon it, but should he not be the owner at the time, or should he retain it and afterwards transfer it to another representing it to be unpaid, the owner at its maturity could again enforce payment from the maker. Therefore one on paying a note should insist that it be surrendered to him, as he has a right to do. Any partial payment should be noted on it at the time the payment is made.

13. Third: Set-Off.—We have seen that ordinary debts

---

* Negotiable paper in the hands of third parties, is, therefore, excepted from the 5th and 6th requisites of a binding contract, but not from the 3d (p. 20). The rest are not applicable. A promise to pay money is of course possible in its nature, and almost always legal; delivery implies assent; and according to its definition it is written.

owed by two parties to each other offset and destroy one another, but this is not always so with negotiable paper before it is due. Thus, let us suppose a note of A payable to B for $100, transferred by B to C, and by C to D. If now at its maturity A has also a claim for $50 against D, it will cancel one half of A's debt to D upon his note. But A may have had claims against B or C during the time they owned the note, yet those claims would not affect it unless it was owned by them at maturity.

14. Fourth: Lost or Stolen Paper.—A negotiable note payable to bearer coming before it is due to one who purchases it believing that the seller has the right to sell it, belongs to him, though stolen from the true owner. We have already considered this rule, and the rule of property to which it is an exception, in connection with all kinds of negotiable securities (p. 89). But it only applies when the security, either originally or by blank indorsement (p. 114, sec. 23) is payable to bearer. If payable to the order of a particular person, he can be deprived of it only by his own consent. The forgery of his name would not affect his rights. Hence if notes, checks, etc., are to be sent by mail, or exposed to danger of loss, it is prudent to have them payable to order. This is the only one of the effects of negotiability which does not apply to order and bearer notes alike.

c.—Conditions of Negotiability.

15. Classes of Conditions.—Not all notes are negotiable, nor are any so under all circumstances. Certain circumstances or conditions must be present, or the transfer will fall back under the rule governing the transfer of other contracts; i.e., one can convey just the rights he has and no others. These conditions are of five kinds: those relating (1) to its form, (2) to the manner of its transfer, (3) to the time of its transfer, (4) to the consideration for the transfer, and (5) to the knowledge about it of the person receiving it. We will consider first the necessities as to form.

16. Five Formal Requisites.—THE FIVE THINGS NECESSARY IN THE FORM OF COMMERCIAL PAPER TO MAKE IT NEGOTIABLE, ARE (1) THAT THE DATE OF PAYMENT BE CERTAIN TO COME, (2) THAT IT HAVE ONE OF THE TWO WORDS, ORDER OR BEARER, (3) THAT THE AMOUNT BE SPECIFIED AND CERTAIN, (4) THAT IT BE PAYABLE IN MONEY ONLY, AND (5) THAT IT BE AN UNCONDITIONAL PROMISE. We shall consider these in order. But many business agreements are in fact drawn in the form of notes, though violating one or more of these rules. They are not on that account void; they may be perfectly valid and binding between the original parties; the only effect is that they are not negotiable. Negotiable notes need not be drawn in precisely the forms given. All are negotiable which have in substance the five requisites named.*

17. Date of Payment.—It is very common to make a note payable a certain number of days or months after date. That renders the date of payment certain, but in such case the note should be dated, as is usually done. So the date is certain where payment is made dependent on an event sure to occur, as where A promises to pay B on the death of some person. But if the time depends on some event which may never occur, as for instance where A promises to pay B when the latter reaches twenty-one, the note is not negotiable. In a demand note the date of payment is certain, for "on demand" means "to-day."

18. Negotiable Words.—The words "order" and "bear-

---

* This is the general rule, though a few States require something further. Thus in Pennsylvania the words "without defalcation" or "without set-off" are necessary; in Missouri the words "value received;" in three or four States it must be payable at a bank.

er" are called negotiable words, because the use of one of them is necessary to confer negotiability.* Thus the note in form 6 may be valid, but it is not negotiable. Fay may enforce it if it represents a legal, real, and honest debt, but if it does not it is void either in his hands or in the hands of any one else.

19. Amount.—It may be for any amount, but the amount must be specified and certain, so that any one can tell just what is due. Thus a promise to pay "$100, and whatever else I owe for repairs to my house," is not negotiable, even though nothing but the $100 was really owed, for a stranger cannot tell what is due. The promise to pay interest does not make a note uncertain, for any one can calculate its amount.

20. Money.—It must be a promise to pay in money. If payable in goods, or any commodity, or even in the money of another country, it is not negotiable.†

21. Unconditionally.—Unless the promise on the note is absolute, and without condition, it is not negotiable. Thus notes having such terms as these, "I promise to pay $100 if I am able," or "to be paid out of the money arising from . . . sales," etc., are not negotiable. And it makes no difference what good reason there is to believe that the conditions will be fulfilled, for if it is possible that one should not be fulfilled, that will produce uncertainty.

Thus it is seen that certainty is the purpose of nearly all these five requisites as to form. Paper which is uncertain in its terms is not suited to the purposes of negotiable paper. Since it is to pass from one to another like other property,

---

* Any other words indicating that the paper was intended to be negotiable would serve the purpose, but those two words are the only ones commonly used.

† In a few of the Western States a promise to pay in personal property is negotiable.

it should have this characteristic of other property, viz.,
that one can tell by looking at it just what it is.

22. Manner of Transfer.—There are two usual modes of
transferring commercial paper, (1) by delivery of the paper alone, (2) by the owner's writing his name upon the
back and then delivering it. The latter is called *indorsement.** Thus in forms 1 or 5, if Fay wishes to sell the
note to some third person, he writes his own name upon
the back and delivers it. PAPER PAYABLE TO BEARER
MAY BE TRANSFERRED BY DELIVERY ALONE. No indorsement is necessary, though it may be made. PAPER PAY-
ABLE TO ORDER MUST BE INDORSED TO BE TRANSFERRED.†
In other words, in paper payable to bearer there is no condition of negotiability as to its manner of transfer: if payable to order, the condition is indorsement.

23. Indorsements are of two kinds, in full and in blank.
A *full indorsement* consists of the owner's name with an
order to pay it to some particular person. A *blank indorsement* is the name without such order, and is usually
the name alone. After a full indorsement the paper is
still payable to order ; the person only is changed. He
must then indorse it if he wishes to transfer it, and he
may indorse in full or in blank. After a blank indorsement the paper is payable to bearer. It is as if over the
name were written "pay the within to the bearer." Thus
an order note may become a bearer note, but the converse
is not true ; a note which is or has become payable to bearer

---

* In another sense the indorsement is the words written. The
word is sometimes written *endorse.*

† That is, and keep its negotiable character. It may be transferred
without indorsement, like any other debt (p. 91, sec. 13), but in such
case it is transferred as a debt or claim only, and not as negotiable
paper, and is subject to all the conditions or defects to which it was
subject in the hands of the person so transferring.

remains so, no matter what the subsequent indorsements are. But one may write over a prior blank indorsement an order to pay to himself. That changes it again to an order note (forms 14, 15, 16).

Note to Teacher.—Draw up notes and have them indorsed by one scholar to another, in the two ways.

24. Time of Transfer.—But negotiable paper ceases to have its peculiar characteristics, at maturity, i.e., the last day of grace. Thereafter it becomes like any other debt or claim. NEGOTIABLE PAPER LOSES ITS NEGOTIABILITY AT MATURITY.* This does not mean that it becomes invalid, but simply that one who receives it after it is due gets only such rights as the one from whom he received it had. There are then two cases, (1) where the person transferring it after it is due has the right to enforce it, (2) where he has not. In the first case the one to whom he transfers it gets the right to enforce, in the second he does not.†

25. Consideration.—ONE WHO RECEIVES NEGOTIABLE PAPER, GIVING NO MONEY OR PROPERTY IN EXCHANGE FOR IT, GETS NO BETTER RIGHT TO ENFORCE IT THAN THE ONE FROM WHOM HE RECEIVES IT HAD. If he gives no consideration for it, he loses nothing by it. The thief or finder of a note, though payable to bearer, cannot enforce it.

---

* This is so as to all notes and drafts due in the future. As to demand notes, though the maker may be sued immediately, yet they remain negotiable for a short time, perhaps two or three months. As to checks, see p. 129, sec. 7.

† Thus suppose form 1 to be an accommodation note: Fay cannot ever enforce it, as we have seen, but he can sell it to another person, and that person can enforce it; and therefore any one receiving it from the latter, whether before or after maturity, can also enforce it; but if Fay keeps it until February 7, 1882, neither he nor any one to whom he should afterward sell it could enforce it. Again, suppose the note was stolen from Fay (after he had indorsed it in blank), and the thief should sell it to a bank, the bank could enforce it if they took it before maturity, but not otherwise.

26. Knowledge.— ONE WHO RECEIVES NEGOTIABLE PAPER, KNOWING AT THE TIME OF ANY INVALIDATING DEFECT, GETS NO BETTER RIGHT TO ENFORCE IT THAN THE ONE FROM WHOM HE RECEIVES IT HAD. The purchase must not only be before maturity, and for good consideration, but it must be in good faith. Thus if I buy a note from a thief knowing, or having reason to know, that it is stolen, I cannot make the maker pay me. So also, if I know it to be already paid, or that it was originally given for an illegal or fraudulent purpose. If, however, I do not hear of the defect until after I have bought it, I may enforce it. But the knowledge that it was an accommodation note is of no effect, and that kind of note is therefore an exception to this rule.

27. The Practical Rules to be drawn from this chapter are as follows:—(*a*) If we are taking a note from the maker its form is unimportant; the contract must have the seven requisites and that is all. (*b*) If we are buying one from some one not the maker, and wish to be sure that we can force the maker to pay it, to be safe we must make sure of one of two things, either (1) that the one from whom we are buying has himself the right to enforce it, or (2) that it is negotiable paper in form, and is transferred to us under all the other necessary conditions of negotiability. The absence of any one condition gives us only the rights had by the one from whom we receive it.

Note to Teacher.—The circumstances under which commercial paper may be bought and sold are, of course, infinite in variety, and only a few examples can be given in a book of this character. But it must be left to the individual teacher—and there is ample opportunity for it—to test the scholar's knowledge and understanding of the rules in the foregoing chapter, by stating cases likely to occur in actual life, and asking for their effect and why, or by having the scholar state a case which shall illustrate one or more of those rules.

CHAPTER XXIII.

DRAFTS AND BILLS OF EXCHANGE.

1. Draft.—A DRAFT IS A WRITTEN ORDER, SIGNED BY ONE PERSON, ORDERING ANOTHER PERSON, TO WHOM IT IS DIRECTED, TO PAY A CERTAIN SUM OF MONEY, AT A CERTAIN TIME, TO A THIRD PERSON (NAMED), OR TO HIS ORDER, OR TO THE BEARER.   The following is a common form:

$1000.   New York, Sept. 13, 1881.

At sight pay to A. B. Runyon & Co. or order, One thousand dollars, value received, and charge the same to account of

A. J. Jones.

To William T. Barber,

New Orleans.

The person ordering [Jones] is called the *drawer*, the one to whom it is directed [Barber] is called the *person drawn upon*, and the one in whose favor it is drawn, i.e., to whom the payment is directed to be made [Runyon & Co.] is called the *payee*.

2. A Bill of Exchange, in common language, is a draft, of which the drawer and the person drawn upon live in different countries, and which is therefore drawn in one country and paid in the other.   In general, the rules governing drafts and bills of exchange are the same, and we shall here use the word draft as meaning either of them. In legal language, in fact, they are both known as bills of. exchange.*

3. Use.—Drafts came into use before notes, have been used now for several centuries, and have been of much benefit to commerce and thus to civilization. It is easily seen that if certain to be paid, they represent like notes so much money, so much property, which may be safely and easily carried or sent from place to place. Thus, suppose Jones in New York owes Runyon & Co. of New Orleans $1000, and that Barber of New Orleans owes Jones $1000; if, now, Jones will draw and send to Runyon & Co. his draft upon Barber, both debts can be thus paid, while otherwise the money itself would have to be transported from New Orleans to New York and back again.

4. Kinds.—Like notes, drafts are made payable to order or to bearer (p. 106). So also they differ as to the time at which payment is to be made, being made payable "at sight," or "on demand," or ".... days after sight," or ".... days after date," etc., according as the parties choose. Of course sufficient time should be allowed so that the draft may be presented to the person drawn upon before or when it becomes due. "At sight" and "on demand" mean when presented, i.e., when the person drawn upon *sees* the draft. (See p. 278 for some forms.)

5. Character.—A note is a promise: a draft is an order. In the transaction in which a note is given, and also on the face of the note itself, there are originally but two parties, the maker and the payee. The contract is complete when

---

* Foreign bills are often drawn in triplicate; three alike, except that they are numbered first, second and third. If the first is lost while being sent for payment the second may be used. Only one is paid in any event (form 9).

it is delivered to the payee. In the giving of a draft there are two persons concerned originally, the drawer and the payee, and the draft is, as we shall see, an implied contract between them (sec. 9), but on the face of the draft three persons are named. But the person drawn upon knows nothing about it: he therefore does not come into the contract, until it is presented to him by the one to whom it is to be paid (sec. 10, 11).

6. Acceptance —The draft, being drawn, is then given or sent by the drawer to the person to whom he wishes the money paid. This one, the payee or bearer, presents it to the one upon whom it is drawn. It need not be presented until it is due, though it is usually done immediately. If when presented to him he agrees to pay it when it becomes due, he is said to *accept* it, and indicates this usually by writing across its face the word "accepted" with his own name (form 10). It is often done by simply writing the name across the face. In some States it may be accepted orally. After he has accepted, the person drawn upon is called the *acceptor*, and the draft itself often called an *acceptance*.

7. When Due.—A DRAFT PAYABLE AT A FUTURE TIME IS NOT DUE UNTIL THE THIRD DAY AFTER ITS SPECIFIED DAY OF PAYMENT. Drafts have three days of grace. Thus, if made payable thirty days from its date, it is not really due until the thirty-third. If payable at sight, or so many days after sight, it must be presented and accepted in order to fix the day of payment. Thus, if a draft drawn payable ten days after sight is presented and accepted July 25th, it becomes due August 7th. If payable "on demand" it has no days of grace, but is due as soon as it is accepted.*

---

* There is some difference in the States as to days of grace on drafts. Thus in a number, drafts payable at sight (called *sight drafts*), have no days of grace.

8. Transfer.—But the person who receives the draft from the drawer may not wish to retain it until it becomes due. He may prefer the money, and will sell it to another. The transfer is made in the same way as in the case of a note (p. 114): if payable to order it is indorsed; if payable to bearer originally, or made so by being indorsed in blank, it is often simply delivered without indorsement. A draft may be transferred in these ways either before or after acceptance, and any one of the intermediate owners may present it for acceptance. When it becomes due the owner of it at that time presents it to the acceptor for payment.*

9. Drawer's Agreement.—A draft is a contract between the drawer and the person to whom it is given. THE DRAWER'S AGREEMENT IS TO PAY THE DRAFT IF THE PERSON UPON WHOM IT IS DRAWN DOES NOT. It is as if he added to its words the following: "And I agree to pay the amount if the person drawn upon refuses to accept or refuses to pay." He is in the position of a surety (Chap. XVI.) or a first indorser (p. 132). If the draft is payable at sight, or a certain time after sight, it should be presented to the person drawn upon as soon as it can be conveniently, or the drawer will be discharged.

10. Acceptor's Agreement before Acceptance.—The person drawn upon does not perhaps know of the draft until he sees it. Therefore until he accepts it he makes no agreement with the owner of it, either to pay or to accept. Therefore THE PERSON DRAWN UPON IS UNDER NO OBLIGATION TO THE HOLDER OF A DRAFT UNLESS HE ACCEPTS

---

* Thus, in the form in sec. 1, Runyon & Co., on receiving it from Jones, may transfer it to S. B. Mapes by writing on the back "Pay to S. B. Mapes or order" and signing the indorsement "A. B. Runyon & Co." Mapes perhaps will present it to Barber and have it accepted, and then transfer it to James Brown. Brown perhaps will retain it until it is due, and then Barber will pay it to him (form 16).

IT. There may be, however, a prior agreement between the drawer and the person drawn upon giving the former the right to draw, and to refuse to accept would be to break that contract. The drawer therefore might have the right to sue him if he refused to accept, but the owner of the draft would not.*

11. After Acceptance THE PERSON DRAWN UPON, I.E., THE ACCEPTOR, IS THE PRINCIPAL DEBTOR AND RESPONSIBLE TO ALL PARTIES. Acceptance changes the nature of the instrument. It then becomes also a contract between the acceptor and the person then owning it, or any one who has owned it or who may own it. It is as if he wrote above his name, "I promise to pay this when due." And this contract is for the benefit of all the other parties whose names appear on it. He becomes primarily responsible; they only if he fails to pay.

12. Principal Debtor.—We have seen that a note and a draft represent in effect a debt, an amount of money owed by some one, and that the transfer of the paper from one owner to another is really the transfer of that debt. The person owing that debt we call the *principal debtor.* In a note the principal debtor is the maker, and his contract is to pay, unconditionally: in an unaccepted draft the principal debtor is the drawer, and his contract is conditional. i.e., to pay if the person drawn upon does not: in an accepted draft the principal debtor is the acceptor, and his contract is to pay, unconditionally. If the principal debtor fails to pay it when he should it is said to be *dishonored.*

13. Negotiability.—DRAFTS ARE NEGOTIABLE BOTH BE-

---

* Thus if A agrees to allow B to draw on him for $500, and B does so in favor of C, but A refuses to accept the draft, the contract between A and B is broken, but there never was any contract between A and C. C's remedy is to compel B to carry out his implied agreement as drawer (sec. 9).

FORE AND AFTER ACCEPTANCE. Negotiability has been already explained (pp. 107, etc.), and we have seen that it only relates to a contract which has been transferred by the first owner to some one else, and to the right of one to enforce it when the one from whom he received it did not have that right; that if the first owner keeps it until it is due, it is only enforceable when it represents a legal, real, and honest transaction, and that if it is enforceable by one party it is also enforceable by one to whom it is transferred by him, whether negotiable or not. But we need not go over these principles again: ALL THE PRINCIPLES OF NEGOTIABILITY APPLY TO DRAFTS, AS TO NOTES.

14. Conditions of Negotiability.—Likewise, to have the quality of negotiability, all the conditions must exist: viz., the five requisites as to the form of the draft, those as to the manner, time, and consideration for its transfer, and as to the knowledge of the person receiving it (pp. 111–116).

> *Note to Teacher.*—Those conditions should be carefully reviewed here, and applied practically to drafts. Sec. 15 and 16 contain some illustrations. In every illustration it would be well to so state it as to bring out its justice, together with the injustice of any other rule. A " why" greatly assists memory.

In other words, if any person receives a draft and any single condition of negotiability is absent, he merely gets such a right to enforce it as the one from whom he received it had. If that was a full right, his is full; if that was qualified, his is qualified; if that was no right, his is no right, and he gets nothing.*

---

* For instance, suppose C is the payee of a draft, and that he transfers it to D. If it be payable to C's order and he transfers it without indorsing it, D gets no better right to enforce it than C had, although D may have paid C a full price for it, and honestly believed it to be valid in all respects. Again suppose C did not sell it until after it became due: then D would get no better right than C's, although he paid for it, and it was regularly indorsed.

But on the other hand, if all the conditions do exist, i.e., if (1) the draft is negotiable in form, and (2) when payable to order it is indorsed, and (3) the person receiving it receives it before it is due, and (4) pays money or other consideration for it, and (5) has no reason to believe it is not valid in all respects, then the person who so receives it has the right to enforce it, whether the one from whom he received it had that right or not. This is illustrated in the two following sections.

15. Accommodation Drafts are of two kinds, (1) where the drawer is accommodated by the acceptor, and (2) where the payee is accommodated by the drawer. Thus, in the first case, if A draws a draft on B, payable to C, when B owes A nothing, but B (willing to accommodate A) accepts the draft, there is no consideration for the promise to pay, which we have seen (sec. 11), B makes by accepting. Nevertheless C can enforce it, provided he received it before maturity and gave consideration to A for it. So also, any one receiving it from C can enforce it, because they receive the same rights he had. But suppose the acceptor B does not pay it when it becomes due, and the owner then compels the drawer A to pay it; A could not then sue B, for the reason that between them there was no consideration for the acceptance.

Taking the second case, suppose C pays nothing to A for it, but A draws it to accommodate him (i.e., in effect lends him the money). There is then no consideration for the promise which, we have seen (sec. 9), A makes in drawing the draft; therefore C could never force A to fulfill that promise.* But suppose that C transfers it to D before it is due and D pays money for it; D could then enforce A's

---

* We are now considering the drawer's agreement only. If B should accept the draft, he would be responsible on it to C and to all others to the same extent as in any other draft.

implied promise. So also could any one else to whom D transferred it, for the reason that he would take D's rights. We see, therefore, that the rule of contracts which accommodation paper is excepted from under some circumstances is that one requiring consideration. It is also excepted from one of the conditions of negotiability, viz., the last one, as to the person's knowledge. It makes no difference as to his rights that the person who receives it knows it to be accommodation paper.

16. Other Examples.—Though the draft should have been originally given for an illegal purpose (e.g., to pay a usurious debt), or though the drawer or acceptor is defrauded into signing the draft, yet the draft can be enforced by one who received it, believing it to be valid, and under all the other conditions. Its being paid before maturity, or its having been stolen, does not affect the right of one who receives it under all the conditions. In the case of the theft, the one from whom it was stolen must lose his money. Thus we see that the important question to ask when we are buying negotiable paper is, Under what circumstances do we receive it? But in all other contracts, the question to ask is, Under what circumstances did the person making the contract make it?

17. Difference in Laws.—The rules which we have given in this and the preceding chapter are the prevailing ones in this country and in England, but in some of the particulars different States have different rules. It would be impossible to state here those differences, but this should be always borne in mind, that A CONTRACT IS GOVERNED BY THE LAW OF THE STATE IN WHICH IT IS MADE. Therefore the maker's responsibility, in a note, is governed by the law of the State where it is drawn; an indorser's, in a note or draft, by the law of the State where he indorses; and an acceptor's by the law of the State where he accepts.

If made payable in a particular State, the law of that State governs it.

> *Note to Teacher.*—Different ways to test the scholar's understanding will easily suggest themselves, upon this subject as under notes, as for instance by varying the names of the parties, their residences, the dates, the forms of the drafts, and asking for the effects, etc., etc., or he might be required to draw up drafts which should have certain stated characteristics, etc., etc.

CHAPTER XXIV.

CHECKS.

1. Definition.—A CHECK IS A DRAFT DRAWN UPON A BANK OR BANKER, AND MADE PAYABLE IMMEDIATELY. The following is a common form:

$245.^{14}/100

New York, Sept. 22, 1881.

STAMP.

Ninth National Bank.

Pay to the order of James S. Fay Two hundred forty-five ^{14}/100 dollars.

No. 54.

A. Y. Jones.

The parties are designated as in a draft. Thus Jones is the drawer, the Ninth National Bank is the person drawn upon, and Fay is the payee.

2. Use.—The purpose of checks is to save the handling of money. Like drafts and notes, they represent so much money or property, and they pass from one to another like money. In the city of New York alone, in a single day, many millions of dollars change hands by means of checks. The operation is as follows: Jones, having a certain amount of money which he does not wish to use immediately, deposits it in a bank, i.e., lends or gives it to the bank with the agreement that the bank will pay any portion of it to any one to whom he may order it to be paid. Jones then orders it paid in such amounts, at such times, and to such persons as he chooses, by means of checks. If he gives Fay a check for $245, Fay may go to the Ninth National Bank and get the money, or if Fay has an account with some bank he may deposit the check with that bank as money, and that bank will collect it from the Ninth National Bank.

3. Like other Drafts.—A check is like other drafts in most respects. It is an order, which the bank is under obligation *to the drawer* to obey, so long as there remains any of the drawer's money on deposit in the bank. There is also an implied contract between the drawer and the payee (p. 120). But the bank knows nothing of it until it is presented; THEREFORE A BANK IS UNDER NO OBLIGATION TO THE HOLDER OF AN UNCERTIFIED CHECK. If it refuses to pay, the holder cannot sue the bank, but only the drawer and indorsers. The drawer may *stop payment*, i.e., order the bank not to pay it, and this is often done when checks are stolen.*

4. Difference in Form.—But there are differences between checks and other drafts. These differences are of two kinds, (1) in form, and (2) in effect. There are two differences in form: (1) a check is always drawn upon a bank, or some person or persons carrying on a banking business; (2) it is always made payable immediately, usually by a simple order without any such words as "on demand," or "on presentation," etc. Unless it has these two elements it is not a check, but an ordinary draft. Thus, if it reads,

---

* Stopping of checks affects only the bank's right to pay. It is a countermand of the order. It does not affect the drawer's implied contract. Thus if payment is stopped, the payee or the holder has the same right he had before.

Note to Teacher.—Apply this principle to the case of stolen or lost checks.

" pay to-morrow," or " pay one day from date," it is not a check.*

5. In Effect, the important difference is that CHECKS HAVE NO DAYS OF GRACE. They are due when presented. They may be presented to the bank and paid as soon as drawn. Other drafts, we have seen, are usually presented for acceptance before they become due, but checks usually are not. They may be, however (sec. 6).†

6. Certification.—A forged check will of course not be paid, nor will one where the drawer has already withdrawn all the money he deposited. To protect one against these risks when a check is offered him by some one whom he does not know about, the practice of presenting checks for certification has arisen. This consists of having it presented to the bank before or soon after receiving it, where the word "certified," or "good," is written across the face of the check by some officer of the bank upon which it is drawn, with his signature, or often the signature alone (form 12). This makes the bank responsible. CERTIFICATION SUBSTITUTES THE BANK FOR THE DRAWER AS THE PRINCIPAL DEBTOR. It is an assent to the order, and a promise to pay, which they must fulfill though the check turns out to be forged, or though the drawer has no funds there. Therefore a bank will not certify a check unless the check is genuine, and the drawer has funds there.

The effect of certification upon the drawer is probably different in different cases. If after receiving it the owner presents it at the bank and it is certified instead of being paid, that releases the drawer. By taking the certifica-

---

* Sometimes checks are dated ahead (e.g., drawn and given on January 4th and dated January 7th). Such checks are still valid checks, but they have no force until the date arrives.

† See p. 136, sec. 13, for another difference between checks and drafts.

tion instead of the money the owner accepts the bank as his debtor instead of the drawer. But the law is not fully settled as to whether the drawer is released, where a check is used which was certified at his own request before being delivered. Probably he is not.*

7. Negotiability.—CHECKS ARE NEGOTIABLE UNDER THE SAME CONDITIONS AS NOTES AND DRAFTS. Therefore the practical rules to be observed in receiving checks are the same (p. 116, sec. 27). Thus, they should be payable either to order, or bearer; if payable to order they should be indorsed. If, then, we receive one before it has been presented to the bank, giving something for it, and have no reason to believe it to be invalid in any way, we may compel the drawer to pay it, or if it has been certified, we may compel the bank to pay it, no matter in what sort of a transaction it originated. Checks, however, do not remain negotiable long. They must be presented for payment as soon as they can be conveniently.

8. Stamp.—A national law requires that every check used shall have placed upon it a two-cent revenue stamp. The absence of such a stamp does not necessarily render it invalid, but subjects the party using it to a penalty of $50. It should be, therefore, affixed to the check before it is used, and cancelled at the same time.

9. A Certificate of Deposit is a certificate issued by a bank, showing that a certain person has deposited a certain amount of money with it. The implied promise is to repay it when demanded, to the one who shall be the owner of the certificate. It is, in effect, a certified check, and is negotiable in the same way (form 13).

---

* The certification of a check is like the acceptance of a draft, in that it always makes the bank responsible: it is unlike acceptance, in that it sometimes releases the drawer, which acceptance never does.

COMMERCIAL NEGOTIABLE PAPER.

I. NOTES.
II. DRAFTS, or BILLS OF EXCHANGE.
III. CHECKS.

CONDITIONS OF NEGOTIABILITY.

I. As to FORM:
1. Certainty of DATE OF PAYMENT;
2. Words ORDER or BEARER;
3. Certainty of AMOUNT;
4. Payable in MONEY;
5. Payable UNCONDITIONALLY.

II. As to MANNER of transfer:
1. If payable to bearer, either
   (1) originally, or   } no condition.
   (2) by blank indorsement. }
2. If payable to order; must be indorsed by one to whose order payable.

III. As to TIME of transfer:
Must be before maturity.

IV. As to CONSIDERATION for transfer:
There must be consideration.

V. As to KNOWLEDGE of defect:
There must be no knowledge (except in accommodation paper).

TRANSFER OF A CLAIM.

SUPPOSE THAT A, REPRESENTING THAT HE HAS A CLAIM UPON C FOR SOME MONEY, TRANSFERS IT TO B:

I. If **A COULD** have enforced it.................**B CAN**:
> Whether or not it be negotiable, or transferred under the conditions.

II. If **A COULD NOT** have enforced it,

because
1. It had no consideration, or only an illegal one, or
2. It had been paid, or
3. C had also a claim upon A, or
4. A had found or stolen it (being commercial paper), or
5. Any similar reason;

  I. In the following cases..............**B CANNOT**:
1. An ordinary debt, not on commercial paper;
2. On commercial, but non-negotiable paper;
3. On negotiable paper, but with some condition of negotiability absent.

  II. In the following case.................**B CAN**:
1. On negotiable paper, and transferred under all the conditions of negotiability;

> *or in other words,*

If it be a note, draft, or check signed by C, and
1. Negotiable in its form;
2. If payable to A, then indorsed by A, either
   1. by blank indorsement, or
   2. in full to B.
3. Transferred to B before it is due,
4. B giving consideration for it,
5. B having no knowledge that A could not enforce it (except in accommodation paper).

CHAPTER XXV.

INDORSER'S RESPONSIBILITY.

1. Two Purposes of Indorsement.—When a person puts his name on the back of a note, or other piece of commercial paper, he becomes an indorser. An indorsement has two distinct purposes, viz., (1) as a means of transferring the ownership, and (2) as creating a new obligation on the part of the person transferring. Thus, taking the forms 1 and 5 (see form 14), when Fay writes "Pay to S. B. Mapes or order" on the back, and delivers the note to Mapes, he does two things: (1) he transfers the contract of Archibald Brothers to Mapes, and (2) he makes a new contract himself with Mapes. INDORSEMENT IS A CONTRACT. We have already considered it as a means of transfer (p. 114). In this chapter we shall consider its meaning as a contract. The rules to be given apply to indorsements upon all kinds of commercial paper, notes, drafts, checks, certificates of deposit, etc.

2. A Transfer without Indorsement DOES NOT RENDER THE PERSON TRANSFERRING RESPONSIBLE FOR THE PAYMENT. Thus, if a check is made payable to bearer, it may pass from one to another, through a dozen hands, without making any one of the successive owners responsible for its payment. Each one takes it at his own risk, and if it is not paid, the final owner can sue only the drawer.

3. Order of Indorsers.—One instrument may have any number of indorsements. The parties are called respectively the first indorser, second indorser, etc., in the order in which they receive the paper and indorse it.* Thus, in

---

* This generally corresponds to the order in which the names appear on the back, but it need not. Brown could write his indorsement

form 14, Fay is the first indorser, Mapes the second, and Brown the third. The payee becomes the first indorser, whether on a note, draft, or check. Where it is made payable to the maker himself, the maker, payee, and first indorser are the same person (form 15).

4. The Contract. — An INDORSEMENT RENDERS THE PERSON WHO MAKES IT RESPONSIBLE FOR THE PAYMENT. This is so whether it is a full or a blank indorsement. It is a guaranty of the debt. Thus, when I write my name on the back of a note I impliedly say, "I agree to pay this note if the maker does not pay it when due;" if it be a draft which has not yet been presented for acceptance, it is, "I agree to pay this draft if the person drawn upon does not accept it, or if he accepts it, but fails to pay;" if it be a draft which has been accepted, it is, "I agree to pay this draft if the acceptor does not pay it when due;" if it be a check, it is, "I agree to pay this check if the bank does not."

5. For Whose Benefit.—This contract is made not only for the benefit of the person to whom I am transferring the instrument, but also for that of any one who may afterwards own it. An indorser is liable to any one who receives it after him.

6. Therefore the person who owns a piece of commercial paper, not paid when it is due, may call upon any one of the following parties to pay it: in a note, the maker, or any one whose name he finds indorsed on the back; in an unaccepted draft or uncertified check, the drawer, or any indorser; in an accepted draft, the acceptor, drawer, or any indorser; in a certified check, the certifying bank, or any indorser.* If any indorser is compelled to pay it, he may

---

above that of Fay. The order of indorsement *in time* makes the distinction between first, second, etc.

* And sometimes drawer (see p. 128).

make any prior indorser pay it to him, until the principal debtor is reached; who, in a note, is the maker; in an unaccepted draft or uncertified check, the drawer; in an accepted draft, the acceptor; in a certified check, the certifying bank. Thus, in the following scheme, each one of the parties is responsible to each one below him:

In a note.	In an unaccepted draft or uncertified check.	In an accepted draft.	In a certified check.
1. Maker.	1. Drawer.	1. Acceptor.	1. The bank.
2. 1st indorser.	2. 1st indorser.	2. Drawer.	2. 1st indorser.
3. 2d indorser.	3. 2d indorser.	3. 1st indorser.	3. 2d indorser.
4. 3d indorser.	4. 3d indorser.	4. 2d indorser.	4. 3d indorser.
Etc.	Etc.	Etc.	Etc.

7. Without Recourse.—But any indorser may restrict his responsibility. If the instrument is payable to the order of some one, in order that he may transfer it and have it retain its negotiability, we have seen that he must indorse it. But he may wish to transfer it without making himself responsible for it. This he can do by adding to his indorsement some such words as "without recourse" (form 17). Such an indorsement, therefore, forms an exception to the rules of this chapter. It is not a contract.

8. Negotiability.—AN INDORSEMENT IS A NEGOTIABLE CONTRACT. When this contract is made, the parties between whom it is made are the indorser himself and the one to whom he transfers the paper. They know all the transaction connected with the indorsement, and why it is made; but those who receive it afterwards may know nothing about it, except what they see on the back of the paper, i.e., the indorsement itself. If, then, they have taken the paper, believing the indorsement to be a valid and complete contract, the indorser should not be allowed to claim that it was not. Consequently, while as between the indorser and the one next to him, it is not an enforceable contract unless it has the seven requisites of a binding contract, and it is intended between them that the indorser shall be responsible, yet as between the indorser and some one else, i.e., some party later than the one next to him, the contract is binding if that party takes the paper relying on the indorsement.*

9. Demand of Payment.—When a note or draft becomes due its payment is demanded. But NO DEMAND IS NECÉSSARY TO MAKE THE MAKER OF A NOTE OR THE ACCEPTOR OF A DRAFT RESPONSIBLE. Thus, the owner may have ascertained beforehand that the note or draft would not be paid. He may sue them as soon as the paper is due, without demanding its payment.

10. But as to Indorsers the rule is different. To MAKE THE INDORSER OF A NOTE, OR THE INDORSER OR DRAWER OF A DRAFT RESPONSIBLE, THE PAPER MUST BE PRESENTED AND PAYMENT DEMANDED OF THE MAKER OR ACCEPTOR ON THE VERY DAY WHEN IT BECOMES DUE. The maker of a note, and the acceptor of a draft, are the primary debtors; the others are sureties, and are entitled to have the demand

---

* Suppose a check made by A to the order of B, indorsed by B to C, by C to D, and by D to E successively. E knows what the agreement was when D indorsed and transferred the check to him; therefore he cannot sue D unless the agreement was that he should have that right. But all he knows about the contract C made with D, or the one that B made with C, is the indorsements of B and C on the back; consequently he can sue them any way. Now suppose he could compel D to pay the check, then the question would arise, could D compel C or B to reimburse him? This would be settled in the same way. He knows the whole agreement between himself and C, but he may not know anything of that between B and C. The same rules of negotiability are applicable to the indorser's contract as to the maker's. (See pp. 108–117.)

made of the primary debtors first, even though it is known that they will refuse to pay. If the paper be payable at a particular place the demand must be made there. So also in a check, the drawer or indorser cannot be sued unless it is first presented, and its payment demanded of the bank.

11. Notice.—But demand alone is not sufficient. IF THE PAYMENT IS REFUSED, NOTICE OF THAT FACT MUST BE GIVEN IMMEDIATELY TO THE INDORSER OR DRAWER OF COMMERCIAL PAPER TO MAKE HIM RESPONSIBLE. If either the demand or the notice is omitted, all the indorsers and the drawer are discharged. The reason is this: that the indorser or drawer, compelled to take up the paper (i.e., pay it), may have the earliest opportunity to protect himself against loss. An owner, knowing that one of the indorsers was well able to pay, might make no haste to sue the maker, but the indorser being notified, may pay it, and sue the maker immediately. After the notice has been given, the owner may delay suing as long as he wishes, without losing his right.*

12. Notice of Non-Acceptance.—In like manner, if the person drawn upon in a draft refuses to accept it, or if a bank refuses to pay an uncertified check, notice must be immediately given to the drawer and indorsers, or they will be discharged.

13. Time of Demand.—It has been already stated that in notes and drafts due at some certain time in the future, the demand must be made on the very day they become due, i.e., the last day of grace. As to notes and drafts which are made due "on demand," to render the maker or acceptor responsible the demand need never be made, but to make an indorser responsible it would be unsafe to delay long, say more than a month or two.

As to checks, demand of payment should be made as

---

* But not beyond six years (Chap. XVII.).

soon as possible. The drawer is not discharged by any delay, unless he can show that he was injured by it, as by the bank's failing in the mean time; but the indorser is discharged, unless it is sent to the bank for payment before the end of the next day after the person to whom he indorsed it receives it.

14. Time of Notice.—THE NOTICE MUST BE SENT BEFORE THE END OF THE NEXT DAY AFTER THE REFUSAL TO PAY OR ACCEPT IS MADE. This applies to all kinds of commercial paper. Thus, if the paper is due on March 8th, and payment is demanded at 10 A.M., the notice must be sent before the close of the 9th. Even though the debtor should promise to pay it in a few days, and the owner of the paper should be willing to trust him to that extent, yet the notice should be sent, for a failure to send it in time discharges a drawer or indorser in any event. These rules as to the time of demand and notice are very strict, and particular care should be paid to them.

> *Note to Teacher.*—It would be useful to take each one of the forms of notes, drafts, and checks on pp. 275 to 280, and state when demand of payment may or should be made, and when the notice should be sent in each case.

15. Manner of Notice.—The notice of non-payment or non-acceptance is usually written. It must describe the paper in such way that the one to whom it is given or sent shall know exactly the instrument referred to. A useful way is to state the amount, date, and parties (form 18). It may generally be sent by mail, and should be sent to the party's usual address, his residence, or place of business.* It is sufficient that the notice be sent, whether it be received or not.

---

* In some States if the parties reside in the same town it is unsafe to use the mail, the notice sent in that way being good only if it is actually received. By *parties* is meant the party sending the notice and the one to whom it is sent.

16. By Whom.—Any one acting for the owner may make the demand and send the notice. Banks often do it for those who keep accounts with them. Usually the owner or his agent notifies all the parties on the paper, and this is the prudent way. It renders all parties responsible to him, and each responsible to each other in their order. But he need notify only such as he chooses to hold responsible to himself. Consequently if any indorser is notified, and indorsers or others prior to him are not, he must himself notify them if he wishes to hold them responsible to him. For such purpose each one has the day on which he received the notice sent to him, and the next day, in which to send his notice.

17. Protest.—This demanding of payment and sending of notice are together often called *protest*, though legally that word has a different meaning. It is commonly done by an officer called a *notary public*, to whom the owner delivers the paper for that purpose. The notary then usually draws up a certificate showing what he has done, and attaches it to the note or draft. On all commercial paper, except foreign bills of exchange, any one may make the demand and serve the notice. On foreign bills a notary should be used.

RESPONSIBILITY

of parties to commercial paper to the owner.*

I. Those **NOT RESPONSIBLE** to the owner;
1. The person drawn upon in a draft, until he has accepted,
2. The bank, in an uncertified check,
3. The drawer, in a certified check (sometimes),
4. Any prior owner, of any kind of paper, who has not indorsed it, or who has indorsed without recourse.

II. Those **RESPONSIBLE WITHOUT DEMAND** being made on the principal debtor on the day of payment;
1. Maker of note,
2. Acceptor of draft.

III. Those **RESPONSIBLE ONLY WHEN DEMAND HAS BEEN MADE** on the principal debtor, and notice given them within the proper time;
1. Indorser of note,
2. Drawer of draft,
3. Indorser of draft,
4. Drawer of check,
5. Indorser of check.

---

* This means the usual responsibility. Of course the parties may make such contract as they choose, to be responsible or not, in any cases.

THINGS NECESSARY

to be done by the owner of any of the ordinary kinds of commercial paper, in order to render the parties upon it responsible to him.

IF IT BE,

I. A NOTE HAVING NO INDORSERS;

Nothing; the maker is responsible without demand.

II. A NOTE HAVING INDORSERS, and due at a specified time;

1. *Present it* to the maker for payment, on the day it is due, and
2. If not paid, *send notice* of its non-payment, to each indorser, on that day or the next.

III. A DRAFT NOT YET PRESENTED FOR ACCEPTANCE;

I. IF DUE AT SIGHT, OR A CERTAIN TIME AFTER SIGHT,

1. *Present it* to the person drawn upon, for acceptance, as soon as possible,
2. If not accepted, *send notice* of its non-acceptance, to the drawer and each indorser, on the day acceptance is refused, or the next day.

II. IF DUE AT A SPECIFIED TIME,

1. *Present it* to the person drawn upon, for acceptance, any time before it is due, and
2. If not accepted, *send notice* of its non-acceptance, to the drawer and each indorser, on the day acceptance is refused, or the next.

(If accepted, see IV.)

or

1. *Present it* to the person drawn upon, on the day it is due, and
2. If not paid, *send notice* of its non-payment, to the drawer and each indorser, on that day or the next.

IV. **AN ACCEPTED DRAFT;**

1. *Present it* to the acceptor, for payment, on the day it is due, and
2. If not paid, *send notice* of its non-payment, to the drawer and each indorser, on that day or the next.

V. **AN UNCERTIFIED CHECK;**

I. To make DRAWER responsible,

1. *Present it* to the bank, for payment, any time, and
2. If not paid, *send notice* of its non-payment, to him, on the day payment is refused, or the next.

II. To make AN INDORSER responsible,

1. *Present or send it* to the bank, for payment, the day it is received from the indorser, or the next day, and
2. If not paid, *send notice* of its non-payment, to the indorser on that day or the next.

VI. **A CERTIFIED CHECK;**

I. To make DRAWER responsible (when not discharged),

1. *Present it* to the bank, for payment, any time, and
2. If not paid, *send notice* of its non-payment, to him, on the day payment is refused, or the next.

II. To make BANK responsible,
Present it to the bank, for payment, any time.

III. To make AN INDORSER responsible,

1. *Present or send it* to the bank, for payment, the day it is received from the indorser, or the next day, and
2. If not paid, *send notice* of its non-payment, to the indorser, on that day or the next.

CHAPTER XXVI.

FORGED PAPER.

1. Forgery is THE FRAUDULENTLY MAKING OR ALTERING OF A WRITTEN INSTRUMENT.—Commercial paper is frequently forged by the forger's making a check, draft, etc., in the name of some responsible person, since it is so easy to obtain the money if the forgery succeeds. An indorsement is itself a written instrument, and therefore if any one having or finding a piece of commercial paper made payable to the order of some one else, should indorse it in his name, without authority to do so, and with a fraudulent intent, it would be forgery. So any material alteration made, with intent to defraud, on a true instrument, is forgery. Thus, suppose the amount in a check were written thus, " *$50.00*," a forgery might be committed merely by erasing the dot.

2. General Principle.—So far, in this book, we have considered only true instruments. All the rules of contracts, notes, etc., apply only to such as are really signed by the one by whom they purport to be, or by some one authorized to act as his agent for that purpose. A FORGED INSTRUMENT IS NOT COMMERCIAL PAPER. Being false, it represents neither a contract nor property, and no rights are gained by its possession or transfer. This general principle is illustrated in the following sections.

3. One whose name is forged CANNOT BE MADE RESPONSIBLE.—The act is not his, and one certainly should not be held responsible for another's acts, which are entirely unauthorized. Thus, if a note is forged in my name as maker, or a draft forged in my name as drawer, or the acceptance forged in my name as acceptor, or my indorsement forged upon any paper, I do not make the contract and therefore cannot be made to fulfill it, i.e., to pay. So, if my name is forged as the drawer of a check, and the bank believing it genuine pays it, the bank must lose rather than I. It makes no difference how careful or honest one is who takes forged paper. He must always take the risk of its being a forgery.

4. Payment under Mistake.—But the rule goes still further. One whose name is forged not only need not pay, but even if he should be himself deceived by the skillfulness of the forgery, and should pay, nevertheless, he may recover his money from the one to whom he paid it. This is but one case of the general principle that MONEY PAID UNDER A MISTAKE MUST BE REFUNDED. Thus, even if the supposed maker, or drawer, or indorser should, after a careful examination, admit his signature to be genuine and should pay, yet the one to whom he paid would have to refund if the signature turned out to be forged.

5. Exceptions.—There are two quite important exceptions to the rule of the preceding section. They both relate to the case where a person drawn upon has recognized the paper as genuine either by paying it, or accepting, or (in a check) certifying it, for a bona fide owner. The cases are (1) where the *drawer's* name is forged, and (2) where the *acceptance* (in a check *certification*) is forged. If in those two cases the person, or bank, drawn upon, accepts or certifies or pays, they must stand by the act.* The reason for this is the convenience of business.

* Thus, in the check on page 126, the Ninth National Bank should be certain that the signature of Jones is genuine before it pays or certifies, for it cannot recall the act. If it should certify it would have to pay the check, and when paid to a bona fide owner it could neither recover its amount back from him, nor charge it against Jones' account. The bank would lose the amount.

Note to Teacher.—Have the scholar apply this rule to the draft on p. 117.

6. Transfer.—Since forged paper is in reality nothing but a piece of waste paper, one who sells it to another in reality sells nothing except so far as it is genuine, even though both believe it genuine as to the whole.* Therefore one who buys forged paper may recover what he loses by it from the one from whom he buys it, because it is money paid under a mistake. Thus if there are a series of real indorsers upon a piece of commercial paper which afterwards turns out to be forged, they are each responsible to each other in the regular order (p. 132) as if it were not forged, and the one who took it from the forger must bear the loss unless he can recover its amount from the forger. Therefore an indorsement may be said to guarantee the genuineness of the paper.

7. Raising Amount.—Paper is sometimes forged by erasing the amount named in a genuine instrument and putting in a larger amount. It is then perfectly valid as to the original sum, but wholly void as to the excess. Even though it is accepted or certified after being raised, the acceptance or certification does not make the acceptor or the bank responsible for any more than the original sum. And if the excess should be paid it could be recovered. The practical business suggestion to be gained from all these rules about commercial paper is that in buying it, unless we are absolutely certain that it is genuine and a valid contract in every respect, we should be careful about those from whom we buy it, so as to have some one responsible to fall back upon if it turns out invalid.

Note to Teacher.—In all cases of dishonored or forged commercial paper there is some one who must sustain the loss finally, some one who is himself responsible, but who has no one else to look to from whom he can make a collection, because the one responsible to him has failed, or has escaped. Have the scholar point out in different cases who must bear the loss.

---

* On the same principle a payment in counterfeit money is no payment.

CHAPTER XXVII.

MONEY.

1. Definition.—Money means those articles which are received and pass from hand to hand among all the people as the representative of so much value. In business it is often called *cash*. All civilized nations have some form of money, and generally it consists either of coin made by the government, or paper money issued or recognized as money by the government. Throughout the United States the money is now substantially uniform, any of it being received as money in every State; but this was not always so.

2. Two Kinds.—The money of the United States is of two kinds, (1) coin, and (2) paper money (often called *currency*). The coin is chiefly of two kinds, gold and silver. The paper money is chiefly of two kinds, United States Notes* and National Bank Bills. There are besides the small copper and nickel coins.

3. Character.—Coin has a value of its own, an intrinsic value as metal, irrespective of its being stamped as coin. But paper money has practically no value, except for what is written on its face. Thus the United States Notes read as follows: "The United States will pay the bearer ten dollars." A bank bill reads as follows: "The . . . . . Bank, of the City of New York, will pay ten dollars to bearer on demand." Each is signed by the proper officers. Paper money, therefore, is merely a promise, a negotiable demand note. In one case the National Government promises, and in the other the particular bank. It only passes current at the same value as the coin, because all believe they can obtain payment in coin whenever they wish.

---

* Popularly called *greenbacks*.—Gold and silver are the safest forms of money. Paper money is convenient, but dangerous, unless its amount is carefully limited.

4. Legal Tender IS THAT KIND OF MONEY WHICH BY LAW CAN BE OFFERED IN PAYMENT OF A DEBT. The creditor may if he chooses take in payment not only any kind of money, but also any other article, such as a draft, or goods. Checks are very commonly used for that purpose. But, if it be insisted on, the person bound to pay must provide legal tender. It is so called because it is what may be legally tendered (i.e., offered) in payment.

5. What is.—Not all money is legal tender. In this country now THE LEGAL TENDER CONSISTS SUBSTANTIALLY OF THE UNITED STATES COIN* AND THE UNITED STATES NOTES. Thus all our money is legal tender except the bank bills, but that distinction is now of little importance, for the reason that the payment of the National Bank Bills is so well secured that they are as readily accepted by all people as any other money.

MONEY

OF THE UNITED STATES.

I. COIN.

1. GOLD COINS,
2. SILVER COINS,
3. SMALL COPPER AND NICKEL COINS (1 *to* 5 *cent pieces*),

II. PAPER MONEY.

4. UNITED STATES NOTES,

} Legal Tender.

5. NATIONAL BANK BILLS..... ..... Not Legal Tender.

---

*Except the trade-dollar, which is not legal tender. The silver coins of less than $1.00 are legal tender up to the amount of $10. The copper and nickel pieces are legal tender up to the amount of 25 cents.

Summary of Leading Rules of Commercial Paper.

I. Notes.

1. A NOTE IS a written promise, signed by the person promising, to pay a certain sum of money, at a certain time, to a person named, or to his order, or to the bearer.

2. There are TWO KINDS of notes, those payable (1) to order, and (2) to bearer.

3. A note payable at a future time is not DUE until the third day after its specified day of payment.

4. In the hands of the ORIGINAL HOLDER of a note it is a binding contract provided it has all the requisites of a binding contract, but not otherwise.

5. NEGOTIABILITY in commercial paper is the quality of being enforceable by one receiving it, though not enforceable by the one from whom it is received.

6. THE CIRCUMSTANCES which, though rendering negotiable paper void in the hands of one party, yet do not affect the rights of others receiving it through him are in general those which do not appear on the instrument itself.

7. The FIVE THINGS necessary in the FORM of commercial paper to make it negotiable are, (1) that the date of payment be certain to come, (2) that it have one of the two words *order* or *bearer*, (3) that the amount be specified and certain, (4) that it be payable in money only, and (5) that it be an unconditional promise.

8. Paper payable to BEARER may be transferred by delivery alone.

9. Paper payable to ORDER must be indorsed to be transferred.

10. Negotiable paper loses its negotiability at MATURITY.

11. One who receives commercial paper GIVING NO MONEY or property in exchange for it, gets no better right to enforce it than the one from whom he receives it had.

12. One who receives commercial paper KNOWING at the time of any invalidating defect gets no better right to enforce it than the one from whom he receives it had (except accommodation paper).

II. DRAFTS AND BILLS OF EXCHANGE.

1. A DRAFT IS a written order, signed by one person, ordering another person, to whom it is directed, to pay a certain sum of money, at a certain time, to a third person (named), or to his order, or to. the bearer.

2. A draft payable at a future time is not DUE until the third day after its specified day of payment.

3. The DRAWER'S AGREEMENT is to pay the draft if the person upon whom it is drawn does not.

4. The person drawn upon is under no obligation to the holder of a draft UNLESS HE ACCEPTS it.

5. AFTER ACCEPTANCE the person drawn upon, i.e., the acceptor, is the principal debtor, and responsible to all parties.

6. Drafts are NEGOTIABLE both before and after acceptance.

7. ALL THE PRINCIPLES of negotiability apply to drafts, as to notes.

8. A contract is governed by the LAW OF THE STATE in which it is made.

III. CHECKS.

1. A CHECK IS a draft drawn upon a bank or banker, and made payable immediately.

2. A bank is under NO OBLIGATION to the holder of an UNCERTIFIED check.

3. Checks have no DAYS OF GRACE.

4. CERTIFICATION substitutes the bank for the drawer as the principal debtor.

5. Checks are NEGOTIABLE under the same conditions as notes and drafts.

IV. INDORSER'S RESPONSIBILITY.

1. INDORSEMENT IS a contract.

2. A TRANSFER WITHOUT INDORSEMENT does not render the person transferring responsible for the payment.

3. An INDORSEMENT RENDERS the person who makes it responsible for the payment.

4. An indorsement is a NEGOTIABLE contract.

5. No DEMAND is necessary to make the MAKER of a note or the ACCEPTOR of a draft responsible.

6. To make the INDORSER of a note, or the INDORSER OR DRAWER of a draft responsible, the paper must be PRESENTED and payment DEMANDED of the maker or acceptor on the very day when it becomes due.

7. If the payment is refused NOTICE of that fact must be given immediately to the indorser or drawer of commercial paper to make him responsible.

8. The notice must be sent before the end of the NEXT DAY after the refusal to pay or accept is made.

V. Forged Paper.

1. Forgery is the fraudulently making or altering of a written instrument.

2. A forged instrument is not commercial paper.

3. One whose name is forged cannot be made responsible.

4. Money paid under a mistake must be refunded.

VI. Money.

1. Legal Tender is that kind of money which by law can be offered in payment of a debt.

2. The legal tender of the United States consists substantially of the United States coin, and the United States Notes.

REVIEW QUESTIONS.

Commercial Paper.

1. Name the three kinds of commercial paper. Why so called?
2. Define a note. Who is the maker? The payee?
3. Explain the usefulness of notes.
4. What are the four kinds of notes in respect to their payee? To how many kinds can they be reduced? What are those kinds?
5. What effect has the name of the payee in form 3?
6. What is meant by "maturity"?
7. What are "days of grace"? When does a demand note become due? The note in form 3? What is the effect if the last day of grace falls upon a Sunday or legal holiday? What are the legal holidays?
8. Who are the two parties first making a contract in an order note? In a bearer note? Explain how other parties may assume relations to the contract.
9. If a note remains in the hands of the party to whom it is first given under what circumstances can he enforce it? Apply the requisites of a binding contract to the maker's contract in a note.
10. How does its character change on being transferred?
11. Define negotiability. What effect does it have upon paper originally enforceable? What effect upon paper void, on account of something appearing upon the paper itself, e.g., a statement that it has been paid, or that it was given for an illegal purpose?
12. What is an accommodation note? When enforceable, and when not? When may a note given for an illegal purpose be _n-forced?
13. Under what circumstances may a maker be compelled to pay a note, when he has already done so once? How may he avoid this risk?
14. Explain how negotiability affects the case of a note held by one who also owes a debt to the maker (case of set-off).
15 Explain how it affects the case of a stolen note. Why is it prudent to make notes, checks, etc., which are to be sent to a distance, payable to order instead of to bearer?

16. Name the kinds of conditions of negotiability. What is meant by a "condition of negotiability"?

17. What are the five requisites as to form in commercial paper, to make it negotiable? Is a note binding on the maker which fails to comply with some one of these requisites? What is the effect of such a note? What is the general purpose of the formal requisites?

18. How is commercial paper usually transferred when payable to bearer? When payable to order? What is indorsement? The two kinds? What is the effect of a transfer without indorsement? How may an order note become payable to the bearer? How may a bearer note become an order note?

19. How long does commercial paper remain negotiable? What is the effect of transferring a note after it is due?

20. If one receives negotiable paper before it is due, and without knowledge of any fault in it, but gives nothing for it, does he get any better right to enforce it than the one from whom he receives it had? Can one who steals a bearer note sue upon it?

21. Can one who buys a bearer note from the thief sue upon it, when he does not know it was stolen? Can he, when he has reason to believe it was stolen?

22. What is a draft? The drawer? The payee? The person drawn upon? A bill of exchange? Explain their use.

23. State some of the different kinds of drafts.

24. Name some differences between a note and a draft.

25. What is acceptance? How is it made? When? Who is the acceptor?

26. When does a time draft become due? A draft on demand? A sight draft?

27. Can a draft be transferred before acceptance? After? How is it usually done?

28. What does a drawer agree in drawing a draft?

29. What is the agreement of the person drawn upon, before acceptance? In accepting? Can the owner of a draft sue the person drawn upon for refusing to accept?

30. Who is the principal debtor in a note? In a draft before acceptance? In a draft after acceptance?

31. Are drafts negotiable before acceptance? After?

32. Is there any difference between drafts and notes, as to the rules of negotiability?

33. What two kinds of accommodation drafts are there? Who is the accommodated party in each? Who is the accommodating party?
34. Can an accommodated party ever sue an accommodating party?
35. By the law of what State is a contract governed?
36. What is a check? The drawer? The payee? In what particulars is a check like a draft? How different in its form? In its effect? Explain the use of checks.
37. Is the bank under any obligation to the holder of an uncertified check? Why? Is it under any obligation to the drawer? Why?
38. What is it to "stop payment"? Its effect?
39. What is the effect of dating a check ahead?
40. What is certification? Its effect upon the bank? Upon the drawer?
41. Are checks negotiable?
42. State the rule as to check stamps.
43. What is a certificate of deposit? What does it most resemble?
44. State in order all the conditions of negotiability.
45. What is an indorser? State the two purposes of indorsement.
46. How is commercial paper, payable to bearer, transferred so as not to make the person transferring it responsible for it? How, when payable to order?
47. Does the order in which their names appear on the back of the paper have anything to do with the parties' being respectively, first, second, etc., indorsers? What is it that makes one the first, another the second indorser, etc.?
48. What is the contract one makes when he indorses a note? An unaccepted draft? An accepted draft? A check? With whom does he make it, i.e., for whose benefit? What is the effect of that?
49. When one owns a piece of dishonored commercial paper which has indorsements of other parties upon it, state whom he may sue, if it be a note? An unaccepted draft? An uncertified check? An accepted draft? A certified check? A certificate of deposit?
50. In each of those cases, whom may each indorser hold responsible to himself? Can a first indorser ever sue a second indorser?
51. What does "without recourse" mean?
52. If the second indorser should agree with the third indorser that

the former should not be responsible to the latter, could a fourth indorser sue the second? Why? Could the third sue the second? Why?

53. What is meant by demand and notice in connection with dishonored paper?

54. Is the maker of a note discharged if the owner neglects to make demand? Is the acceptor of a draft? The drawer? An indorser? Who is?

55. To whom must notice be sent? What is the effect of not sending it?

56. What is notice of non-acceptance? The effect of omitting it?

57. What is the effect if the owner sends notice to some indorsers and not to others?

58. When must demand be made, in paper due at a particular time? In checks? Upon whom must demand be made, in a note? In a draft? In a check? By whom may the demand be made?

59. When must the notice be sent? How may it be sent? To where? What should it say?

60. When an indorser receives notice of the dishonor, what should he do to protect himself?

61. What is protest?

62. What is forgery? Is an alteration forgery? Is an accidental alteration forgery?

63. What is the effect of a forgery upon the one whose name is forged? If he recognizes the forgery as genuine and pays the money, can he recover it from the one to whom he pays?

64. State the two cases in which one is bound by his recognition of a forged signature as genuine.

65. If one transfers forged paper without indorsing it, has he any responsibility with regard to it afterwards?

66. What is the effect of paying a note where the amount has been raised by forgery? Of accepting a raised draft? Of certifying a raised check? Of paying a raised draft or check?

67. What is money? The kinds in the U. S. ?

68. What is the difference between money and legal tender? What part of our money is legal tender?

DIVISION III.

MISCELLANEOUS CASES.

CHAPTER XXVIII.

AGREEMENTS FOR PERSONAL SERVICES.

1. Kinds.—The agreement to work for another, i.e., to render services for wages, or a salary, or other compensation, is a very common kind of contract in business life. These contracts may, for our present purpose, be divided into two general classes, agreements (1) to do some particular thing, and (2) to do whatever the employer may direct. Brokers, commission merchants, lawyers, tradesmen,* and many others belong to the first class; clerks and all others employed to do general work belong to the second class. The act of employing in both classes is a contract, in which each party, the employer and the employé,† agrees to do certain things. The following sections of this chapter will show the important elements of such a contract.

2. Compensation.—Every agreement to employ contains an agreement to pay for the services. This is the most important part of the employer's agreement, and it is either express or implied. If the parties fix the compensation themselves beforehand, that controls; but where nothing is said about whether the services will be paid for, or how much will be paid, nevertheless such a contract is al-

---

* Who make or repair articles, as, for instance, a jeweler employed to repair a watch.

† Using these terms with reference to both classes.

ways implied. WHEN SERVICES ARE REQUESTED THERE IS ALWAYS AN IMPLIED CONTRACT TO PAY WHAT THEY ARE WORTH, i:e., the usual amount paid for such services elsewhere. This is similar to the rule in sales (p. 91). Unless there is a special agreement for payment in advance, the person employed is entitled to no pay until the whole service has been rendered.

3. Employé's Agreement.—The person employed must fulfill his agreement, but if anything else is asked of him he need not do it. IT IS AN IMPLIED PART OF EVERY AGREEMENT TO RENDER SERVICES THAT THE WORK WILL BE DONE WITH ORDINARY SKILL, CARE, AND DILIGENCE. If the person employed fails to carry out his contract in any respect ; if, for instance, the jeweler fails to repair the watch as soon as he agreed to or does it carelessly, he is entitled to no compensation, no matter how much he has done. (See p. 23, sec. 9.) In ordinary commercial transactions, if I agree to do a thing, it is fulfilling my agreement to get some one else to do it ; but, of course, I am responsible for all my agent does, and for his want of skill, care, or diligence.

4. Skill.—Any one by engaging in any kind of business represents that he and his clerks or workmen have the degree of skill ordinarily required in that business. He does not therefore agree to use all possible skill, but only such as is ordinarily possessed.

5. Care.—This rule as to care applies particularly to cases where the person employed is to render some services in connection with certain property belonging to the other party, such as those who repair articles, or warehousemen, who take goods on storage, or forwarding merchants, etc. The care required in handling the property is ordinary care, i.e., so much as an ordinarily careful person takes of his own property. It is therefore not enough to take as much care of others' property as you take of your own, unless you are a careful person.

6. Loss or Injury.—When one has another's property in his possession and through his carelessness it is lost or injured, the careless one is not only entitled to no compensation for what he has done, but must compensate the owner for his loss or injury. But if the loss or injury occurs in spite of ordinary carefulness, then the owner must not only bear his own loss but must pay for whatever services were rendered.*

7. Lien.—ANY ONE HAVING THE PROPERTY OF ANOTHER IN HIS HANDS UPON WHICH HE HAS DONE WORK MAY KEEP IT UNTIL HE IS PAID FOR HIS WORK. In other words, he has a lien† upon it for his pay. Thus, a bookbinder may retain books that he has bound, a warehouseman may retain goods stored with him, each until his charges (if correct) are paid. Machinists, carpenters, jewelers, and all kinds of manufacturers and repairers have this right. This kind of lien applies to one who carries on a regular trade or business, and it exists under three conditions only, (1) when he has possession of the property, and (2) has performed some service in connection with it at the owner's request, and (3) it has not been paid for. If he lets it go he loses his lien. If he has not done the work as ordered he has no lien. If payment is made the lien ends.

8. Length of Employment.—In the second class of cases, where one is employed to perform a general class of duties, the time for which he is hired is an important element. This may be for any time, a day, a month, a year, or longer.

---

* Thus, if a jeweler repairs my watch, but before I call for it his store is entered by burglars and my watch is stolen, I must bear the loss (unless the store were carelessly left unprotected), and must also pay his charges for the repairs.

† For other illustrations of *lien* see pp. 93, 99.

Very often no time is specified in so many words.   In such
case, the time when payment is to be made will indicate the
length of employment.   Thus, if a clerk, messenger, etc.,
is hired for no fixed time but at so many dollars a week, or
a month, it is a hiring for a week or a month respectively.
If the work goes on the next week or month in the same
manner, it is a new contract on the same terms.   Thus, it
is as if the employer said at the beginning of each period,
"I agree to pay you .... dollars if you will work this week
[or month]," and the employé answered, "I agree to work
this week [or month]."   When the contract ends, i.e.,
when the week or the month expires, each party may do as
he chooses.   There is no obligation to renew it.

9. Discharge.—We have just seen that an employé may
be discharged at the end of his time, without any cause, and
without notice.   Thus, if hired at so much a week and for
no definite time, he may be discharged at the end of any
week.   He may also be discharged during the week or other
period, and has no right to insist upon working after he is
discharged.   But in that case if the discharge is without
good cause, i.e., if he was properly performing what he
agreed to, he is entitled to payment for the whole period.
If, however, there was good reason for the discharge, arising
from his own fault, he is entitled to no pay for any of that
period.

10. Leaving.—Similar rules apply where the employé
leaves of his own accord.   He can leave at the end of the
time without giving notice.   But if he leaves before the
time has expired he is entitled to no pay for that period, no
matter how much of it he had worked there.   Thus, if he
agreed to stay a month and left at the end of three weeks,
he would be entitled to nothing.   In short, each party must
keep his contract if the other does, but need not if the other
does not.

CHAPTER XXIX.

TRANSPORTATION OF GOODS.

1. The Business of the transportation of freight from place to place is, in this country, of great importance. Those who transport goods for others are called *carriers,* and since all the business is done under contract, such contracts are very numerous. They are contracts for personal services. Generally, all the rules of contracts which we have already considered apply to them, with a few exceptions, which will be mentioned in this chapter. The rules of agency are peculiarly applicable here, for in almost every case the actual work is done, not by the carrier but by his agents, i.e., workmen, clerks, etc.

2. Common Carriers.—Those engaged in this business are also called *common carriers.* A COMMON CARRIER IS ONE WHOSE BUSINESS IS TO TRANSPORT FROM PLACE TO PLACE THE GOODS OF ANY ONE WHO MAY EMPLOY HIM.* The most common ones are the railroad, steamboat, steamship, and express companies. Truckmen and others, in cities, who offer their services to the public generally, are also common carriers. There are two elements necessary to constitute one a common carrier, (1) his following it as a business, and (2) his offering his services to the public generally. Thus, a carman who works only for a particular person is not a common, but a *private carrier.*

3. Obligation to Take.—A COMMON CARRIER IS OBLIGED

---

* The word "he" is used in this chapter for convenience's sake. It is meant to include individuals, firms, and corporations alike. Thus a railroad company is a common carrier, its officers, engineers, brakemen, etc., being its agents.

BY LAW TO TAKE ANY GOODS THAT ARE OFFERED TO HIM
FOR TRANSPORTATION TO ANY POINT ON HIS ROUTE, provided his usual compensation is offered him in advance.
Ordinarily people are free to make or not to make contracts
with whom they choose (p. 18), but this exception is made
for the benefit of the public.   But where the carrier's cars
or other conveyances are full he may refuse to take more ;
so also he may refuse to take freight of a dangerous character, such as explosives.

4. Compensation.—Ordinarily carriers may establish such
rates, or make such contracts, as they choose.   The large
corporations, like railroad companies, usually have established schedules of rates.   These they can change from
time to time, but they must accept the goods of all persons at those rates.   They cannot demand more from particular persons than from others, but must treat all alike.
Very often the State provides a maximum rate, which they
are not allowed to exceed.   It is now a debated question
whether the railroads of the country should be left free to
compete or combine with each other, or should be brought
more under the control of law as to their rates.

5. Who must Pay.—Though common carriers may demand their pay (often called *freight*) in advance, yet it is
common for them to transport the goods and collect the
freight from the person to whom they are transported.   But
if he refuses to pay then the question may arise, Who is
responsible to the carrier for the freight, the sender or the
one to whom they are sent?   This question is solved by asking, With whom did the carrier make his contract?   Now,
usually the contract is made only with the sender ; the
other party makes no contract with the carrier.   Therefore
the carrier can only sue the sender.   Thus, if Jones in New
York takes goods to a railroad depot and asks the company
to carry them to Brown & Co. in San Francisco the only,

contract is the one between Jones and the company.* But sometimes the sender is acting as the agent of the person to whom they are to be sent, and then the company may sue the latter, for the contract is made with him.†

6. Carrier's Lien.—But common carriers have still another way to obtain their pay. COMMON CARRIERS MAY KEEP THE GOODS THEY HAVE TRANSPORTED UNTIL THEIR CHARGES ARE PAID. In other words, they have a lien upon the goods. Thus there are three ways in which a carrier may enforce payment of his freight: (1) he may refuse to take the goods unless payment is made in advance; (2) he may transport them and then keep them until paid; and (3) he may transport and deliver them, and then sue the person with whom he made his contract.

7. Loss or Injury.—COMMON CARRIERS ARE RESPONSIBLE FOR ANY LOSS OR INJURY OCCURRING TO GOODS WHICH THEY ARE TRANSPORTING. Ordinarily, as we have seen, (p. 157, sec. 6), a person having the goods of others in his possession is not responsible for the loss unless it is caused by his negligence or that of his servants, but with the common carrier the rule is more strict. He has complete control over the goods as if they were his own, and if while in his possession they suffer injury it is his loss. It makes no difference how much care he takes, nor what the cause of the loss may be. If any injury occurs he must pay for it,

---

* This contract is often written, and is called a *receipt* or *bill of lading.* (See p. 163 for the kind used in marine business.)

† This question, Whom may the carrier sue, is not the same as the one, Who is finally responsible for the freight? The latter is wholly a matter of agreement between the sender and the one to whom they are sent. That one must finally pay who between them has agreed to, and the ordinary rule is that where one buys goods and orders them to be sent to him, he impliedly agrees to pay for the transportation. Thus if Brown & Co. had agreed with Jones to pay, and the company had compelled Jones to pay, he might sue Brown & Co.

unless it occurs through the fault of the sender, as on account of careless packing, etc. Yet if a package is of very great value, as for instance a package of money, the carrier must be informed beforehand of its value or he will not be responsible for its loss.

CHAPTER XXX.

SHIPPING.

1. In General.—By *shipping* is meant any kind of vessel, whether navigating the ocean, or rivers, or lakes, and whether propelled by sails or steam. There are two classes of persons concerned in the law of shipping, (1) the owners of vessels, and (2) the owners of the goods shipped. Since shipping is the transportation of goods by water, ship-owners are carriers: those who send their goods are called *shippers.* Sometimes the owner of a ship instead of sending it out himself lets it to another person. The latter is said to *charter* the vessel, and the contract made between him and the ship-owner is called a *charter-party* (form 23, p. 288). He then becomes the carrier in place of the shipowner.*

2. Common Carriers.—Those who offer to carry the goods of any one are, as we have seen, common carriers. Where ship-owners or charterers offer to do this, their rights and responsibilities are the rights and responsibilities of common carriers, which need not be repeated here.

The rules of law governing shipping are therefore chiefly

---

* If a person carries his own goods in his own ship, or one he has chartered, he is of course his own carrier.

those governing transportation by land, and in this chapter we will only notice a few rules peculiar to shipping.

3. **A Bill of Lading** is a document delivered by the master (or owner) of a vessel to one sending goods by it (called the *consignor* * or shipper), acknowledging that they have been received upon the vessel for transportation. It constitutes the contract between the shipper and the carrier. The shipper then sends the bill of lading to the person to whom the goods are to be transported (called the *consignee* *), and it serves as evidence of his right to receive the goods when they arrive. When he receives the goods he delivers up the bill of lading (form 24, p. 288).

4. **Its Transfer.**—The bill of lading stands as the representative of the goods, and in a certain sense it may be considered property itself, belonging to the consignee. Like commercial paper the consignee may indorse it and transfer it to some one else, even before the goods arrive, and the goods then belong to the one to whom it is transferred. TRANSFER OF THE BILL OF LADING CARRIES THE OWNERSHIP OF THE GOODS. Thus in form 24, Willoughby may indorse it in full or in blank, and the final holder of the bill may demand the goods when they arrive.

5. **Loss or Injury.**—According to the general rule as to common carriers, carriers by sea would be responsible for any loss or damage which the goods might suffer on the voyage, whether it was caused by the negligence of their agents, the master and crew, or not (p. 161, sec. 7). But they are an exception to this rule in one respect, viz., CARRIERS BY SEA ARE NOT RESPONSIBLE FOR DAMAGES WHICH OCCUR THROUGH SOME EXTRAORDINARY PERIL OF THE SEA. Thus, if I ship goods on a vessel and they are lost through a violent storm, or piracy, or fire at sea, the

---

* Pronounced *con-si-nor*, *con-si-nee'*.

carrier is not responsible to me. I took the risk of *extra-ordinary* perils, and must bear the loss unless I have insured my goods (Chap. XXXII.).

6. General Average.—The occasion will sometimes arise upon a voyage when it becomes necessary to sacrifice some part of the cargo, or vessel, in order to save the rest. Thus, perhaps in a storm the vessel must be lightened by throwing overboard some of the cargo, or the spars must be cut away. Now, it would be highly unjust to let those who owned the part sacrificed to bear all the loss, if by means of it the rest was saved. If the cutting away of the spars saved the ship and the cargo, the owners of the cargo ought to share in the loss, since they share in the benefit. Therefore, the law is that IF ANY PART OF THE VESSEL OR CARGO IS VOLUNTARILY SACRIFICED TO SAVE THE REST, ALL THE OWNERS OF BOTH VESSEL AND CARGO MUST BEAR THAT LOSS IN PROPORTION TO THEIR INTERESTS. Such a loss is called *general average.** Instead of a loss of property it may be an expense incurred for the benefit of all, which all must share. †

7. Three Conditions.—But it must be noted that it is not every loss which is thus distributed. Three conditions are essential to make it a general average: (1) the sacrifice

---

* *Average* in this connection means *loss*. A general average is one distributed among all: a particular average, one which is not of a nature to be distributed.

† Suppose A owns a vessel worth $50,000, which has on board a cargo worth $50,000, owned by the following persons: B $10,000, C $20,000, D $5000, and E $15,000. Suppose that $10,000 worth of C's goods are thrown overboard: A, B, D and E must pay their share of the loss to C; i.e., A must pay $5000, B $1000, D $500, and E $1500, making altogether $8000, which leaves C's final loss $2000. In other words the whole vessel and cargo being worth $100,000, and the loss being $10,000, each owner, including C, loses one-tenth of his property.

must be *necessary;* (2) it must be made *voluntarily;* and (3) the design must *succeed,* i.e., the rest of the vessel or cargo must be saved by it. If an incompetent captain should throw over goods when it was not necessary, the carrier might be responsible, but the owner of the goods would have no general average claim against the owners of other goods on board. So also, if they-are washed overboard, or if after a voluntary sacrifice is made it proves to be of no avail, there is no general average claim.

8. Salvage relates to property abandoned at sea. On land the finder of an article must surrender it to the owner, and is entitled to nothing for his services; but ANY ONE SAVING PROPERTY WHICH HE FINDS ABANDONED AT SEA IS ENTITLED TO LARGE COMPENSATION FOR HIS SERVICES. This compensation is called *salvage,* and its object is to encourage such services, which are usually attended with danger. The amount of salvage varies according to the difficulty, sometimes amounting to one-half of the value of the vessel and cargo saved. All who take part in the saving have a share of the salvage, viz., the master, crew and owners of the saving vessel. When a vessel is found in great distress, though not actually abandoned, and aid is rendered, salvage is allowed.

CHAPTER XXXI.

FIRE INSURANCE.

1. **Insurance** is a contract; an agreement by which one assumes a certain risk which another would otherwise bear. Thus the owner of property risks its destruction by fire, and the insurance company assumes that risk by agreeing

to pay for any loss. FIRE INSURANCE IS A CONTRACT TO INDEMNIFY THE OWNER OF CERTAIN PROPERTY IF IT IS DAMAGED OR DESTROYED BY FIRE. Any one may make that contract, and it may be either oral or written, but the business is now almost universally carried on by companies, incorporated for the purpose, using written contracts called *policies.* The company issuing the policy is called the *insurer* or *underwriter;* the one to be indemnified is called the *insured.**

2. The Contract has two parties, (1) the owner of the property, and (2) the company. The chief elements of it are as follows: The owner agrees to pay to the company a certain sum of money called the *premium*, in any event; and the company agrees to pay him whatever his damage amounts to if there is a fire, unless the damage exceeds a certain amount, which is named in the policy (sec. 8). That amount far exceeds the premium. Thus, if there is a fire the company may have to pay many times as much as the premium it received; but on the other hand if there is no fire it gains the whole premium (form 25, p. 289).

3. The Time for which the insurance is to last is always specified in the policy. It may be made for any time, but is usually made for one, two, or three years. At the end of the time a *renewal* is often issued (p. 290). This is merely to save the labor of issuing a new policy, and it has just the same effect as a new policy.

4. The Risks.—The policy reads, "The ...... Company do insure Edward A. Bradford against loss or damage *by fire.*" This includes not only damage done by the fire itself, as by burning, charring, cracking, etc., but also all that results directly from the fact of there having been a fire. THE COMPANY IS RESPONSIBLE FOR ALL DAMAGE

---

* *Assure* means the same as *insure.*

DONE BY THE FIRE, OR DONE IN PUTTING OUT THE FIRE. Very frequently the water used to put it out causes more damage than the fire itself; that is covered by the policy, even though the fire is not in the same building. The fire is the cause, because the damage would not have been done if there had been no fire.

5. Payment of Premium.—The parties may make any agreement they choose as to when the premium shall be paid. It is quite common for the policy to provide that it shall not go into effect until the premium is paid, and in such case, though one has his policy, yet he has no insurance until the company is paid the premium.* But without such a provision the policy is binding before payment is made. The company may sue for it, and if there is a fire before it is paid, it is deducted from the amount of the loss. In other words, each party must keep his agreement.

6. Ownership.—One may insure property which he owns, and also any in which he has any interest, as by holding a mortgage upon it. But in the latter case it is quite common for the owner to obtain the insurance and have the policy provide that the loss, if any, shall be paid to the one holding the mortgage. If a person sells property covered by a policy of insurance, the person buying it does not get the benefit of that policy unless the company is notified of the sale and assents to a transfer of the policy.

7. Change of Risk.—When a company issues its policy insuring certain property, the amount of premium is based upon the degree of danger there is of fire. If that danger could be increased by the owner of the property, the company might be subjected to a greater risk than it would have assumed for that premium. Consequently it is not

---

* If the owner of the property pays the premium to his broker, as is often done, that is not paying the company until the broker pays it over to the company. (See sec. 13.)

allowed to an owner to increase the risk. If the risk is increased by anything he does his policy becomes void. Even the repairing or altering a house, or, if personal property, changing it from one place to another, may under some circumstances make the policy void. THE PRUDENT RULE IS ALWAYS TO OBTAIN THE COMPANY'S CONSENT TO ANY CHANGE IN THE PROPERTY, ITS POSITION, OR ITS OWNERSHIP. Having given their consent they cannot complain afterwards.

8. The Amount of the policy may be any which the parties choose. Its effect is to limit the liability of the company to that amount in any event. Some owners will prefer to be fully insured, i.e., to have the amount of insurance equal to the value of the property; some will take some risk themselves. In any case the company pays only the amount of the loss, and never more than the amount of the policy. THE AMOUNT TO BE PAID IN FIRE INSUR-ANCE IS THE AMOUNT OF THE LOSS, UNLESS THAT EXCEEDS THE AMOUNT OF THE POLICY, AND THEN ONLY THE AMOUNT OF THE POLICY. Thus, if the policy is for $2000, and the loss is $50, it pays $50, and the policy becomes one for $1950 for the remainder of the time. If the loss is $3000, it pays $2000, and the policy is wholly discharged. But many companies will not issue policies of more than $5000 or $10,000 in amount on the same property, and if a person wishes to insure some property (as for instance a large building) for more than that, he must often obtain separate policies from several companies.

9. Insurance in Several Companies.—In that way a person may obtain full insurance, however valuable his property is. If a fire occurs where the property is insured in several companies, and the damage is more than the amount of all the insurance, each company must pay the amount of its policy; but if the damage is less than the amount of the insurance, then the question arises, Which company shall pay? This is usually provided for in the policies themselves, and the ordinary rule is that IN FIRE INSUR-ANCE EACH COMPANY, WHERE THERE ARE SEVERAL, MUST PAY THAT PROPORTION OF THE LOSS WHICH ITS POLICY BEARS TO THE WHOLE AMOUNT OF INSURANCE. It is of no moment which policy was issued first. But in no event can any company be compelled to pay more than the amount of its policy.*

10. Negligence.—It is ordinarily the rule in law that a person must himself bear the consequences of his own negligence, or that of his employés, but in fire insurance we find this rule modified. Perhaps most fires occur through the negligence of some one, and it is just the result of that possible negligence which the owner of property wishes to insure himself against. Consequently the company must pay even though the fire was caused by carelessness. That is what it agrees to do. But one cannot intentionally burn his own property for the sake of getting the insurance. That is fraud. Nor can one allow his property to burn after a fire has started. His policy becomes void unless he does all he can to save the property.

11. Any Misrepresentations at the time the policy is made, as to the character of the property, or the danger of fire to which it will be exposed, make the policy void. This is only an application of the rule that no fraudulent contracts are binding (p. 22).

12. Additional Agreements. — Every policy contains

---

* Thus, if property worth $50,000 is insured in one company on January 9th for $10,000, and in another on July 15th for $15,000, and a fire occurs on July 17th, in which $25,000 or more is lost, the first company pays $10,000, and the second $15,000; if the loss is $5000, the first pays $2000 and the second $3000; if the loss is $40,-000, each pays the amount of its policy (form 25, clause (4)).

agreements or conditions additional to the main agreement of insurance, which act as restrictions upon the owner; as for instance that no gunpowder or kerosene oil shall be kept on the premises insured, or, if a house, that it shall not become vacant, or that the company shall be notified of any other insurance obtained (see p. 289). These are all a part of the contract, and must be strictly observed. When a loss occurs notice must be given immediately to the company.

13. Agency.—The rules of agency are especially important in insurance. The companies sometimes have their agents in different cities, who issue the policies and do all the business there: owners very frequently do their part through insurance brokers. The company must abide by all its agent does, and the owner by all his broker does.

CHAPTER XXXII.

MARINE INSURANCE.

1. The Business of marine insurance relates to vessels and their cargoes. MARINE INSURANCE IS A CONTRACT TO PAY THE OWNER OF CERTAIN PROPERTY A CERTAIN PROPORTION OF HIS LOSS IF IT IS DAMAGED OR DESTROYED WHILE ON THE SEA. Like fire insurance, it is carried on almost exclusively by companies incorporated for the purpose, who issue written policies, the owner paying a premium in proportion to the amount insured. The premium is often paid by a series of notes called *premium notes*. Form 27 on page 290 gives only the main part of such a policy.

2. The Time for which the insurance is to last differs in different cases. Sometimes it is specified, as for instance for a year. That is a common way to insure vessels. Sometimes it is for a particular voyage, no matter how long it may last. Both vessels and goods may be insured in that way. A third way in which goods are insured is to specify a time (e.g., a year), the policy to cover all goods which the party may ship during any portion of that time. Such a policy is often called an *open policy*, and it requires the greatest good faith. The shipper must give notice to the company whenever any goods are shipped, and the shipment is indorsed on the policy or noted in the company's books.

3. The Risks.—In fire insurance the risk assumed is of fire; IN MARINE INSURANCE THE RISKS ASSUMED ARE NOT ALONE THAT OF FIRE, BUT ALSO ALL THE OTHER EXTRAORDINARY PERILS ATTENDING A SEA VOYAGE.* Among others usually enumerated in the policy are those of *the perils of the sea, fire, piracy, capture, general average* and *salvage.*

The *perils of the sea* mean the risks of navigation, of injury from a violent storm, of a wreck, of a collision, etc. The company must pay for loss or damage so caused. *Fire* and *piracy* need not be explained. *Capture* means capture by the ships of war of another nation. In a war between two nations all property belonging to the citizens of one and taken on the sea is liable to capture and confis-

---

* On p. 163, we have seen that the carrier by sea is not responsible for damage to the goods he carries when it is caused by the extraordinary perils of the sea. Now it is in general just those perils which marine insurance covers; so that if I ship goods and they are lost or damaged by the ordinary perils of the sea, such as could have been provided against, the carrier is responsible to me, but if caused by the extraordinary perils, the insurance company pays me, if I am insured.

cation by the war-ships of the other. This is the risk insured against in that word. We have seen what *general average* is (p. 164); its connection with insurance is as follows. When there has been a general average loss, no goods are really lost except those thrown overboard, but the other owners must contribute their share. Each one, therefore, loses something. That is the risk assumed by the company under that phrase. In the same way, when property is rescued we have seen there is a claim for salvage which the owner must pay, though the property itself is not lost. Therefore when property is insured against the risk of general average or salvage, and its owner has to pay a claim on account of either one, the company must pay him what he has to pay.

4. Payment of Premium.—The policy is equally valid, whether the premium or the premium notes are or are not paid when they become due, unless the policy itself otherwise provides. The premium is a debt like any other debt. The premium is said to be *earned* if the vessel or the goods insured are upon the sea during any of the time mentioned in the policy. But it may happen that after a policy is issued, it is decided not to undertake the voyage, or not to send some of the goods. In such case the premium, or that part of it corresponding to the goods not shipped, is not earned. It need not be paid, or if paid must be returned.

5. Ownership.—As in fire insurance the owner is the person to be indemnified in case of a loss. But goods are often sold after being insured: in such case the new owner should ordinarily obtain the consent of the company, or the policy will be void. This is sometimes obviated by making the policy " for the benefit of whom it may concern at the time of loss." Then the policy remains in force whoever owns the goods. Sometimes the company issues a certificate with the policy, which certificate may be transferred from one owner to another, the policy remaining in force all the time and being payable to the final holder of the certificate (form 28).

6. Deviation.—Where the property is insured for a certain voyage, all such policies on the vessel or cargo are rendered void if the vessel deviates from that voyage, except from necessity. To deviate is to change the risk (p. 167, sec. 7), and it makes no difference whether the deviation increases the risk or not. The proper course for that voyage must always be followed. Thus in a voyage from New York to Rio Janeiro, it would be a deviation for the vessel to go to New Orleans unless the policy allowed it. But if the deviation was necessary, as to make repairs or to save life, the policies would remain in force.

7. The Amount of the policy may be any fixed by the parties. But its effect is very different from the effect of the amount named in a fire policy, for it establishes what proportion of any loss the company shall be responsible for. THE AMOUNT TO BE PAID IN MARINE INSURANCE IS THAT PROPORTION OF THE LOSS WHICH THE AMOUNT OF THE POLICY BEARS TO THE VALUE OF THE PROPERTY. Consequently the company does not pay the whole of any loss unless the amount of the policy equals the value of the property. If the party has property which he only insures to half its value, the company only pays half of any loss that may occur. He is his own insurer for the other half.* (See p. 168, sec. 8, for the rule in fire insurance.)

---

* Taking the same example that we did in fire insurance, suppose the policy is for $2000 and the property is worth $3000. If now a loss occurs of $50, the company pays two-thirds of it ($33.33), and the owner loses the remainder; if the loss be $1500, it still pays two-thirds ($1000); if the loss be $3000, i.e., if the property is entirely lost, it still pays two-thirds of the loss ($2000), which would be the ·

8. Insurance in Several Companies.—If the property to be insured is of large value (e.g., a vessel), policies are often obtained in several companies, as in fire insurance. But there is not here, as there is in fire insurance, any difference between the shares of any loss to be paid by a company, when its policy is the only one, and when there are others. In either case it pays only its proportion. Whether there are one or many policies the amount to be paid by any one company is found by the following proportion: as the value of the property is to the amount of its policy, so is the amount of the loss to the share it must pay.*

Note to Teacher.—It should be noted that though the rules of fire and marine insurance are different as to the proportion of any loss to be paid, their results are the same when either the insurance is full insurance, or the loss is total. The difference appears only in a case of partial loss, where there was but partial insurance.

9. Value.—If the property insured is lost or damaged it becomes important to know its value, for that is one of the elements to determine the amount to be paid. Sometimes the place for the valuation in the policy is left blank, and in that case the value must be determined at the time of

---

amount of the policy. Therefore if one wishes to free himself from all risk he must obtain *full insurance*, i.e., the amount of his policy or policies must equal the value of his property.

* Taking again the same example as in fire insurance, if property worth $50,000 is insured in one company for $10,000 and in another for $15,000, the first company will pay one-fifth and the second three-tenths of any loss. Thus if the lost be $25,000, the first pays $5000 and the second $7500; if the loss be $5000, the first pays $1000, and the second $1500. (See p. 169, foot note.)

In form 27 the clauses relating to prior and subsequent insurance, and beginning "Provided always," have to do only with a case where the insurance is more than the value of the property. We will not examine that subject.

the loss. But very often a value is inserted, and when it is, that value is controlling upon both parties. The policy is then called a *valued policy*. Thus if goods are valued in a policy at $500 and half of them are lost, the loss is $250, no matter what the goods were really worth. The company pays only its proper proportion of $250. An owner may use this method to determine the amount of insurance he will get. If in the above case the goods are really worth $500, and his policy is for $500, he is fully insured, but if they were worth $1000 he is only half insured.

10. Misrepresentation and concealment with regard to any important fact make this contract void, as they do all others. They are fraud. Thus a fraudulent over-valuation in a policy would make it void.

11. Additional Agreements.—In almost all policies there are several additional agreements or conditions, all of which are binding ; but it is impossible to review them here. The important principle to be kept in·mind is that whatever agreement a person makes, that is binding upon him. Marine insurance is a business in which there are also many customs, which have the force of implied agreements and therefore of law (p. 32).

12. Seaworthiness.—It is always an implied condition that the vessel insured, or on which the goods insured are shipped, shall be seaworthy.* The person insured, not the company, must take that risk. If the vessel is not seaworthy the insurance is void, though both the company and the insured were ignorant of the fact.

---

* *Seaworthy* means able to withstand the ordinary dangers of the sea, and fully equipped with all the things usually needed on such a voyage as she is intended to take. Thus she is not seaworthy if so out of repair that a slight gale can cause her to spring a leak, or if she is without the ordinary equipment of spars, sails, boats, anchors, fuel, charts, nautical instruments, etc., appropriate to such a vessel.

13. Lost or not Lost.—These words occurring in a policy have no reference to the case where the property is insured before it goes to sea, but only to that insured while it is on the sea, about which neither the owner nor the company know but that it is already lost. The words mean that the company take that risk also, and will pay the insurance though the property is already lost at the time the contract is made.

14. Abandonment.—Property insured may be wholly lost, or only partially lost or damaged. If wholly lost, the company pays the whole amount of its policy. If the partial loss be less than half the value of the property, the company pays its due proportion of the amount of the loss. But IF THE LOSS IS PARTIAL BUT AMOUNTS TO MORE THAN HALF THE PROPERTY IN VALUE, ITS OWNER HAS THE RIGHT TO GIVE UP TO THE COMPANY WHAT REMAINS AND CLAIM THE FULL AMOUNT OF THE POLICY. This is called the right of *abandonment*. The company cannot refuse to take it.* But the policies sometimes provide that this right shall not exist. They should then contain some such phrase as this, "without right of abandonment."

Note to Teacher.—The similarities and dissimilarities between corresponding rules of fire and marine insurance should be noted all along It would not ordinarily be difficult to obtain blank forms of policies in actual use.

---

* Thus if property worth $1000 is insured for that amount, and it is all lost, the company must pay $1000; if one-third of it is lost, the company must pay $333.33; if it is damaged so that what is left is worth only $400, the owner may keep it and claim $600 from the company, or he may give it up to the company and claim $1000.

CHAPTER XXXIII.

LIFE INSURANCE.

1. The Business of life insurance is also usually carried on by companies incorporated for the purpose, using written policies. The risk assumed is the death of some person. LIFE INSURANCE IS A CONTRACT TO PAY A CERTAIN SUM OF MONEY ON THE DEATH OF A CERTAIN PERSON OR WHEN HE REACHES A CERTAIN AGE. The premium is a fixed sum paid by the person insured annually or semi-annually. The object of life insurance, when properly conducted, is to give those who are dependent upon a certain person some means of support if he should suddenly die (form 29, p. 292).

Note to Teacher.—Explanations and illustrations might be given at this point showing how all insurance is merely a means of distributing a loss among many which would otherwise be borne by one, or a few. The loss to the world at large still remains.

2. The Parties.—Here also the parties to the agreement are two, (1) the person agreeing to pay the premium, and (2) the company. But there is also a third person concerned, viz., the one upon whose death the money is to be paid. Very often that person and the one who makes the contract are the same, and he is then said to insure his own life. He may make it payable to himself, and if it is payable at his death it then forms part of his estate; or he may make it payable to his wife or children, or any one else he chooses. If payable to another it cannot be touched by his creditors, nor can he in his will deprive the other party of its benefit.

3. The Contract is not to indemnify, but to pay a certain sum, and in this respect differs from the contract in fire or marine insurance.   A person may insure his own life in as many companies as he chooses, and to any amount that he chooses, provided he is willing to pay the premiums.

4. Who May Insure.—The most common case is where a person insures his own life.   But the money may be made payable on the death of some other person, and he is then said to insure the life of that person.*   In that kind of insurance ordinarily a person must have some pecuniary interest in the life of the one on whose death the money is to be paid, or the policy is void.   Thus a wife may insure the life of her husband, or a child the life of his father, because they are dependent for support on that life.   So also a creditor may insure the life of his debtor.   But one may not insure a life in which he has no such interest.   That would be only a wager.

5. Payment of Premium.—THE INSURANCE CEASES IF THE PREMIUM IS NOT PAID WHEN DUE.   This is so even though it was accidentally forgotten, and that only for a day.   This is practically very important where the policy has been running for several years, for by that time, the person being older, the yearly premium on a new policy would be larger.

6. Assignment.—Policies are frequently assigned.   Thus, instead of a creditor's obtaining a policy on his debtor's life, the debtor may obtain it on his own life and assign it to the creditor.   IN EVERY ASSIGNMENT THE PRUDENT RULE IS TO OBTAIN THE COMPANY'S CONSENT.   Sometimes the policy provides that it shall be void if it is assigned without consent.

7. Misrepresentation.—This subject is of great importance in life insurance.   The companies before issuing a

---

* Though properly we should say that he is insured against the death of that person.

policy require a written application, in which the party must make answer to a large number of questions with regard to his health, occupation, etc. Those questions must all be truthfully answered. No deception can be practiced in any way, or the policy is void.

CHAPTER XXXIV.

INTEREST AND USURY.

1. Interest is MONEY PAID FOR THE USE OF MONEY. Where one borrows money of another promising to repay it with an additional amount, the sum borrowed is called the *principal*, the additional amount *interest*. It is usually stated as so much *per cent*, i.e., so many dollars of interest for every hundred dollars of principal. All profits are not interest. It must be a return for another's money lent or retained. Thus the profits upon money invested in a business, or dividends on stock, are not interest. One may receive profits or dividends to any amount.

2. On What Allowed.—There are three general classes of cases in which interest accrues: (1) where it is expressly contracted for, (2) many cases where such an agreement is implied, and (3) where a debt has become due but remains unpaid. The most common instance in the first class is where money is borrowed by one of another. The debtor usually expressly agrees to pay the debt and interest. But in many cases where the money of one is borrowed or detained by another, the agreement to pay interest is implied from the nature of the business or the usual custom. That is the second class. The third class relates to the interest accruing after the debt becomes due, and it is a general rule that one who fails to pay money due must also pay interest upon it up to the time he does pay.

3. Usury.—Many of the States forbid any one to give or receive more than a certain rate of interest. This rate differs in the different States, varying from six to twelve per cent. The taking of a higher rate than that allowed by the law is usury; thus USURY IS UNLAWFUL INTEREST.[*]

4. Legal Rate.—But every State establishes a certain rate which shall be the rate of interest in all those cases where the parties have not fixed their own rate. This is called the *legal rate*, and in most of the States it is six per cent per annum. Thus, a promise to "pay $100 and interest" means interest at the legal rate of the State in which the payment is to be made. The legal rate very often, but not always, is the same as the rate mentioned in the preceding section, i.e., the highest rate of lawful interest.

5. Effect of Usury.—Some penalty is inflicted upon the one who takes usury, i.e., upon the lender, not upon the borrower. This penalty varies greatly in the different States, but generally it is one of these three kinds: (1) the forfeiture of the usurious interest, i.e., all above the lawful rate; (2) the forfeiture of all the interest; or (3) the forfeiture of both principal and interest. Thus, in a State where the first rule is adopted, the lender who has lent at a usurious rate may recover the principal and interest at the legal rate; where the second is adopted, only the money he lent; and where the third is adopted, not even that (p. 24, sec. 3).

---

[*] It is thought by many that usury laws are necessary for the reason that if there were none the lenders (i.e., the rich) would oppress the borrowers (i.e , the poor) by charging exorbitant rates. But, on the other hand, the opinion has of late grown that this is a mistaken policy, and that it would be better for the community at large to allow parties to make such contracts as they choose. Consequently a few States, doing that, have no usury laws.

CHAPTER XXXV.

PLEDGING OF PROPERTY.

1. Security.—A creditor is said to have security for his claim or debt when he has something to rely upon besides the mere promise of the debtor. That security may be the guaranty of some third person, as, for instance, when some one beside the maker indorses a note. It may also be some particular property of the debtor appropriated to secure that particular debt. If it is real property it is done by way of mortgage (p. 225); if personal property, by way of pledge.

2. A Pledge is therefore security for the payment of a debt. We may define it thus: A PLEDGE IS AN AGREE-MENT BETWEEN A DEBTOR AND CREDITOR BY WHICH THE FORMER GIVES THE LATTER CERTAIN PERSONAL PROPERTY AS SECURITY FOR THE DEBT. The word *pawn* means nearly the same thing, and both words are often used to mean the property pledged, as well as the agreement. Thus we see a pledge is a contract. These three elements are essential to it: (1) a debt, (2) an actual delivery to the creditor of the property pledged, and (3) an agreement that it shall stand as security.

3. Collateral.—The words *collateral* or *collateral security* are often used in the sense of pledge. Thus, when banks loan money they often require security, and government bonds, the stock and bonds of railroads, etc., are often used as pledges for the debt, and are then called collateral. The bank is said to *loan on collateral.*

4. Creditor's Rights.—THE CREDITOR MAY KEEP THE PROPERTY PLEDGED TO HIM UNTIL THE DEBT IS PAID, OR IF NOT PAID WHEN DUE HE MAY SELL THE PROPERTY. Thus he has two rights, the right to *keep* (i.e., a lien) and a right to *sell*, but the latter does not arise until the debt is due. If it is sold the creditor then may deduct from the proceeds the amount of his debt, giving the surplus, if there is any, to the debtor. If it does not sell for enough to pay the debt, the creditor has his claim for the balance against the debtor.

5. Demand and Notice.—But before the pledge can be sold a demand for the payment of the debt must be made upon the debtor, and notice must be given him of the time and place of sale. But often the parties originally agree that no notice need be given to the debtor, and in such case it need not.

6. Debtor's Right.—Until it is sold the property belongs to the debtor, the creditor simply having the right to hold it in his own possession. When the debt is paid the creditor loses all right, and the property is then said to be *redeemed*. THE DEBTOR MAY AT ANY TIME BEFORE IT IS SOLD REDEEM HIS PROPERTY BY PAYING THE DEBT.

7. Negotiable Paper, like other personal property, may be pledged. The two parties will themselves know that the transaction is only a pledge, and that the creditor is not the owner. Consequently the rights of the parties as to each other are governed by the principles of this chapter. But to others the creditor may appear to be the owner of the property. Therefore, if he should act as owner, as by pretending that he had the right to sell when he had not, the rights of those others would be governed by the law concerning negotiable paper (pp. 107–117).

8. Pawnbrokers are those who make it a business to loan money (generally in small sums) on pledges of articles of personal value, such as clothing, jewelry, musical instruments, etc. They are not brokers in the sense in which the word is used in Chapter XXI., for they act for themselves. Their rights and duties are those of parties with whom property is pledged. They are often allowed by law to charge more than the ordinary rate of interest for the money they loan.

9. Chattel Mortgages.*—Property cannot be pledged without being delivered into the possession of the creditor. Yet a person will often desire to use his personal property as security and yet retain it in his possession, as, for instance, if it is a stock of goods from which he is selling. This may be done by his giving a *chattel mortgage* (form 34), which must be filed in a certain public office. A chattel mortgage is like a pledge in that the debtor may become entitled to the property by paying the debt: they are unlike in that in a chattel mortgage, if the debt is not paid, the property becomes the creditor's, and the debtor is not entitled to any surplus. A chattel mortgage is a conditional sale of the property to the creditor, the property becoming the creditor's if the debt is not paid. (See p. 87, sec. 3.) A pledge is not a sale to the creditor, but only gives him the right to sell the property to some one else if the debt is not paid.

CHAPTER XXXVI.

BANKING.

1. In General.—Banking as a business, is dealing in money. It consists mainly of two branches, (1) the receiving of money on deposit, and (2) the loaning of money at interest. Thus A, B, and C deposit some money with the bank; the bank takes that money and lends it to D and

---

* A *chattel* means a piece of personal property.

E.   It pays no interest (or a low rate) to A, B, and C, but charges D and E interest.   There are therefore two classes of people with whom the bank has dealings, (1) those who deposit their money with the bank (called *depositors*), and (2) those who borrow from the bank.   Banking is often carried on by individuals or firms, but most extensively by banking corporations.*

2. Deposits.—A deposit is substantially a loan to the bank.   The depositor may withdraw his money or any part of it at any time he chooses.   The act of opening an account with a bank makes a contract.   On the part of the depositor, this contract is that the bank may use as its own whatever money he deposits with it; on the part of the bank, the contract is that it will pay back to him the money or any part of it whenever he calls for it.   He calls for parts of it from time to time by means of checks (p. 126).

3. Discounts.—One way in which a large part of the lending of a bank is done is by *discounting commercial paper*.   Its depositors, or others dealing with it, often obtain notes or drafts not yet due, but upon which they wish to obtain the money immediately.   If, believing them to be certain of payment, the bank is willing to buy them, it does so and the notes and drafts are transferred to it, and it pays for them, deducting a certain interest.   Thus a discount is in reality a sale, the property sold being the note or draft.   But its effect is that of a loan, with the interest paid in advance.†

Note to Teacher.—The foot-note gives an example in which the transaction is in the nature of a loan.   If the bank should take the note without the indorsement of the other party, or should buy it in the market, it would be more in the nature of a sale.

---

* As the word *bank* will be used here, it will include bankers.

† Suppose A has B's note for $500 due in six months.   If he wishes the money immediately he applies to the bank to discount it.

4. Other Business.—Banks loan money in other ways besides by discounting paper. Nor is the lending of money the only business done. They are allowed to pay out and use as money bank bills, which we have seen are really their promissory notes (p. 145). They also buy and sell gold, stocks, bonds, etc., or receive valuable articles into their vaults for safe-keeping. But we need not consider these things, for the laws governing their transactions are not peculiar, but are the ordinary rules of sales, commercial paper, pledge, etc.

CHAPTER XXXVII.

HOTEL KEEPERS.

1. Definition.—A *hotel keeper* * is one engaged in the business of supplying board and lodging to travelers. It is essential that we should know just what constitutes one a hotel keeper, for his rights and his duties are peculiar in some respects. As we shall see in the following sections, he has greater obligations, especially with regard to the property of his guests, and more extensive rights, than a person ordinarily has who has the property of another in

---

The bank takes it, with his indorsement, and pays him (say) $485, i.e., $500 less six months' interest. Thus A gets his money six months sooner than he would have if he had kept the note; and the bank (when B pays the note) gets $500, which is all it paid and interest. Another way to make the loan is, for A to make his own note, and have the bank discount that.

* "Innkeeper," or "tavern-keeper," means the same as "hotel keeper," and a hotel, tavern, or inn is a house where any one may obtain food or lodging. The term *public-house* expresses the idea well.

his possession. The constituting elements are three: (1) his following it as a business, (2) his offering his services to the public generally, and (3) his providing both food and lodging, (p. 159). Thus one who received private guests in his own private house, or one who even received strangers now and then for a compensation (but not as a business), would not bear towards them the responsibility of a hotel keeper to his guests. Neither would one who kept only a restaurant, even though it was open to all the public.

2. Obligation to Receive.—The rights and duties of hotel keepers are in some respects similar to the rights and duties of common carriers. One similarity is this: they offer their services to the public, and they must render them to whoever chooses to accept of them. A hotel keeper on being paid a reasonable compensation is obliged by law to receive any one who comes to his house until the house is full. He, therefore, is an exception in this particular, to the rule allowing one to contract with whom he pleases (p. 18). But intoxicated or disorderly persons he need not receive, and if they are there he may require them to leave. The amount of compensation is not regulated by law, but left to agreement between the parties.

3. Lien.—A hotel keeper may detain the property of a guest placed in his care until the charges against the guest are paid. This lien is like the lien of a common carrier (p. 161). Thus the trunks of a traveler, or his horse which has been stabled at the inn, may be detained until he pays his bill. If one is traveling with a family or servants, this will include the board and lodging of all.

4. Loss of Property.—If the property of a guest is lost while he is at a hotel, the hotel keeper is responsible for it, unless it were lost through the fault or carelessness of the owner himself or of those with him. As in the case of the common carrier, it makes no difference whether or not the hotel keeper exercised due care. Thus if other guests or burglars from outside should steal it, or if it should be destroyed by fire in spite of every precaution upon the hotel keeper's part, yet he would still be responsible for it.

But the guest must place the property where he is requested to, in order that the proprietor may have the opportunity to protect it, or else he must take all the risk himself. Very often in large hotels safes are provided, in which the guests are requested to place their money, jewelry and other valuable property. If they neglect to do so and in consequence the property is lost, the hotel keeper is not responsible.

5. Boarding-Houses.—A boarding-house is different from a hotel in two particulars: (1) it is not intended for transient guests, but for permanent boarders, and (2) it is not open to the public. Those and only those are received there whom the proprietor chooses to accept. The peculiar rights and duties of a hotel keeper do not pertain to one who keeps a boarding-house. The latter is under no obligation to receive any one who applies for board; he has no lien upon a boarder's property; and he is not responsible for the loss of that property unless such loss has been caused by his negligence. The same person may be a hotel keeper to some and a boarding-house keeper to others. Thus if one lives at a hotel for some time under an arrangement agreed upon beforehand, as to him the proprietor is not a hotel keeper.

LIENS.

| Those having the right to retain others' property which is in their hands. | How long it lasts. |

I. A **SELLER** of goods, ... Until price is paid.
    (unless selling on credit).   (p. 93).

II. A **COMMISSION MERCHANT** ;
    1. As to the buyer he is a seller . . . . .See I.
    2. As to his principal,
        He may keep any of the latter's
        goods in his hands . . . . Until all commissions,
                                          advances, and expenses
                                          due are paid (p. 95).

III. One who holds property,
    to render **PERSONAL SERVICES**
    in connection with it, . . . Until his charges are paid.
    as to repair it, keep it   (p. 157).
    on storage, etc.

IV. A **COMMON CARRIER** . . . . Until the freight is paid.
                                          (p. 161).

V. A person holding it
    as a **PLEDGE** . . . . Until the debt is paid.
                                          (p. 181).

VI. A **HOTEL KEEPER** . . . . Until his charges are paid.
                                          (p. 186).

[This list does not include all the liens there are, but only some of the more important ones.]

CHAPTER XXXVIII.

TELEGRAPHS.

1. Parties to the Contract.—The business of telegraphy is carried on by corporations, and like other business consists of the making and performing of a system of contracts. The parties to this contract are two, (1) the sender of the message, and (2) the telegraph company. Each of these two parties agrees to do certain things, and each must keep his (or its) agreement. Consequently if the company fails to do what it agreed, the sender can compel it to pay for any loss resulting. But there is no contract ordinarily between the company and the one to whom the message (called a *dispatch*) is sent, and consequently it is not responsible for any loss he may suffer.*

2. The Contract.—To ascertain, therefore, the duties of the two parties to the contract we have simply to inquire, What did they agree? The ordinary telegraph blank sometimes constitutes that contract. The sender says to the company, "Send this message," i.e., he requests it to do so, and such a request is in effect an offer to pay for the service if it is done. The company by taking the message agrees to send it, i.e., accepts the offer. The request and compliance, or as we may say, the offer and acceptance, make the contract. This is an agreement for personal services (Chap. XXVIII.), and the company is as it were a special messenger.

3. Its Terms.—The main parts of this contract are these: (1) the sender agrees to pay for the message at the regular

---

* Thus, suppose A sends a telegram to B, but through the fault of the company in not sending it promptly both A and B suffer loss. A can compel the company to pay him, but B cannot.

rate, and the company may refuse to take it unless he pays in advance; (2) the company agrees to send the message by telegraph with promptness, deliver it to the person addressed, and not to reveal its contents to any one else. But the liability of the company for mistakes is often limited by its blanks, the blank being drawn in such a way that it is a contract.

4. Accuracy.—The message must be sent as it is given. Hence the operator cannot correct evident mistakes, such as mistakes of grammar, nor add, nor omit anything, nor make any change in it.

5. Promptness.—The message must be sent as soon as it can be, and different messages must be sent in the order in which they are received. Even an hour's unnecessary delay might make the company responsible.

6. Secrecy.—A telegraph company is a confidential messenger. It has no right to reveal the message to any one, except the one to whom it is addressed.

CHAPTER XXXIX.

PATENTS.

1. A Patent is a written instrument issued by the National Government, securing to an inventor the exclusive right to his invention within the United States.* Every one always has the right to make, or use, or sell anything he invents. That right does not need a patent. But without a patent any one else can also make it. A patent secures

---

* The word is also used to mean a deed of lands granted by the Government, but in this book we speak of patents for inventions only.

to him the *exclusive* right, or in other words, the right to keep all others from making, using, or selling the thing. It does not, therefore, grant the inventor any new right; it simply takes away that right from every one but him. A patent lasts for seventeen years, and after that any one may make, use, or sell the thing patented.

2. Its Object is to encourage inventors and increase their number, by greatly increasing the profit to be made if the invention is successful. Without the exclusive right an inventor might make nothing out of his invention. The more useful it was the more eager others would be to make, use, or sell it, and thus he would not only be deprived of a large portion of the market, but he would be exposed to competition which would greatly lessen, if not take away, his profits. But with the exclusive right the inventor not only has the whole field but also can fix his own prices.

3. How Obtained.—To obtain a patent an application must be made to the Commissioner of Patents, accompanied by carefully prepared papers and drawings describing the invention. The government officers then make an examination to see if the case is a proper one for a patent, and if it is the patent (also called *letters patent*) is signed and sent to the inventor. Foreigners may obtain patents here.

4. What may be Patented.—Almost anything may be patented, provided it is a new invention, and is suited to some useful purpose. The inventor must be the very first one who has ever known of it. Patents are very often granted for complete machines, which are entirely new, involving some wholly new principle,* or for a manufactured article itself, the article being entirely new in its

---

* For example, the Morse patents for the electric telegraph, or the Howe patent for the sewing machine.

nature.* But the great majority of inventions are for some small improvement upon an old machine or process. In such case the inventor gets his patent, not for the new machine he makes, but only for his improvement. Thus, if A invents a steam engine, and B afterwards invents an improved valve to go with it, B cannot make, use, or sell the engine without A's consent, nor can A make, use, or sell the valve without B's consent.

5. The Sale of a Patented Article by the inventor carries with it the right to use, to repair, and to sell that particular article until it is worn out, but not to make another like it. The patented article, once sold by the inventor, goes into the world's stock in trade, and may be sold and resold indefinitely.

6. The Sale of the Patent is a different thing, and means the transfer of the exclusive right, or some portion of it. Thus if I buy a newly-patented pen, I may use, or repair, or sell that one pen anywhere; if I purchase the patent, I may make, use, or sell any number of these pens. Inventors often sell the exclusive right in certain portions of the territory, as by granting to one the exclusive right to make, use, and sell the invented article in the Eastern States, to another the same right in the Pacific States, etc.

7. Infringement is the making, using or selling the patented article without the permission of the owner of the patent. Its consequences are twofold: (1) the infringer must pay to the owner of the patent whatever damages the latter suffers through the infringement, equivalent usually to the profits which the infringer has made; (2) the court will compel the infringer to stop. These are the two methods by which the exclusive right is enforced (sec. 1).

---

* For example, the Goodyear patents for vulcanized rubber, or some patents for patent medicines.

8. Validity of Patent.—Patents are not necessarily valid because granted. We may never certainly know whether a patent is valid until some court has decided it to be so. Thus, it may be for an invention that was not really new, though thought to be at the time; or, the papers may be drawn incorrectly. In any such case it is altogether void. If, when one is sued for infringement, he can prove that the supposed inventor was not really the first inventor, the patent is declared void, and every one may disregard it.

9. Mark.—Every patented article, before it is sold, must be marked *patented,* so as to give notice to every one that it is patented.

CHAPTER XL.

COPYRIGHTS.

1. A Copyright is the exclusive right to print and sell what one has written or drawn; or, in other words, the exclusive right to make copies. This means, as we have seen with patents, not the right to make copies, but the right to keep all others from doing so. Thus a copyright is the same as a patent right applied to articles which may be printed. This right is granted to authors by the National Government upon proper application, and continues for twenty-eight years, with the privilege of fourteen years longer if it is then desired.

2. Its Object is to encourage the writing of books, by securing to the author the sole profit. Patents and copyrights increase inventions and books. The general purpose of both, therefore, is the improvement of the knowledge and condition of mankind.

3. How Obtained.—A copyright for a book is obtained by simply sending to the Librarian of Congress a copy of the title page of the book before it has been published, and two copies of the complete book when it is published. No examination is made, as in the case of patents.

4. What may be Copyrighted.—Books are the most frequent subjects of copyright, but maps, charts, engravings, musical compositions, etc., may be protected in the same way.

5. Sale.—The sale of the copyrighted book carries with it the right to use and to sell that particular book forever. The copyright may also be sold, and that carries with it the right to publish and sell any number of copies of the book.

6. Infringement is the making or selling of the copyrighted article without the permission of the owner of the copyright. Its consequences are substantially the same as in the case of patents (p. 192), viz., the liability to be sued for damages by the owner of the copyright, and to be ordered by the court to cease printing the article.

7. Foreign Works.—The books of authors not residing in this country cannot be copyrighted here. Thus any one may publish or sell here the work of an English author without his permission.

8. Mark.—Each copyrighted article must be marked "copyright," so that all people may have notice that it is copyrighted. In a book this must be printed upon the title page or the page following.

CHAPTER XLI.

TRADE-MARKS.

1. A Trade-Mark is a device or name used by a merchant or manufacturer as a symbol to denote his own goods. It is usually attached to them. It may be a peculiar or manufactured word, such as "Cocoaine," or "Vegetable Pain-killer," or it may be any sort of picture or design.

2. The Right Acquired in a trade-mark is the exclusive right to use it, or, in other words, the right to keep others from using that trade-mark. It may be acquired by a citizen or a foreigner, and lasts as long as the trade-mark is used.

3. Its Object is to protect both the owner and the public against imitations of an article which has acquired a good reputation. Were it not for the exclusive right others might put on their goods the same mark, and thus deceive the public into believing they were manufactured by the same persons. This might deprive the one who had built up the trade of the results of his industry or skill, or it might defraud the public into buying an inferior article.

4. How Acquired.—The exclusive right to use a trade-mark is acquired simply by its adoption and use. No application is made to either the State or National Government. In 1881 Congress passed a law which gives additional protection to trade-marks used in foreign commerce, provided they are registered in the Patent Office. But for ordinary trade-marks used only in this country, no registration in any public office is ordinarily necessary.*

5. Infringement of a trade-mark is prevented in substantially the same way as in the case of patents (p. 192), viz., by a suit against the infringer for damages, and for an injunction to compel him to cease using it.

---

* The law of Congress of 1870, which was much broader than the law of 1881, and which purported to require registration in all cases, has been decided to be unconstitutional and void.

I. PATENTS

    I. Are **FOR** new **INVENTIONS**;
   II. Are **GRANTED** by the National Government,
        1. After an examination, and
        2. To citizens or foreigners;
  III. **SECURE** the exclusive right to
        (1) *Make*, (2) *use*, and (3) *sell* the patented article;
  IV. **CONTINUE** for 17 years.

II. COPYRIGHTS

    I. Are **FOR** new **BOOKS**, maps, engravings, etc.;
   II. Are **GRANTED** by the National Government,
        1. Without any examination, and
        2. To a citizen or resident of the U. S. only;
  III. **SECURE** the exclusive right to
        (1) *Print*, (2) *publish*, and (3) *sell* copies of the copyrighted article;
  IV. **CONTINUE** for 28 years, with a right to 14 years more.

III. TRADE-MARKS

    I. May be attached to **ANYTHING** one makes or sells;
   II. Are **ACQUIRED**,
        1. By use simply, and
        2. By a citizen or foreigner;
  III. **SECURE** the exclusive right to use them, and
  IV. **CONTINUE** as long as used.

CHAPTER XLII.

BANKRUPTCY.

1. Bankruptcy is, in a general sense, the same as insolvency, and a bankrupt or insolvent is one who is unable to pay his debts as they become due.   A person in commercial life who finds himself unable to pay his debts, usually has a number of creditors, and also has some property remaining. There is in nearly every State a system of law, called the *bankrupt law, insolvent law,* or *assignment law,* which has one or both of these objects; (1) to distribute the remaining property of the bankrupt among his creditors, and (2) to release him from his debts, so that he may have opportunity and incentive to devote himself to business again.

2. National Law.—From 1867 to 1878 there was a national bankrupt act, operating the same in every State; but that has been repealed and now (1882) each State regulates the matter as it chooses, the systems being quite different in some respects.

3. General Assignment.—A debtor may pay first any creditor he chooses, even if after so doing he has not enough property left to pay the rest.   If he desires to pay all the creditors a portion instead of leaving some unpaid, that is often done by means of a *general assignment,* which is a paper signed by the debtor, in which he assigns or transfers all his property to some one else, called the *assignee* or *trustee,* to distribute it among the creditors (form 30).   After the assignment the sheriff cannot levy upon the property, nor has the debtor any control over it.

Note to Teacher.—It may be asked why the debtor himself cannot sell his own property, and distribute the proceeds equally.   For this reason: Any creditor may sue, and on obtaining judgment have the sheriff seize any of the property and satisfy his own claim fully out of it, without·regard to any other creditor. Thus, it is a race between creditors. An assignment stops this.

4. The Assignee's Duties are (1) to notify all the creditors to present their claims to him, (2) to sell all the property of the debtor and convert it into cash, and (3) to distribute all the money thus obtained among all the creditors in proportion to the amount of their respective claims. Thus if all. the debts are $50,000, and all the money $20,000, each creditor receives 40 per cent of his claim. In many States the assignee is subject to the supervision of some court, and the proceedings are in effect court proceedings.

5. A Preference in a general assignment is a provision in it that certain creditors shall be paid in full before any others are paid at all. This makes an unequal division of the property. Some States entirely forbid preferences.

6. Involuntary Process.—Some States have a process by which a failing debtor's property may be taken from him without his consent in order to be distributed among the creditors equitably.

7. Discharge of Debtor.—So far we have considered only the first object of a bankrupt law, the distribution of the property; let us now consider the second, the discharge of the debtor. The making an assignment, i.e., giving up all his property, does not discharge him from his debts unless they are paid. The discharge is granted by a court under certain conditions. but there is no uniformity in the different States. In some, it is granted if a certain proportion (30 to 70 per cent) of the debts are paid ; in others, if a certain proportion of the creditors consent to it ; in others no discharge is ever granted.

8. Effect of Discharge.—The residence of the creditor is of great importance in determining the effect of a discharge under a State law. In general, if he lives in the State where the discharge is granted, the discharge cancels the debt, as if it were paid ; if he lives in any other State, the debt is not affected. A National law is superior to a State law chiefly because it affects all debts alike.

9. Release by Creditors.—Any creditor may release his debtor from the debt. Thus, by obtaining a release from each creditor, the debtor may accomplish his own discharge without reference to where they live. This is perhaps the most common method pursued, and is called a *compromise.* The debtor agrees to pay some percentage of the debts, and the creditors agree to release him, believing that they could get no more in any other way. Should the debtor, in such a case, secretly agree to pay some creditor more than his proper share, in order to get him to consent to it, such agreement would not only be void but would render the whole release by the other creditors void.

Summary of Leading Rules.

I. Agreements for Personal Services.

1. When services are requested there is always an IMPLIED CONTRACT TO PAY what they are worth.

2. It is an implied part of every agreement to render services that the work will be done with ordinary SKILL, CARE, AND DILIGENCE.

3. Any one having the property of another in his hands upon which he has done work MAY KEEP it until he is paid for his work.

II. Transportation of Goods.

1. A COMMON CARRIER IS one whose business is to transport from place to place the goods of any one who may employ him.

2. A common carrier is OBLIGED by law TO TAKE any goods that are offered to him for transportation to any point on his route.

3. Common carriers MAY KEEP the goods they have transported until their charges are paid.

4. Common carriers are RESPONSIBLE FOR ANY LOSS or injury occurring to goods which they are transporting.

III. Shipping.

1. Transfer of the BILL OF LADING carries the ownership of the goods.

2. Carriers by sea are NOT RESPONSIBLE for damages which occur through some extraordinary peril of the sea.

3. If any part of the vessel or cargo is voluntarily SAC-

RIFICED TO SAVE the rest, all the owners of both vessel and cargo must bear the loss in proportion to their interests.

4. Any one SAVING PROPERTY which he finds abandoned at sea is entitled to large compensation for his services.

IV. FIRE INSURANCE.

1. FIRE INSURANCE IS a contract to indemnify the owner of certain property if it is damaged or destroyed by fire.

2. The company is responsible for all damage done by the fire, or done in PUTTING OUT the fire.

3. The prudent rule is always to OBTAIN the company's CONSENT to any change in the property, its position, or its ownership.

4. The AMOUNT TO BE PAID in fire insurance is the amount of the loss unless that exceeds the amount of the policy, and then only the amount of the policy.

5. In fire insurance each company where there are several must pay that PROPORTION of the loss which its policy bears to the whole amount of insurance.

V. MARINE INSURANCE.

1. MARINE INSURANCE IS a contract to pay the owner of certain property a certain proportion of his loss if it is damaged or destroyed while on the sea.

2. In marine insurance the RISKS ASSUMED are not only that of fire, but also all the extraordinary perils attending a sea voyage.

3. The AMOUNT TO BE PAID in marine insurance is that proportion of the loss which the amount of the policy bears to the value of the property.

4. If the loss is partial but amounts to more than half the property in value, its owner has the RIGHT TO GIVE UP to the company what remains and claim the full amount of the policy.

VI. LIFE INSURANCE.

1. LIFE INSURANCE IS a contract to pay a certain sum of money on the death of a certain person or when he reaches a certain age.

2. The insurance ceases if the PREMIUM is not paid when due.

3. In every assignment the prudent rule is to OBTAIN the company's CONSENT.

VII. PLEDGING OF PROPERTY.

1. A PLEDGE IS an agreement between a debtor and creditor by which the former gives the latter certain personal property as security for the debt.

2. The CREDITOR MAY KEEP the property pledged to him until the debt is paid, or if not paid when due he may sell the property.

3. The DEBTOR MAY, at any time before it is sold, REDEEM his property by paying the debt.

REVIEW QUESTIONS.

1. What is an agreement for personal services? State the two kinds, with examples of each.
2. What is the consideration in such an agreement?
3. When nothing is said about price or payment at the time of employment, what (if anything) is due? Why? When must services be paid for in advance? When not?
4. State the substance of an employé's agreement, as to what care, etc., must be taken. Is one who agrees to do certain work and who gets others to do it for him, responsible for what those others do or neglect to do? Why? Is it always enough to take as good care of others' goods as one takes of one's own? Why? If one, through carelessness, loses goods, is he entitled to compensation for work he has done on them? Is he, when lost without his fault? In each case who bears the loss of the property?
5. When, and for how long has one, who has done work upon something belonging to another, a right to keep that article?
6. When one is hired for three months at so much a week, when does the employment end? When hired at so much a week but for no particular time? In the first case, when may the employer discharge the employé? When in the second? What is the effect of a discharge before the time has expired? The effect of the employé's leaving before the time has expired?

---

7. What is a common carrier? Name some. A private carrier?
8. May a common carrier refuse to take goods offered? Why? May he charge different rates to different parties?
9. With whom does a carrier contract, the sender or receiver? State three ways the carrier has to obtain payment.
10. State the rule as to a carrier's responsibility for loss or injury to goods.

---

11. To what kinds of vessels does the law of shipping apply? What is a shipper? A charter-party? When a ship is chartered by one, who is the carrier, he or the ship-owner?

12. What is a bill of lading? A consignor? A consignee? State how and by whom a bill of lading may be transferred. The effect of such transfer.

13 How does the responsibility of a carrier by sea, for loss or injury to goods, differ from that of a carrier by land?

14. Describe general average. The three conditions under which it is allowed. Give examples of some losses where there would, and some where there would not, be any general average claim.

15. What is salvage? Its amount? To whom given?

16. What is fire insurance? An insurer? An insured? An underwriter? A policy? May an insurance contract be oral? Is it usually? What is the premium?

17. For what time is fire insurance usually made? What is a renewal? Its effect?

18. For what kinds of damage is a company liable under a fire policy?

19. If a policy provides that it shall not be binding until the premium is paid, and a fire occurs before the premium is paid, is the company responsible? How would it be in that case, if the owner had paid the premium to his broker but the latter had not paid it to the company? Is a policy ever binding without payment of premium?

20. If property is sold after being insured, does the buyer get the benefit of the insurance? What is the effect upon the policy of increasing the danger of fire? Of what changes should the owner notify the company?

21. If in a fire the damage is less than the amount of the policy what amount must the company pay? If it be more than the amount of the policy? What is it to be fully insured?

22. Explain how two or more companies which have insured the same property ordinarily share the loss when there is a fire.

23. Is the company responsible when the fire is caused by carelessness? Is it when the owner purposely set the property on fire? Is it when the owner does not try to put out the fire?

24. The effect of misrepresentations at the time the policy is made? Of what more general rule is that an illustration?

25 Are all the provisions of a policy binding?

26. How does marine insurance differ from fire insurance, as to the property insured? As to the risks? Name the usual perils insured against in marine insurance, and explain, as to each, how there may be a loss under it.

27. State two ways in which marine policies are drawn as to the time the insurance is to last. State two ways as to the property to be insured.

28. In what case is the policy void until the premium is paid? When is the premium said to be earned?

29. When property insured is sold, how can the buyer obtain the benefit of the insurance?

30. If property is insured for a particular voyage, and the vessel deviates from its course, what is the effect upon the policy?

31. The effect of the amount of insurance named in the policy? What does the insurer pay in case of partial loss? In case of total loss?

32. Explain the proportions of the loss to be paid by several companies which have insured the same property.

33. The effect of inserting the value of the property in the policy.

34. State the rule as to misrepresentations.

35. What is seaworthiness? If an insured vessel is lost because it is unseaworthy, who bears the loss, the owner or the company? If insured goods are lost upon an unseaworthy vessel, is the company responsible?

36. What do the words "lost or not lost," in a policy, mean?

37. What is abandonment? When has the owner that right?

---

38. What is life insurance? In what particulars different from fire and marine insurance?

39. Can one insure his life for his own benefit? For the benefit of any one else? If one insures his life, the amount to be paid to his wife, have his creditors any claim upon it? What is it to insure the life of another? May one insure any other person's life?

40. The effect of non-payment of a premium?

41. What should be done in case of assignment of a policy?

42. State the application to life insurance, of the rule as to misrepresentations.

---

43. What is interest? Difference between interest and dividends?

44. State the three general classes of cases in which a debtor must pay interest.
45. What is meant by the legal rate? What is the most common legal rate in the United States? Is it always usury to take more than the legal rate?
46. Who is punished for usury, the borrower or lender? Name the three most common kinds of penalties.

---

47. What is a pledge? Can lands be pledged? State the three elements necessary to constitute a pledge. State some other kinds of security besides pledge. What is collateral?
48. What are the creditor's rights over the property he holds in pledge? What must he do before he can sell?
49. Who owns the property while it is pledged, the creditor or the debtor? Who owns negotiable paper while it is pledged? Can pledged negotiable paper be sold before the debt is due so as to make any one else the owner? Can other property?
50. What right has the debtor up to the time the property is sold?
51. What is a pawnbroker? What is the difference between a pledge and a chattel mortgage?

---

52. What are the two branches of banking as a business? What is the contract made between a bank and one who deposits money with it?
53. Explain the discounting of paper, when it has the nature of a loan, and when of a sale.

---

54. What is a hotel keeper? State the three elements.
55. Can a hotel keeper refuse to receive any one who comes to his hotel? When?
56. What is the hotel keeper's lien?
57. State the rule as to a hotel keeper's responsibility for the loss of a guest's property.
58. What are the differences between a hotel keeper and a boarding-house keeper as to their rights and duties?
59. State six common kinds of lien, and how long each lasts.

---

60. In the sending of a telegram, between whom is the contract made? What does each agree? State the rule as to accuracy.

As to secrecy. Is the company responsible for a loss to the person receiving a dispatch, occasioned by its carelessness? Why?

61. What is a patent? What does it secure? The object of granting patents? How obtained? For what? For how long? Can foreigners obtain them?
62. If one person obtains a patent for an improvement on a machine already patented, does it give him the right to use the latter with his improvement?
63. Explain the difference between the sale of a patent and of a patented article; what rights does each carry?
64. What is infringement? How prevented?
65. Is there such a thing as a void patent? How is the question settled in any case? How is notice given that an article is patented?

66. What is a copyright? What does it secure? The object of granting copyrights? How obtained? For what? For how long? Can foreigners obtain them?
67. How is infringement prevented?
68. Can the work of a foreign author be published by any one here without his permission? How is notice given that a book is copyrighted?

69. What is a trade-mark? What does it secure? Can any one but the owner of the trade-mark make articles like those to which it is attached? State two objects in allowing trade-marks. How acquired? How long does the right last? Can foreigners obtain them?
70. How is infringement prevented?

71. What is a bankrupt? An insolvent? State two general objects of a bankrupt law.
72. What is a general assignment? Has a debtor always the right to pay one creditor and not another? What are an assignee's duties under a general assignment? What is a preference? Is it legal?

73. Does the making of a general assignment discharge the debtor from his debts? How is the discharge obtained? Has a debtor always the right to a discharge?

74. Is there any national bankrupt law now? What is the effect of a discharge under some State law upon debts due to creditors living in that State? Upon other debts?

75. Is there any other way for a debtor to become released from his debts? If in a compromise and release the debtor secretly agrees to pay some creditor more than the rest, is that promise binding? What is its effect?

ADDED CHAPTERS

ON

REAL ESTATE.

CHAPTER XLIII.

KINDS OF INTEREST IN REAL ESTATE.

1. Real Estate.—All property is divisible into two kinds, *real estate* (also called *real property*), and *personal property*. Real estate means land and everything growing or built upon it, such as trees, houses, etc. Or we may say that real estate means land, and that the houses, trees, etc., are a part of the land. Personal property includes everything else. Thus, all the capital stock of railroad companies and other corporations is personal property, even though the property of the corporation consists only of land. A note, draft, or claim upon a debtor is personal property. Some kinds of real property may become personal under some circumstances. Thus trees growing, and coal in the mine, are real, but when the trees are cut down, and the coal is mined, they become personal. In the same way when a post is set upon land it changes from personal to real.*

2. Kinds of Interest.—There is much variety in the kinds of interest or ownership which may be had in real

---

* The word "real" in the phrase does not have the sense of true, for personal property is just as truly property, but refers rather to its fixed, immovable character. Personal property, on the other hand, is in general movable property. So far in this book we have been concerned only with personal property.

property.   It may be full and absolute ownership, or it may
be conditional, to end if a certain event happens, as when
a widow receives property which she is to lose if she marries
again, or as when a railroad company is given land on condition that its road is built within a certain time.   Again, the
ownership may be given to one without limit as to the time
for which it is to last, or it may be limited to his lifetime,
after which the property is to go to some one else who is
named (sec. 4).   Again, one may have an interest or kind
of ownership in property, while his right to use it is de-
ferred until some future time (sec. 5).   Still again, one
may have the right to use certain property for a certain
definite period, as for a year.   That is a tenant's interest,
but it is not called an ownership.   In this chapter we shall
consider only the kinds of ownership. (See Chap. XLVIII.)
More than one person may have the same kind of ownership in the same land at the same time (sec. 6).   It will be
seen that two persons may also have different kinds of
ownership in the same property at the same time, as where
one owns a life interest and another a future interest. (See
also sec. 7.)

3. Full Ownership.—In this country by far the greater
part of the real estate is owned in full absolute ownership
—in legal terms, it is owned in *fee-simple.*   One may do
what he chooses with property he owns in full.   He may
use it, sell it, or give it away, or at his death give it by will
to whomsoever he chooses.   He may, if he wishes, destroy
any of it, as for instance by tearing down a house.   He injures no one else by doing so, because no one else has any
ownership in it to be injured, and his power over it is un-
limited so long as he inflicts injury on no one but himself.

But yet there is a certain limitation upon his use of it,
which is embodied in the rule that no one has a right to use
his own property in such a way as to injure others or their

property.* Thus, no one has a right to maintain upon his property something which is a public nuisance, such as a very offensive trade, etc. If A and B are adjoining owners and A digs a cellar for his house, he must not dig it in such a way as to cause any of B's land to fall into the pit.

4. Life Ownership.—Property may be given to one to hold and enjoy as long as another person lives (e.g., to A to own during B's life), but ordinarily where there is a life limitation it is for the life of the person himself (i.e., to A to own during his own life). In a life ownership the owner may, during that time, use the property as he sees fit, and is entitled to all the profits arising from it. He may use it himself or rent it to others. Thus his rights are, as to a proper use, the same as those of a full owner. But we may notice three particulars in which his rights are less than those of a full owner: (1) he cannot sell or mortgage the property; (2) he cannot control the disposition of it at his death; and (3) he can do nothing with it which will decrease its value, as by taking down buildings, cutting down trees, etc.

As to selling, a life owner cannot sell the property itself so as to give the buyer the full ownership, for that would be selling what he has not himself. But he can sell or mortgage what he has, viz., his life ownership, and in that case a buyer would obtain the right to use it so long as the first party lived. Thus if A had a life ownership and sold it to B, B would own it during A's life. In the same way the creditors of a life owner can never take the property, but only A's interest in it. If he rents it the tenant must give it up at his death. As to willing away the property, it must be seen that if a life owner had such a power his interest would extend beyond his own life. As to decreasing

---

* Law is, to a very large extent, the balancing and adjusting of rights.

its value he cannot do that because others have an interest in it (sec. 5). He may use it, but not abuse it. The life owner must pay the ordinary taxes laid upon the property.

A life ownership may arise in several different ways. The following ways are some of the most common. (1) A full owner may, during his life or at his death, give a life ownership to one for whom he wishes to provide but to whom he does not care to give the power to dispose of the property (e.g., a father and a spendthrift son). (2) A widow is by law entitled to a life interest in one-third of all the lands which her husband has owned since their marriage, unless he has conveyed them away and she has joined in the deed with him. That is called her *dower*. (3) In many States a widower is entitled to a life interest in all the lands which his wife has owned since their marriage, provided a child has been born, and unless he has conveyed them away with her.

5. Future Interest.—By this we mean an ownership where the right to use the property itself depends upon some future event. In a sense, the person having such a future interest is an owner now. Thus, there is always a future interest connected with a life interest, for there is some one else who is to take the property when the life owner dies. Neither of them can affect the other's ownership. The owner of a future interest has no right to any use of the land until the event happens, and then his interest is in some cases full ownership, in others life ownership, etc. The interest of a child during his parent's life in the latter's property is not a future interest in land, as we here use the term. It is not a legal claim or right. The parent may sell or lose the land, or leave it to others by his will. But a future interest is itself property, which no one can deprive the owner of without his consent.

6. Joint Ownership is where two or more persons together

own and possess the same property at the same time. It
is different from the case of a present owner and the owner
of a future interest (sec. 5), for in joint ownership each
has a present and equal right to possession. The relation
may arise in several ways. It arises when property is given
by deed as a single piece to two or more. On the death of
a person without a will his heirs become joint owners of
his real estate. Each joint owner is said to have an un-
divided share of the whole, and the shares may be sometimes unequal. But unless the will or the deed or the law
creating the joint ownership specially designates the proportions, the shares are all equal. All may use the property together, and each is entitled to a proportionate share
of the profits. Each may sell to any one his individual
share. If all sell together to the same person he becomes sole owner. Joint owners may divide the property
among themselves, and thus make themselves separate
owners of the separate parts. If they cannot agree, any
one of them may bring a suit, and the court will divide the
property among them according to their relative interests.

7. **Trusts.**—It is sometimes desired to give one the benefits arising from the ownership of certain property (the income), but without the right to manage or dispose of it, as
where a parent is providing for children too young to be
able to manage property themselves. This is done by
giving the property to a third person, who is called the
trustee, and laying upon him the duty of managing the
property and applying the profits to the use of the person
to be benefited. A trust is a holding of property for
another's benefit. The powers of the trustee over the
property are governed by the deed or will creating the
trust, and are different in different cases. Sometimes his
only duty is to collect rents and pay them over; sometimes
he has power to sell the land and invest the money other-

wise. The position is one requiring perfect good faith. The trustee can do nothing with the estate to benefit himself. The person for whose benefit the property is held has no power over it, and in many cases cannot even transfer to another his right to receive the income.*

8. Law of State.—Contracts with regard to personal property, we have seen (p. 124), are governed by the law of the State where they are made, but the rule of real estate is entirely different. All contracts and other matters affecting real estate are governed by the law of the State where the land lies. Hence all deeds, mortgages, leases, etc., must be made to conform to the law of the State in which the real estate is situated, no matter where the parties live, or where the deed or other contract is made.

CHAPTER XLIV.

RIGHTS INCIDENT TO OWNERSHIP.

1. Two Kinds.—There are two kinds of rights which an owner of certain land has or may have in connection with his ownership, and dependent upon it, (1) rights concerning that land itself, or things upon it, and (2) rights to be exercised over land belonging to another owner. Those of the first kind do not have to be specially acquired, but always exist. They are implied in the term ownership. But those of the second kind do not exist unless they have been specially acquired. We shall in this chapter give

---

* Some of the statements of this chapter will apply also to personal property. Thus, there may be a life ownership, or future ownership of it, but they are not common. It is, however, often rented, and held in trust.

some instances of the two kinds separately (sec. 2–9). The word *appurtenance* means a minor article or right belonging to certain real estate. All the rights belonging to the second kind are called appurtenances, and some of those in the first (sec. 2).

a. Rights over One's Own Property.

2. In General.—A person who owns land owns not only the surface but also everything below and above it. His property extends downward to the center of the earth and upward indefinitely. Thus he owns all the metals, stone, oil, coal, water and everything else which he may find underneath the surface, and has the sole right to extract them. He owns also everything above the land which is affixed to it, such as houses, trees or crops. Even if houses are built upon land, or other additions made to it by one not the owner, they become the property of the owner of the land.* Such things as these, houses, minerals, trees, etc., being always firmly planted or imbedded in the earth itself, are considered as a part of the land. The use of the word "land" includes all such things upon or in it. But there are also certain other things to which the word appurtenances applies, and which are also considered as a part of the property even when away from it. They are such things as the keys, doors, windows, and blinds of a house, unless they have been permanently separated from it.

The rights of an owner over his own property are exclusive. No one else may even come upon it without permission. An owner, or one having the right to possess land, has the right to use all the force necessary to put off and keep off any one whom he wishes to.

---

* But see p. 239, sec. 10, for an exception to this rule.

3. Highways.—An owner of property bounded by a road or street usually owns the property to the center of the street. The public has the right to pass over it, to use it as a road, but does not own it. The adjoining owner may use it in any way which does not interfere with that right, though there are perhaps few ways in which he could make use of it without obstructing it, or otherwise interfering with its use by the public, or its regulation by the public authorities. If, however, it should be abandoned as a road it would then belong to him again.*

4. Streams.—The owner of property has the right to use a stream which flows through his land, so far as that use does not perceptibly diminish its volume, or change its course, or in any way prevent a similar use of it by other owners upon it. Thus he may use it to water his cattle, or irrigate his land, or to run a mill with, provided it flows out of his land at the usual point, and substantially as large as it has customarily been at that point. Each owner has all these rights, but each must exercise them in such a way as to injure no other owner (p. 210, sec. 3). An owner may build a dam upon his own land, but not so high as to cause the water to set back upon his neighbor's land, unless with the latter's permission. If a stream is the boundary line between two owners, each owns to the center, and they have an equal share in the use of it.†

---

*Sometimes streets in cities belong not to the adjoining owners but to the city itself. In such case the owner has no greater right over the land on the street than any other citizen.

† With navigable rivers the rule is different. The State owns the river, and owners whose lands adjoin them have no greater rights in them than the rest of the public.

b. Rights over Another's Property.

5. Right of Way.—We come now to the second kind, viz., those rights which an owner of land, or as we may say the land itself, may have over certain other land. They also are said to be appurtenant to the land which owns them. Such a right may be of almost any character. A common one is a right of way, i.e., a right belonging to one owner to pass over another owner's property at a certain place; in other words, a private road or path over one piece of land, leading to and belonging to another piece of land. Such a right may be very essential, for if it is land not bordering upon some public road its owner without such a right has no way to get upon it, for no one has the right—unless it is given him—to even step upon another's land. Such a way must be used only for its original purpose.- Thus, if the right granted be only a foot-path, it cannot be used for horses. But it may be used as often or by as many as the owner of the right chooses to allow.

6. Other Rights, analogous to a right of way, are, the right of the owners of one piece of land to go upon other land to fish, to cut and take from it a certain amount of wood, to draw water from a spring, etc. One owner on a stream may acquire the right to build a dam and thus overflow another's land. Under some circumstances one owner may even acquire the right, as against the owners of adjoining land, to maintain a nuisance, such as a noxious trade, on his own land.

7. Party-Walls.—A party-wall is a wall used jointly by two estates. It is usually one built on the dividing line between the estates, half on one side and half on the other, and it is frequently the case in cities that both of the side walls of a house are of this character. In a party-wall each owner owns that part which is on his own land, and also owns the right to have the rest of the wall stand though it is not on his land. Neither has the right to take down even that part which is his own, without the other's consent.

8. Restrictive Rights.—The rights which the owners of one piece of land may have over other land are of two kinds, (1) active, and (2) restrictive. The examples we have already given have been of active rights, i.e., rights to use the other land in some way, or to take something from it. Restrictive rights are those which prevent the owner of the other land doing something which he otherwise might do. They may be of almost any nature. A common example is where the owner of certain property has acquired the right to prevent certain other property being used for particular purposes, such as that no buildings shall be placed upon it, or only dwelling houses costing a certain amount. (See p. 224, sec. 11, and foot-note.)

9. The Transfer of a piece of land carries with it all the appurtenances and rights of whatever nature connected with that land, whether they are mentioned in the deed or not. Though it is common in deeds to mention appurtenances (see form 38, clause *d*), yet it is not necessary. Each successive owner of the land has the same rights, and each owner loses those rights as he parts with the land. It is thus convenient to say, as we have done, that they belong to the land. That is what is meant by "appurtenant." And if any land is subject to any such right belonging to other land, its transfer from one owner to another cannot affect the right.

10. Acquisition of Right.—Rights of the first kind, those over one's own land, we have said, do not have to be acquired. If I own property I have all those rights over it, unless I or some prior owner has granted them away. But those of the other kind, rights over others' land, must be acquired and can be acquired in only one of two ways : (1) by being at some time expressly or impliedly granted by the owners of the other land, or (2) by being exercised for twenty years uninterruptedly. But once acquired they last forever, unless surrendered.

CHAPTER XLV.

DEEDS.

1. **Definition.**—A deed of real estate is a written paper transferring the ownership from one person to another. It is when delivered a contract. Like a sale of personal property it is an executed contract, an agreement that something is done, not that something will be done hereafter. (See p. 86.) But there may be a contract for the future sale of land. The land does not however become the property of the buyer's until a deed is given. All transfers of land by one owner to another are done by deed.

2. **Necessity.**—A deed is necessary to every such transfer. Thus if A should sell land to B, and B should take possession of it without a deed, nevertheless it would not be a transfer of ownership. The property would still belong to A. No matter how full and how clearly proven the oral agreement was it would be of no avail. A contract for the future sale of real estate must also be in writing. The reason for this is the same as that which requires writing in other cases, viz., that the act is so important a one that the evidence of it should be something more certain and enduring than spoken words (p. 22).

3. **Contents.**—The forms of deeds in use in the different States differ from each other in some particulars. In each

State also we shall find two or three different forms in use. Again, most deeds contain clauses which, though valid and binding agreements upon the parties, are not necessary parts of the deed, as a deed (sec. 11). But there are certain provisions which every deed must contain in order to be a deed and transfer the ownership. These are five in number: (1) the name (or other identification) of the party to whom the property is transferred, (2) an adequate description of the property, (3) some appropriate words of transfer, (4) the signature of the owner, and (5) a seal. On p. 298 is given a form of what is called a full covenant and warranty deed. It has been in use many years, and contains many words which in very many cases would be of no use. The clause *a* down to the words "in consideration," the clauses *b* and *c*, the signatures, and the seals, comprise all that is strictly necessary to transfer the ownership. We will consider the five essentials in order.*

4. Party.—The party who is to take the property must be named. This does not mean that his full name must necessarily be used (though that is best), but simply that some one must be specified in the deed. A deed to no one is a nullity. If the place for the name is left blank, it must be filled up before the deed is delivered. If full ownership of the land is to be given it is necessary in a few States to add to the name the words, "and his heirs" (clause *b*).

---

*That part of *a* beginning "in consideration" is useful and for some purposes, which we will not consider here, is necessary. Clause *d* is superfluous because a grant of the land in most cases includes all the things there named (p. 218, sec. 9). In clause *e* is usually inserted the provision showing what sort of ownership is to be given. Thus, if a life ownership is to be given, it should read at the end "for the term of his natural life" instead of "forever." As it stands in the form it simply repeats the last part of clause *b*.

5. Description.—The property must be described with sufficient distinctness to be distinguished from all other property. Yet the description need not be as exact as in the form given (clause *c*). In country property it is usual to describe it with reference to the property of neighbors, e.g., "five acres bounded westerly by the land of Mr. B., northerly by land of the late . . . ," etc. Any description which identifies it is sufficient. Thus, "my farm on the Bronx" would suffice, unless I owned two farms on the Bronx.

6. Words of Transfer.—The words of transfer commonly used are "grant, bargain, sell and convey," oftentimes with others. Probably in most cases the use of one word, such as "grant," would be sufficient, though it is advisable always to use all of them and to follow the forms. One form of deed which is used without covenants (called a quit-claim deed) has the words "remise, release and quit-claim." They have substantially the same effect as the other words given. The deed should also specify the kind of ownership to be given, whether full ownership, life ownership, etc., whether absolute or conditional, etc. Full and absolute ownership would ordinarily be implied unless it expressly provided otherwise.*

7. Signing.—In most of the States a deed must be signed, with the owner's name. It need not be signed by the one receiving the land. If the person cannot write he must make his mark, and his name must be signed by some one else. Instead of being done personally it may be done by an agent, but his authority to do so must be in a written instrument signed by the owner himself. The wife or

---

* In deeds, as in all contracts, the kind of language used, whether English, German, or any other, and whether good or bad in spelling or grammatical construction, is of not the slightest consequence legally, provided that the meaning can be gathered from the paper.

husband of an owner should sign it with him or her, for we have seen that they have a possible future interest in each other's property (p. 212, sec. 4). In many States, also, one or two witnesses must sign the deed.

8. Seal.—A seal is a necessary part of a deed in most States. It may be a piece of paper wafered or gummed to the instrument, and in many States it is sufficient if a circle or scrawl is made with the pen opposite the signer's name. Any one may attach the seal provided it is done before the deed is delivered.

> *Note to Teacher.*—In matters of detail concerning the form and execution of deeds, mortgages, etc., there is much diversity among the States. For particulars in those respects reference should be had to the Statutes of the particular State, and to the blank forms to be obtained at the stationer's.

9. Delivery.—Delivery of the executed deed to the party to whom the property is transferred is the last and most important act of all, and without it there can be no transfer. It is the act which gives efficacy to all. The conveyance takes effect from the time the delivery is made. Thus after the deed is drawn and signed, it may be destroyed or kept in the signer's possession; the property still remains the former owner's. But if finally delivered, even though it should be years afterward, the ownership would immediately change. After delivery the loss or destruction of the deed would not change the ownership. Delivery may be made to the party himself or to any one authorized to receive it for him, and a person may be so authorized orally. We may add, that to make a transfer the deed must also be accepted. No one can be made an owner by deed without his consent.

10. Acknowledgment is not generally necessary to make a deed complete and binding upon the person signing it, but it is mentioned here because it is commonly practiced, and is very useful and essential for some purposes (see p. 234 sec. 7). It is made before delivery of the deed, and consists of two acts: (1) The party's going before a certain officer to whom he is known, and acknowledging to him that the deed is his own deliberate act, and (2) that officer's attaching to the deed his certificate that the party has done so. Each State designates certain officers before whom acknowledgments of deeds and other instruments affecting land in that State may be made. Notaries Public and Commissioners of Deeds are the most numerous classes. The exact form of the acknowledgment and of the certificate differs in the different States (form 42). In some States an affidavit made before the officer by a witness who has signed the deed will take the place of an acknowledgment (form 43).

11. Covenants.—So far we have considered the essentials of a deed; but many deeds contain additional agreements called *covenants*. They, though not a part of the deed as a deed, being merely personal agreements relating to the land, are often very valuable to the purchaser as security, their purpose being to secure him in the possession of the property or to reimburse him if some one with a prior right takes it from him. The six covenants, f, g, h, i, j and k, in the form, are all used together in some States; others use only some of them; and very frequently only the last one, k, is used.

The clauses f, g, h and k have nearly the same legal effect, and we will consider them together. In every sale of personal property the seller impliedly guarantees his ownership, i.e., agrees to reimburse the buyer if the property turns out not to be his (p. 95). But there is no such implied agreement in the sale of real estate. By simply granting the land without covenant the seller only grants such right as he has, and if some one else proves himself to have a better right or a prior claim to the property or any of it, the buyer must stand the loss. But with one of those four covenants in his deed he has a right to claim reimbursement from the seller. Each one is an agreement that he shall not be injured by the loss of the property, through the seller's not having the right to grant all he professed to. The clause *i* means this, that if there are any taxes or other charges against the property the seller will pay them. The covenant *j* is another one with the same general purpose, viz., to secure to the purchaser the full and absolute right to the property which he is buying.

Deeds not infrequently contain other covenants with various objects. One, sometimes found in deeds of city lands and called a covenant against nuisances, has for its object the keeping of that property or of all the property within a certain locality free from certain objectionable trades.*

---

* Thus, suppose that an owner of a block of land, who was selling portions of it from time to time to different parties, desired that no part of it should be used for such purposes, in order that it might be suitable for residences. He might insert in every deed a covenant such as that given in form 39. Again, the buyer of a lot under the same circumstances might desire to protect himself against having such trades established on the remaining portions of the block. In such case the covenant would read to the same effect, substituting the name of the seller for that of the buyer, and describing the property to be subject to the covenant, i.e., on which the trades should not be permitted. These rights would then form appurtenances belonging to the respective pieces of land (p. 218, sec. 8).

CHAPTER XLVI.

MORTGAGES.

1. Definition.—A mortgage * of real estate is, in effect, substantially a pledge of the real estate for the performance of some act, usually for the payment of a certain amount of money. The person owning the property, borrowing the money, and giving the pledge, is called the mortgagor.* The person lending the money, and receiving the pledge, is called the mortgagee.* A mortgage is not a transfer of the property, but only a security. The borrower remains its owner, and when he repays the money the mortgage is wholly discharged. It is different from a pledge of personal property in some particulars. In the latter the creditor takes the property and has two rights, a right to keep, and a right to sell (p. 181), but in a mortgage in this country the mortgagor usually keeps possession of the property and the mortgagee has only the right to sell it or to take it, if the debt is not paid when due. The mortgagor rents it, uses it, takes all the profit or income arising from it, and exercises all the other rights of ownership; the mortgagee exercises none.†

2. Bond.—When the mortgage is given to secure the repayment of a loan it is usual for some instrument to be

---

* Pronounced *mor'-gaje, mor-ga-jor', mor-ga-jee'*.

† The laws of the different States are not uniform upon the subject of the exact legal character of mortgages, and in some of them the mortgagee may perhaps be considered the owner of the property conditionally. But sec. 1 represents correctly the practical effect in most of them.

given to represent the loan, some promise to repay it. This in some States is in the form of a bond (form 40), in others simply a note. The wording of a bond is rather peculiar. The one in form 40 represents a loan of $10,000. On its face it is a promise to pay $20,000 unless $10,000 (the real debt) is paid. But even though the debt should not be paid the larger amount would not be due. Only the actual amount due, i.e., the debt and interest, could ever be demanded. In other words the bond has just the same effect as a note for the smaller amount would have. A mortgage would be good without a bond or note, provided that a real debt existed.*

3. Contents.—A deed is very different in its effect from a mortgage, for the former transfers the ownership, and the latter does not. But when we come to examine the form of mortgage generally in use we find it to be in form a deed. The main clauses in the two are the same (compare clauses *b*, *c*, *d*, and *e* in forms 38 and 41). But there is one important difference, viz., that in the mortgage there is an additional clause, providing that the grant shall be of no effect if the money is paid (clause *f*), and that is the clause which changes the paper from a deed into a mortgage.†

A mortgage of real estate must be in writing. Being in

---

* Yet the debt, i.e., the claim, is the real thing owned by the mortgagee. The mortgage is something incidental to it. For this reason one to whom a mortgagee is about to transfer a mortgage should be careful to obtain the bond or note also. It might happen in some States that if the bond was transferred to one and the mortgage to another the latter would receive nothing.

† Thus a real estate mortgage in its form is similar to a chattel mortgage (compare forms 34 and 41). It is not however a conditional sale (p. 183), and the property does not immediately belong to the mortgagee when the mortgagor fails to pay the debt, as is the case with a chattel mortgage.

form a deed, it must contain all the essentials required in a deed (See Chap. XLV., sec. 3–9). It should contain also the additional clause providing that it shall be void if the money is paid as agreed, or some clause showing that it is not intended as an absolute transfer. It must be delivered to be effectual. It ought to be acknowledged. All these requirements being the same as those we have considered in the chapter on deeds, and having the same limitations, it is necessary here only to refer to them.

4. Additional Agreements.—A mortgage does not usually contain the covenants found in deeds (p. 223, sec. 11),though there is no reason why it should not. It does, however, often contain additional agreements, which are binding in every respect, though not necessary parts of the mortgage as a mortgage. Clause *i* in form 41 is an example of one. A common agreement often inserted in the bond, but which might be put in the mortgage instead, is this, that if the borrower shall fail to pay interest regularly on the money borrowed, the whole amount of the debt shall become due immediately. Thus in form 40, if the interest due upon February 1, 1883, remained unpaid until March 4, 1883, the $10,000 would immediately become due. This enables the mortgagee to enforce his rights by foreclosure as soon as the first default in payment of interest is made, without waiting for the time to expire for which the loan was made.

5. Foreclosure.—A mortgage gives to the mortgagee a certain claim against the land. Foreclosure means the method of enforcing that claim, or in other words the method by which the land is appropriated to satisfy the debt. Its result is to deprive the mortgagor of his ownership. Foreclosure cannot be resorted to unless the debtor fails to keep his agreement or some part of it, as by not paying the debt when it becomes due, or in case of a bond and mortgage like the ones in forms 40 and 41 by not paying the interest regularly.*

The methods of foreclosing mortgages in the different States are various, and some States allow of more than one method. The most common course is for the mortgagee to bring a suit, in the course of which it is decreed that the property be sold at auction. Out of what is obtained for it upon the sale the mortgagee is paid the amount of his claim, and the surplus (if any) is given to the mortgagor. If it does not bring sufficient to pay the mortgagee a judgment is rendered against the mortgagor for the deficiency. After such a sale the mortgagor has no further ownership in the property. Thus it is that the final effect of the mortgage is a sale.

6. Transfer.—Both the mortgage and the property mortgaged can be sold. Thus if A owes B \$5000 to secure which he has given B a mortgage upon certain property, B owns the debt secured by the mortgage, and A still owns the property, subject to the mortgage however. Either may sell what he owns, and the purchaser will obtain just the rights which the seller had and no others. Thus if B sells his bond (or note) and mortgage to C, C obtains the right to foreclose if the debt is not paid when due. On the other hand, A may sell the property, but no matter how many hands it passes through it still remains subject to the mortgage. Thus if A sells it to D and D to E, E must see to it that the interest is paid regularly, and that every other agreement of the mortgage is carried out, or the owner of the mortgage will have the right to foreclose. A

---

* Mortgages upon which the interest is regularly paid are very often allowed to stand for years after the principal becomes due, because, the principal being secure, interest is all the creditor wants. But he has the right to foreclose at any time if the debt has become due.

change of ownership in either the mortgage or the property does not change the relative rights of the parties.

7. Assuming Mortgage.—When property upon which there is a mortgage is sold, that fact is usually mentioned in the deed, and in one of the two following ways, (1) in words which simply call attention to the fact, and (2) in words which imply an agreement on the purchaser's part to pay the mortgage. The first way is where such words as these are used, "subject to a certain mortgage." The second is where the deed says "subject to a certain mortgage which is hereby assumed," or "subject to the payment of a certain mortgage," for those words imply an agreement to pay. So far as the mortgagee's rights to satisfy the mortgage out of the property are concerned, it makes no difference which way is followed, for, for that purpose, the mortgage need not be mentioned at all (sec. 6), but the two ways have very different effects upon the purchaser's responsibility. If the first is used, i.e., if the deed simply states that the property is subject to a certain mortgage, that does not bind the purchaser to pay it, but if the purchaser agrees in his deed to pay it, then he must pay it all. If the property was certainly worth more than the amount of the mortgage it would make no difference to any one which way was taken, but if it was not, and a sale of it upon foreclosure did not bring the amount of the mortgage, the purchaser would be liable for the deficiency if the second way had been used, but not if the first had been used.*

8. Other Liens.—A person may after mortgaging his property to one, mortgage it again to another. The second mortgagee then obtains all the rights of a mortgagee, but

---

* Thus if property mortgaged for $5000 sells upon foreclosure for $4000, $1000 of the debt remains due. A purchaser who had bought it "subject to the mortgage" would not be responsible for the $1000; one who had "assumed the mortgage" would be.

subject to the rights of the first mortgagee. In other words the second mortgage is a mortgage of the value remaining above the first mortgage. A second mortgagee may foreclose, but the sale is a sale subject to the first mortgage, and if the property is worth more than the amount of the first, the second obtains the surplus; if it is not, the second obtains nothing. There are other charges or liens * which may exist against real property. One kind is a judgment for money (p. 41). If a judgment is filed against a person in a county in which he owns real estate, it is a lien against that property for a certain period (a few years); in other words the creditor may have that property sold to satisfy the judgment at any time within the period, whosoever may meanwhile have come to be its owner. Where there are several liens against the same property they take precedence of each other in the order of time in which they arose. Taxes form an exception to this rule. They are a first lien without reference to when they became due.†

---

* A *lien* or a charge upon real estate means substantially a right to sell it to satisfy some claim, no matter into whose hands it may come. A lien upon real estate is different from a lien upon personal property. Each means substantially a right to sell the property to satisfy the claim, but in the latter there is also a right to keep (p. 181). The former may exist without the person who owns it having the property, the latter cannot.

† Thus, let us suppose a piece of property mortgaged to B for $5000, on January 5th, to C, for $3000, on July 8th, that there was a judgment obtained against its owner on July 7th, for $500, and that taxes upon it to the amount of $250 became due on November 27th. If now the owner of the first mortgage should foreclose, and the property should sell for $7000, the different liens would be paid in this order, (1st) the taxes, (2d) the first mortgage, (3d) the judgment, and (4th) the second mortgage. Thus the second mortgagee would lose a part of his claim. If the second mortgagee foreclosed, he could only sell the land subject to the prior liens.

9. Searching the Title.—We thus see that when one is purchasing real estate he should be careful to ascertain beforehand what mortgages or other liens exist against it. The process of doing so, and of examining the successive deeds of the property to ascertain whether they have been drawn and executed properly, is called *searching the title*, and forms one part of a lawyer's occupation. Every real estate lien, to be available as such, must be recorded in a certain public office, and these records are accessible to any one who chooses to consult them.

CHAPTER XLVII.

RECORDING OF DEEDS AND MORTGAGES.

1. Should be Recorded.—After a deed or mortgage has been signed, sealed and delivered, there is one thing more usually done with it, which though not necessary to make it a complete deed or mortgage, is necessary to make the purchaser or mortgagee secure: that is to record it in the proper office. Each county has an office in which are kept books for the recording of the deeds and mortgages of land in that county. Into these they are copied in full, the originals being returned when copied to their owners. An instrument is considered to be on record from the moment it is handed in to the office. It is not recorded when recorded in the wrong office.

2. Object of Record.—The object of the laws with regard to record, which exist in every State, is to prevent fraud, by affording a way by which any one who intends to buy land can ascertain whether the seller has the right to sell.

Such fraud might be committed in different ways. Thus, one might pretend to own property that he did not, or that he had recently sold, or an owner might mortgage his property to one person to-day and to another to-morrow, concealing the first mortgage from him. In such cases it might happen that a person would have little opportunity to protect himself beforehand, unless there were some office, open to the public, where he might find all the papers affecting the property. But if such a paper is recorded that is notice to all the world that it exists and of its contents, for any one by searching can find it. Recording is therefore giving notice. *

3. Not Essential as to Signer.—But one who signs a deed or mortgage does not need any notice of it. Consequently, recording is not essential as against him. An unrecorded deed is valid as against him, and so far as he is concerned makes the other party the owner just as fully as if it had been recorded. Having given a deed he can never claim the land again; or if he has given a mortgage he can never maintain that the land is not subject to it. An unrecorded instrument has its full effect also against the heirs of the signer, for, giving nothing for the land themselves they cannot be defrauded. Recording is meant to protect only those who part with something, or bind themselves to

---

* Recording protects against the fraud of one who pretends to have what he has not, but not against the fraud of one who pretends to be a person that he is not. Against that there are two means of protection, the acknowledgment (see p. 234, sec. 7, and form 42), and the law against forgery. It may be asked why there is not a system of recording transfers of personal property, as well as of real estate. Two reasons are, (1) its impracticability owing to the frequency with which it changes hands, and is divided up, and even changes its character, and (2) because, personal property being movable, there arises more of a presumption of ownership from its mere possession.

do so, upon the faith of there being no unrecorded instruments.

4. The Effect of not Recording.—Thus it is third parties who are to be protected. The way in which the protection is accomplished is this: the record shows them all instruments that have been recorded, and the law provides that all that have not been recorded shall be of no effect as to them. No unrecorded instrument can affect the interest of one who holds a recorded one from the same party, even though the other is prior to his. Hence the effect of not recording a deed or mortgage is to make it void so far as it would affect the interest of all parties who subsequently acquire an interest in the land either by way of ownership or of lien. It is therefore greatly to the interest of one receiving such a paper (not to the other) to have it placed on record immediately. The recording law, while protecting him against other prior unrecorded instruments, must also protect subsequent parties against his.*

5. Examples.—The following cases will illustrate the principles of the last two sections:

(1) If A sells to B and B neglects to record his deed, and A afterward sells to C, C becomes the owner. B's deed becomes wholly void. (2) If A gives a mortgage to B, which B neglects to record, and A afterward sells to C, C takes the land free from the mortgage. Thus the mortgage may be void, but A's debt to B still remains. (3) If A sells to B, and B neglects to record his deed, and A afterward gives a mortgage to C, C's mortgage is valid and effectual against the land, but B still owns the balance of the property, for A himself could never dispute the unrecorded deed. It is valid as to him. (4) If A gives B a

---

* In some States a certain time is allowed in which to make the record (fifteen days to three months), and yet obtain all its advantages. In others it should be made immediately.

mortgage which B neglects to record, and afterward gives C another mortgage, C's mortgage takes precedence of B's, but B's would still be valid against A as if recorded.

> *Note to Teacher.*—By giving a value to the property, and amounts to the mortgages, the amount of interest which one may have in recording a paper may be brought out in a strong light. It should be remembered also that though a neglect to record does not always result in loss yet the danger always exists.

6. Good Faith.—We have seen that only those are to be protected who have parted with something (sec. 3). So also only those deserve protection who have acted in good faith. Therefore any one who acts with knowledge of any unrecorded deed or mortgage cannot take advantage of the fact of its not being recorded. To allow him to do so would be to allow fraud. If he knows of it his claim will always be subject to it, though his own deed or mortgage is recorded first. Possession of land is also notice to all others that the possessor has some right in it, and in some States one who takes a deed or mortgage from one who is not in possession (i.e., not using it, renting it, etc.) takes it subject to the claim of the one in possession, even though the latter's deed is not on record.

7. Acknowledgment is an essential pre-requisite to the right to record, and unless the instrument is properly acknowledged its record is a nullity. Proof by a subscribing witness will in some States supply its place.* For this purpose, then, every deed and mortgage should be acknowledged. Its object is to make sure that only genuine instruments go upon the record. Since the officer before whom it is made must be acquainted with the parties who make the acknowledgment or proof, his certificate is evidence to the recording officer that the instrument is entitled to be recorded and is not a forgery.

---

* See p. 222, sec. 10, for explanation of acknowledgment and proof by witness.

CHAPTER XLVIII.

LANDLORD AND TENANT.

1. The Relation.—In Chapter XLIII. we considered the different kinds of ownership of real property, and we there saw that one incident of ownership was the right to use, and one method of use was the granting of that right to others. When the right is granted temporarily for a consideration it is called a *renting.* A *tenant*, then, is one to whom the owner of real estate has granted the sole and full use of it for a time, for a consideration to be paid by him. The owner is then called his *landlord.* This relation arises as much when the letting is of a single room in a house as when it is of a whole house and grounds. But it only arises from agreement. I cannot force one to become either my tenant or my landlord against his own consent. Since a tenant has the sole use of the land he can exclude any one else from it, even the landlord himself. Having the full use, it must be without burden(except such as he agrees to take), and hence the landlord must pay all taxes due upon the land, and the interest of mortgages upon it. The tenant, on the other hand, pays the landlord for this right (sec. 4), and the obligation to pay rent arises even though he did not expressly agree to do so.

2. Duration.—The time for which the relation is to last depends altogether on the contract. That usually specifies a definite time, e.g., a month, a year, five years, fifty years, etc. Where no definite time is specified and no rent is to be paid, either party may end the tenancy at any time; but if rent is to be paid, it is in most places the law that neither party can terminate the tenancy until the termination of a year from its commencement, and only then when some prior notice of his intention has been given to the other party (see sec. 11). The parties may of course end any tenancy by mutual agreement at any time. The surrender of the premises by the tenant and their acceptance by the landlord would accomplish this. So also would the making of a new agreement inconsistent in its terms with the old one.

3. Lease.—The agreement to rent is called a *lease*. Leases must be in writing and signed if the time for which the tenancy is to last is more than three years,* but need not in general be sealed. If the time be less than that, an oral lease is valid. But where one has had the use of certain land, though under a void lease, he cannot avoid paying for that use. (See form 44.)

4. Rent is something rendered by the tenant to the landlord in return for the use of the property. Usually this is a certain amount of money, due periodically—so much a month or a quarter. Its amount and when it is due are regulated by the lease. If the agreement is silent on those points the amount is what the use of the property is reasonably worth, and the time of payment is governed by the custom of the vicinity. The time for the payment of rent has nothing to do with the length of the lease. Thus it is quite common to make it payable monthly or quarterly during the period for which the lease is to last. Unless the lease specifies that rent shall be paid in advance it is not due until the end of the particular month or quarter. But no custom can override an express provision of the lease.

5. Sale of Property.—The renting of property by an owner does not take away any of his rights, except just those rights which it gives the tenant, viz., the right to

---

* In a few States, if more than one year.

possess and use. Consequently the owner can still sell his ownership to another. The new owner by such sale obtains all the rights which the seller had, and no others. One of these was the right to receive rent from the tenant. Therefore on a sale the tenant must pay the rent to the new owner. On the other hand, a sale does not lessen or change a tenant's rights in any way. A lease holds good not only against the original landlord, but also against any one who afterwards obtains the property, whether by sale from him or through his death. Thus, if after renting the land the landlord should mortgage it, the mortgagee's rights would be subject to those of the tenant, and a sale on foreclosure could not disturb the tenant's possession. But if the mortgage was made before the renting, the case would be reversed.*

6. Assignment by Tenant.—The tenant also may transfer his rights to others. He may transfer them entirely, in which case he is said to *assign his lease*, or he may transfer but a portion of them, as by renting to another a part of the premises, in which case he is said to *sublet.*† The difference in effect between a sublease and the assignment of a lease is this: in the first case the subtenants bear no relations to the original landlord, and are not responsible to him for rent, the tenant being their only landlord; but in the other case, the new tenant becomes a tenant of the landlord, and must pay him the rent. In the first case the landlord can sue only his original tenant: in the second he can sue both the original tenant and the new one, having the right, however, to obtain his rent but once. But in neither case does the landlord lose any rights. If the rent is not

---

* These rules are only applications of the simple proposition, that when I have already given a thing (or a right) to one person, I cannot give it to another. (See also p. 229, sec. 8.)

† *Sublease* and *underlease* mean the same.

paid, and if the lease gives him the right in such case to take the land, he may do so, although the subtenants have paid their rent to their landlord. But to protect themselves in such case the subtenants may pay their rent to the original landlord, and that will deprive their immediate landlord of the right to sue them for it.

7. Distress for rent was the forcible taking by the landlord of any personal property found upon the land, in order to enforce payment of the rent. This proceeding, being so harsh, has been generally discontinued, and in many of the States the right to take it has been abolished by law.

8. Destruction of Property.—Where there is an express agreement to pay rent the destruction of a part of the property—as, for instance, by a fire or flood—does not relieve the tenant from any part of his rent. Having entire charge of the property he must take the risk of its destruction. Thus, if a house is burned down the rent is still due, for the land still remains.* Neither the landlord nor the tenant is obliged to rebuild houses accidentally destroyed by fire.

9. Repairs.—A landlord is under no obligation to his tenant to make any repairs to the property rented, unless he has specially agreed to do so. Neither can the tenant make the repairs and deduct the amount from the rent, for that is in effect compelling the landlord to do it. On the other hand the tenant must deliver up the premises when his lease has expired, in as good condition as that in which they were when he received them, except that he will not be chargeable with the ordinary wear and tear. Therefore he must make all ordinary repairs, such as the keeping of

---

* This rule is harsh where the building forms the principal part of what is rented, and is therefore changed to some extent in some States.

fences in order, replacing broken doors and windows, etc. But those which cannot be called ordinary, such as the supplying of a new roof, or repairs necessitated by an accidental fire, he need not make.

10. Improvements.—We have seen that anything added to land becomes a part of it, and belongs to its owner (p. 215). Thus if a tenant builds upon the land, or places any improvements upon it (which when finished are affixed to the land, and are not merely pieces of movable personal property *), he must leave them there, and can be allowed nothing for them, unless there was some arrangement to that effect. Thus if he built new buildings or fences, or made repairs, such as the laying of floors, or papering of walls, he could not remove them or obtain an allowance for them without an agreement. But to this rule there is an exception. A tenant may remove from rented property articles which he has built upon it or affixed to it if they were placed there for use in some trade or for domestic purposes. The first class might include such things as steam-engines, or other machines built into the ground or house, or even buildings themselves when used for manufacturing purposes. The second class might include such articles as furnaces, shelves, pier-glasses, gas-fixtures, etc.

11. Notice to Quit is a notice from the landlord to the tenant that he desires to end the tenancy at a certain time. Where the renting was for a definite time no notice from either party to the other is necessary.† The landlord has the

---

* A tenant can of course take away any of his personal property. In sec. 10 we are speaking only of those articles which are firmly affixed to land or a building in such manner as ordinarily to form a part of it.

† A short notice to quit is, however, sometimes necessary before a landlord can regain possession of leased premises by the summary method mentioned in sec. 13.

immediate right to possession as soon as the time expires. The tenant also has the right to go then without notice. It is only when the parties have not fixed a definite time that a notice is necessary, and its object is to prevent either party from injuring the other by any sudden change. The length of the notice required varies in different cases, being very often as long as six months.

12. Eviction means* a turning out, or in other words a landlord depriving his tenant of the property. This he has the right to do when the tenancy has expired, and also whenever the tenant does, or omits to do, anything for which the lease provides the landlord shall have the right to " re-enter." To re-enter means to evict the tenant. Leases often provide that he shall have the right † whenever the tenant fails to pay any instalment of rent due, though he does not have it for that cause unless the lease does so provide. If the landlord deprives the tenant of the property without right it relieves the latter from paying rent. If some third party, having a better right to the property than the landlord, should deprive the tenant of it, that would also relieve him from paying rent. That result would occur if a mortgagee, whose mortgage was given before the property was rented, should foreclose. Any one whose right to the land is superior to that of the landlord can, of course, deprive the tenant of it.

13. Recovering Possession.—When a landlord or any one else has the right to the possession of land, and can take it himself peaceably, he may do so. Thus when the landlord has the right to evict he may do it himself if he can accomplish it without force. But the law does not allow one to use force for the purpose. If the tenant or other person in possession refuses to leave, resort must be had to the

---

* In a popular sense.   † But not by force (see sec. 13).

courts, and in many States there is a speedy process by which a landlord can be put in possession in a few days. That applies especially to the case of a tenant failing to pay his rent, or holding over after the period of the tenancy has expired.

REVIEW QUESTIONS.

1. What is real estate? Personal property? To which kind does the stock of corporations belong? Give instances of property changing from one kind into the other. What is the distinguishing difference between real and personal property?
2. Explain the difference between full ownership and life ownership. Is there any limitation upon the right of a full owner to do what he pleases with his property? What three limitations are there upon the power of a life owner over the property? Can he rent it? Which must pay the taxes upon it, he or the person who is to take it after him?
3. How may life ownership arise? What is dower?
4. Explain what is meant by a future interest in land. How does it differ from an expected interest, such as that of an heir? Can the present owner of land in which another has a future interest affect the other's ownership?
5. What is joint ownership? State some ways in which it may arise. Are a life owner and the one who is to take the property on his death joint owners? What are the rights of joint owners as to use of the property? As to its division?
6. What is a trust? A trustee?
7. Where land is situated in one State and its owner lives in another, by the law of which State are transactions with regard to it governed? How does that differ from the ordinary rule as to contracts?

---

8. State the two kinds of rights connected with the ownership of real estate. What is an appurtenance? What is included in the word "land" besides the surface?

9. What right over the highway has an adjoining owner of land? What right has the public? When a road is abandoned to whom does the land in the road belong?

10. What rights has an owner of land over a stream flowing through it? Can he diminish it? Why? When can he dam it?

11. What is a right of way? Has the owner of a way the right to use it after he has sold the land to which it leads? Name some other rights analogous to right of way. What is a party-wall? What are the rights of the respective owners? Name some restrictive rights.

12. Why is it appropriate to say that certain land may own rights over other land?

13. Must the appurtenances belonging to land be described in a deed of it? Why?

14. How are rights over one's own property obtained? Rights over other property? How long do they last?

---

15. What is a deed? How different from an agreement to sell?

16. Can property be granted by one to another without a deed? Why? Is an oral contract for the future sale of real estate binding?

17. State the five essentials in the contents of a deed.

18. May a deed be signed by an agent? How may one sign who does not know how to write? Who besides the owner should sign?

19. Is a seal necessary to a deed? What is it? Who must attach it? When?

20. At what moment precisely does the transfer of ownership take place? What effect has the destruction of a deed before it is delivered? After delivery? Must it be delivered to the party himself?

21. What is the acknowledgment of a deed? Is it necessary to a transfer?

22. If after a sale the property turns out not to have belonged to the seller, in what case can the buyer call on him for reimbursement?

23. What is a covenant? State the effect of the usual covenants in a deed. State the object of a covenant against nuisances.

---

24. What is a mortgage in effect? In form? How does it differ in effect from a pledge of personal property? How in form from

a deed? Define mortgagor. Mortgagee. After a mortgage has been given which party owns the property?

25. What is a bond? Is it (when secured by a mortgage) personal or real property? Is a mortgage valid without a bond or note? Why?

26. State the essential contents of a mortgage. Must it be in writing?

27. What is foreclosure? The most common method? State the circumstances under which the bond and mortgage in forms 40 and 41 might be foreclosed. What is the effect of foreclosing as to ownership of the property? As to payment of the debt?

28. May mortgaged property be sold? What is its effect upon the mortgage?

29. May a mortgage be sold?

30. In what case does one buying mortgaged property become responsible for the debt, and in what case not? When is it of importance, and when not? Why?

31. What other liens may there be on real estate? The difference between a lien on personal property, and one on real estate?

32. In what order do liens upon the same property take precedence of each other? What exception is there to that rule?

33. What is the effect upon a first mortgage of a second mortgagee's foreclosing?

34. What is "searching a title?" Its object?

35. What is it to record a deed? Is it legally recorded until fully copied? Is record necessary to a transfer? What instruments should be recorded?

36. What is the object of recording?

37. What is the effect of not recording an instrument? May the one who gave it claim it is void if unrecorded? May his heirs? Why? Who may? Why?

38. To whose interest is it to see that the record is made? Why?

39. If a second mortgagee takes his mortgage knowing that there is one prior to his but unrecorded, which takes precedence? Why? State the rule.

40. Name one thing necessary to the right to record, besides a signed instrument. If a deed is recorded without it, is the record good? What may take its place in some States?

41. What is a landlord? A tenant? Renting? Rent? A lease?

42. May a tenancy for a definite period be terminated by one party without the other's consent? May it by agreement?

43. In what case must a lease be written? Must it have a seal?

44. What circumstances regulate the time when rent is to be paid? If the provisions of a lease differ from the custom of the neighborhood, which controls? When is rent due in advance?

45. What is the effect upon a tenant's rights of a sale of the property? The effect upon his rights of the foreclosure of a mortgage which was made before his lease? The effect, if his lease was made first? Why, in each case?

46. May a tenant lease the property to others? What is a sublease? An assignment of a lease? Is a subtenant responsible for rent to the original landlord? Is one to whom a lease is assigned?

47. What is distress for rent? Is it generally resorted to in this country?

48. Does a destruction of a part of the property relieve a tenant from paying any of the rent? Why?

49. Which party is under obligation to make ordinary repairs to rented property, the landlord or the tenant? Can a tenant make repairs, and deduct it from the rent? Is a tenant obliged to make extraordinary repairs?

50. If a tenant makes improvements to property is he entitled to allowance for them? Can he in general remove buildings he has built? Can he remove articles of his own not fastened to the land or building?

51. What two kinds of articles may a tenant remove, though in a sense they are part of the land or building?

52. In what case is it necessary for a landlord to give notice to quit to a tenant?

53. What is eviction? When has a landlord the right? How is it exercised? May a landlord ever evict a tenant by force? Has a landlord always the right to the possession of the land if the tenant fails to pay any instalment of rent due?

EXERCISES

IN THE

DRAWING OF PAPERS.

THE purpose of the following exercises is to aid in familiarizing the scholar with the forms of some of the more common business papers and contracts, by requiring him, on a statement of certain hypothetical facts, to draw up the paper appropriate to the case. The cases would thus be presented to him just as they might arise in real life. The exercises given will serve merely as examples or suggestions, which may be amplified or multiplied according to the ideas of the individual teacher.

In those papers which have no established invariable form there will be room for choice in the use of language. But let the pupil remember that in legal papers the one great object to be striven for is clearness. Let the full meaning be expressed, and in such terms as to provide as far as possible against all future differences of opinion. It is better to make a long clear paper than a short ambiguous one. Common words also should be used, those which will most naturally express the idea. It is a rule of law that in all contracts the words are to be interpreted in their ordinary signification. They do not have one meaning popularly and another legally.

COMMERCIAL PAPER.

I. NOTE.

On September 18th, 1883, Samuel S. Hoyle lends $500 to Franklin Grant, the loan to be paid in six months, with interest at six per cent, the borrower agreeing to give his note for it.

Draw the note in the following different ways:

1. *Make it payable to the order of the creditor;*
2. *Make it payable to bearer;*
3. *Make it payable to the maker's order, with his indorsement to the order of the creditor;*
4. *Draw one that will not be negotiable.*

II. NOTE.

On April 5th, 1884, the firm of John Livingston & Company buy of the firm of Martin Spinney's Sons $652 worth of dry goods on credit, $200 to be paid in two months, $200 in three months, and the balance in four months, without interest.

1. *Draw three notes to represent those three payments to be made, making each one payable to order and negotiable.*
2. *Draw the third note in such a way as to give Livingston & Co. the right to pay it, either in money or, if they choose, by returning to Martin Spinney's Sons an equal amount of the goods bought at the prices at which they are bought.*

III. NOTE.

Addison Howland is indebted to B. K. Curran & Co. in the sum of $52.75. Not being able to pay it at the time, they ask him on January 4th, 1886, for his note payable to their order on demand.

Draw the note.

IV. NOTE.

On September 10th, 1885, Charles H. Laudon asks Charles K. Page to lend him $300 for a month. Page is willing to do so, but cannot conveniently get the money just then. However, knowing that he will have the money at the North Western Bank in a month, he offers to give Laudon his note for the amount, due in one month, which Laudon may get discounted or use as he wishes.

1. *Draw the note, payable at the North Western Bank.*
2. *Draw Laudon's note, payable to Page's order, due in one month, to represent the loan from Page to him.*

V. DRAFT.

Packard & Company, of Milwaukee, Wis., make a draft June 25th, 1885, on the Merchants' Union Bank of Hartford, Conn., for $1500, in favor of Robert P. Field, payable on presentation.

Draw the draft.

VI. DRAFT.

Pease & Ashley, of Rochester, bought of A. R. Kimball, of New York, $4500 worth of goods on July 7th, 1884, on a credit of six months. At the time the bill becomes due Kimball makes a draft on them payable to his own order, thirty days after sight.

Draw the draft.

VII. BILL OF EXCHANGE.

Henry O. Jewell, of Brooklyn, N. Y., owes B. T. Hobbs, of London, England, $3000. Wishing to pay the debt, he buys of Yeoman & Young, bankers, of New York, a bill of exchange drawn by them upon the International Bank, of London, payable to the order of B. T. Hobbs, and to be paid as soon as presented.

Draw the bill of exchange.

VIII. ACCEPTANCE.

Take the case stated in Exercise VI.

Draw the draft as it will be after it has been presented to the persons drawn upon and accepted by them.

IX. CHECK.

Arthur K. Archer, living in Boston, Mass., wishes to send $29.40 to O. P. Martin, who lives in Galveston, Texas. He does it by sending a check for that amount upon the Bay National Bank, dated August 14th, 1884.

1. *Draw the check in such a way that it can safely be sent by mail.*
2. *Draw it in a number of ways which would be unsafe, were it to be sent by mail.*

X. CERTIFIED CHECK.

Take the same case.

Draw the check as it would be when certified.

XI. INDORSEMENT.

Take any one of the notes drawn under Exercise II., and suppose that the firm to whose order it is drawn, instead of keeping it until it is due, get it discounted at the Eighth National Bank, indorsing it themselves.

1. *Place the proper indorsement upon it to make them responsible upon it, and to keep it still payable to order.*
2. *Place the proper indorsement upon it to make them responsible, but to render it payable to any one.*

XII. Indorsement.

Take the note drawn under Exercise IV., No. 1: suppose that the payee sells it to Christian Sackett, indorsing it so as to make himself responsible, and so as to make the note payable to any one; that Sackett sells it to Joseph J. Hubbard & Co., indorsing to make himself responsible; and that Joseph J. Hubbard & Co. sell it to the Ninth National Bank without guaranteeing it; and that the bank collects it when due.

Draw the note with the proper indorsements as it will appear when due.

XIII. Indorsement.

Take the note drawn under Exercise IV., No. 2, and make the same suppositions as in Exercise XII., except that Joseph J. Hubbard & Co. make themselves responsible upon it.

Draw it with the indorsements as it will appear when due.

XIV. Indorsement.

Take the draft drawn under Exercise V.; suppose that the person in whose favor it is drawn transfers it to Thomas Dumont, making it payable to Dumont's order, but relieving himself from responsibility, and that Dumont transfers it to D. P. Marion without guaranteeing it, but making it payable to any one.

Draw it with the indorsements.

XV. Indorsement.

Suppose that Samuel Jones draws a check upon the Bank of the United States for $725.18, in order to pay a bill of that amount which he owes to Abraham Jones; that he draws it to his own order and gives it to Abraham Jones; that Abraham Jones transfers it to John Jones; John Jones to William Jones; William Jones to Charles Jones; Charles Jones to Amos Jones, who collects it at the bank; that each one indorses it in full, except the last, who indorses in blank; and that all indorse so as to make themselves responsible, except Charles Jones.

Draw the check with its indorsements.

MISCELLANEOUS PAPERS.

XVI. RECEIPT.

Mrs. E. A. Scott owes William B. Waters & Son $524. On January 17th, 1881, she pays $100, on February 6th, 1881, $250, and the remainder on February 8th, 1882.

Draw three receipts to represent the three payments.

XVII. GUARANTY.

Take one of the notes drawn under Exercise II.

Draw on its back a guaranty of its payment by George K. H. Inness.

XVIII. NOTICE TO INDORSERS.

Take each one of the papers with its indorsements, drawn under Exercises XI., XII., XIII., XIV., and XV., and suppose that in each case the paper was not paid at maturity.

1. *Draw in each case a proper notice to be sent to the indorsers.*
2. *Draw a draft which had been transferred and indorsed before it was presented for acceptance, and on which acceptance has been refused, and then draw a proper notice of non-acceptance to be sent to the indorsers.*

XIX. MEMORANDUM OF SALE.

A. Robert Wolf, sells on July 23d, 1883, to Robinson & Company, 1000 tons of coal, at $3.50 a ton, payment to be made in three months.

1. *Draw a memorandum of the sale, signed, sufficient to make it binding.*

2. *Suppose that instead of a sale on July 23d, 1883, it was an agreement made on that day, to sell that amount, at that price, any time within six months: draw that.*

XX. Contract of Employment.

On March 19th, 1884, the firm of Mason & Mattling, employ Job B. Bellows as a bookkeeper for one year, commencing April 1st. They agree to pay him $1500 for the year, payments to be made on the last day of each month. They also agree that if Bellows during the year is offered any other situation by any one, and wishes to leave, he shall be at liberty to do so, and his salary shall be paid him up to the time he leaves. The parties also agree that if before the end of the year the firm should be dissolved in any way, or Bellows should die, then the employment should terminate.

Draw the agreement so as to be binding upon both parties.

XXI. Contract of Partnership.

Stephen Mills, Ezekiel B. Warren, and Alonzo C. Carman enter into partnership August 8th, 1875, upon the following terms:

1. Mills contributes $5000 to the capital, Warren $3000, and Carman agrees, as his share, to allow the firm the use of the building 345 Wall Street, rent free;

2. The firm name is to be Mills, Warren & Co.;

3. The business is to be the manufacture and selling of paper;

4. Mills is to devote himself solely to the manufacturing branch of the business, and the other partners are to take charge of every other department;

5. All the partners are to devote all their time to the business;

6. The partnership is to continue three years;

7. The profits are to be divided in the following proportions: to Mills one-third, to Warren one-fifth, and to Carman seven-fifteenths;

8. The losses are to be borne in the same proportions;

9. No partner is to draw from the firm more than $1500 the first year.

Draw articles of copartnership embodying those conditions.

XXII. Notice of Insurance Loss.

Take the case supposed in form 25 (p. 289), and suppose that on the 14th day of December, 1874, a fire occurs destroying a large number of books.

Draw a proper notification to the Insurance Company.

XXIII. Power of Attorney.

Andrew P. Wilson owns 245 shares of the American East Coast Improvement Company. He wishes to give Stephen W. Mack, of Ottawa, Canada, a written paper showing that the latter is authorized to sell and transfer the stock to any one as his agent.

Draw the power of attorney.

XXIV. Broker's Notes.

Take the case stated in Exercise XIX., and suppose that instead of the sale being made by the parties themselves it is made through the firm of C. B. Rice & Carberry as brokers.

Draw two notes, for the brokers to send to the buyer and seller respectively.

XXV. Dissolution of Partnership.

Take the case stated in Exercise XXI., and suppose that after the business has been carried on for three years Warren desires to withdraw from the firm, and that the other two partners, wishing to continue the business, are willing to pay him, and he is willing to receive, $4000 for his interest, to be paid as follows : $2000 immediately, $1000 at the end of another year, and $1000 at the end of two years, the two remaining partners to agree to assume all the debts of the firm.

1. *Draw such a contract to be signed by all three of the partners.*
2. *Draw such a notice as Warren ought to send to those who have dealt with the firm, and such a notice as he ought to publish, in order that he may not be made responsible for future debts of the firm.*
3. *Draw a short contract of partnership for the two remaining partners, by which they agree to carry on the business on the same terms as before for five years longer, except that each is to receive half the profits and bear half the losses.*

A Table of Definitions.*

Abandonment.—See under *Insurance*.

Acceptance (of a draft).—Two meanings:

1. The agreeing of the person drawn upon to pay it.
2. The draft after it has been accepted.

Acceptor (of a draft).—See under *Parties to Commercial Paper*.

Accommodation Paper.—Commercial paper for which no consideration exists as between the original parties.

> BUSINESS PAPER.—Commercial paper for which there is a consideration given when it originates.

> ACCOMMODATION DRAFT.—Two kinds:
>
> 1. One in which there is no consideration for the drawing (i.e., for the drawer's agreement); therefore, one by which the drawer accommodates the payee.
> 2. One in which there is no consideration for the accepting (i.e., for the acceptor's agreement); therefore one by which the acceptor accommodates the drawer.

> ACCOMMODATION INDORSEMENT.—One for which the indorser receives no consideration.

> ACCOMMODATION NOTE.—One in which there is no consideration for the making (i.e., for the maker's agreement); therefore one by which the maker accommodates the payee.

Acknowledgment (of deeds, etc.).—The signer's going before a certain officer and acknowledging to him that the deed is freely and voluntarily given, and the officer's attaching his certificate that the signer has done so. The word is sometimes used to mean the signer's act alone, or the officer's certificate alone.

---

* It is not intended in this table to give a list of words in legal use, but only the exact meaning of many words in common use. Those relating to the same general subject are grouped together, with cross-references, so that words with contrasted meanings may be compared.

Advances (made by a commission merchant).—Money paid by a commission merchant to his principal, before any sale of the goods, as a part of what they will probably sell for.

Agency.—The relation existing between two parties by which one (called the agent), is authorized to do certain acts for the other (called the principal), with other parties.

> PRINCIPAL.—A party for whom another is authorized to do certain acts with third parties.

> AGENT.—A party authorized to do certain acts for another, with third parties.

> THIRD PARTY.—A party with whom an agent does certain authorized acts for his principal.

> AUTHORITY.—The power granted by a principal to his agent to do certain acts for him with other parties.

> APPARENT AUTHORITY.—The power which a principal has allowed his agent to seem to have, to act for him.

> SUB-AGENT.—The agent of an agent.

> ATTORNEY.—In one meaning another word for *agent.* Used chiefly in connection with important matters.

> POWER OF ATTORNEY.—A written instrument by which a principal grants to the agent authority to act for him with others.

Agent.—See under *Agency.*

Agreement to Sell.—See under *Sale.*

Apparent Authority.—See under *Agency.*

Appurtenance (to real estate).—A minor article or right connected with the property, and passing with it from one owner to another.

Articles of Association. ⎫
Articles of Incorporation. ⎬ See under *Corporation.*

Articles of Copartnership.—See under *Partnership.*

Assignee (in insolvency).—See under *Bankruptcy.*

Assignment, General.—See under *Bankruptcy.*

Assignment (of a claim).—The transfer of its ownership by one person to another. It is generally used of a written transfer, and in connection with claims not founded on commercial paper.

Assignment of a Lease.—See under *Lease.*

Assure.—Means the same as *Insure.*

Attorney.—Two meanings:

> 1. A lawyer.

> 2. An agent. See under *Agency.*

Authority.—See under *Agency.*

Average (in insurance).—See under *Insurance.*

Bank Bill.—See under *Money.*

Bank Note.—Means the same as *Bank Bill.*

Bankruptcy.—The condition of one who is unable to pay his debts as they fall due.

> FAIL.—To become unable to pay one's debts as they become due. Used only of persons in commercial life.

> GENERAL ASSIGNMENT.—A transfer by a failing debtor of all his remaining property to some one for the purpose of having it distributed among his creditors.

> ASSIGNEE (in a general assignment).—The person to whom the failing debtor transfers all his remaining property for the purpose of having it distributed among his creditors.

> PREFERENCE (in a general assignment).—A direction that certain ones of the creditors shall be paid their entire claims, though nothing is left for the rest.

> COMPROMISE.—An agreement between a debtor and his creditors by which they agree to accept a certain proportion of the amounts due, and discharge him from the remainder.

Barter.—See under *Sale.*

Bill and Note Broker.—See under *Broker.*

Bill of Exchange.—See under *Commercial Paper.*

Bill of Lading.—A document delivered by a carrier to one sending goods by him, acknowledging that they have been received by him for transportation to a certain place. It is both a receipt and a contract.

Blank Indorsement.—See under *Indorsement.*

Bond.—A written instrument by which one agrees to pay to another a certain amount of money, unless something else specified therein is done.

> BOND (for the payment of money).—A written instrument by which one agrees to pay to another a certain amount of money, unless a certain smaller amount is paid. It is in effect an agreement to pay the smaller amount.

> BOND OF INDEMNITY.—An agreement in the form of a bond by which one agrees to indemnify another for all loss in a certain matter.

Broker.—An agent to make contracts.

> BILL AND NOTE BROKER.—One who acts for others in the buying and selling of commercial paper.

INSURANCE BROKER.—One who acts for the owners of property in obtaining insurance upon it.

MERCHANDISE BROKER.—One who acts for others in the buying and selling of merchandise without having it in his possession. See *Commission Merchant.*

REAL ESTATE BROKER.—One who acts for others in the buying, selling, mortgaging and renting of real estate.

SHIP BROKER.—One who acts for others in the buying, selling, and freighting * of vessels.

STOCK BROKER.—One who acts for others in the buying and selling of the stocks and bonds of railroads and other corporations.

Business Paper.—See under *Accommodation Paper.*

Capital (of a corporation).—See under *Corporation.*

Capital (of a firm).—See under *Partnership.*

Capital Stock.—See under *Corporation.*

Carrier.—One who transports the goods of others, or transports passengers, from one place to another.

COMMON CARRIER.—One engaged in the business of transporting from place to place goods or passengers for the public generally.

PRIVATE CARRIER.—One who transports goods or passengers, but only casually, or only for particular persons.

Certificate of Deposit.—See under *Commercial Paper.*

Certificate of Stock.—See under *Corporation.*

Certification (of check):

1. *In form:* The signature of the proper officer of the bank written across its face, sometimes with and sometimes without the word "certified," or "good."

2. *In legal intent:* A recognition of the check by the bank as good in two particulars, viz., (1) that the drawer's signature is genuine, and (2) that he has that amount of money in the bank.

Charter (of corporation).—See under *Corporation.*

Charter (a vessel).—To hire or let a vessel or a part of it.

Charter-Party.—The written instrument by which the owner of a vessel lets it, or a part of it, to another.

---

* Obtaining goods to be transported upon a vessel, or taking charge of a vessel and her cargo when she arrives at a certain port.

Chattel.—A piece of personal property. *Chattel* includes not only merchandise, but also animals, and leases of real estate.

Chattel Mortgage.—A conditional sale of personal property, i.e., one which is to become void if a certain thing happens. Chiefly used as a security for the payment of money. See also *Pledge.*

Check.—See under *Commercial Paper.*

Civil Remedy.—See under *Remedy.*

Coin.—See under *Money.*

Collateral.—See under *Pledge.*

Commercial Paper.—Written evidences of indebtedness in common use among merchants.

> NOTE.—A written promise, signed by the person promising, to pay a certain sum of money at a certain time to a person named, or to his order, or to the bearer.

> DRAFT.—A written order, signed by one person, ordering another person, to whom it is directed, to pay a certain sum of money at a certain time to a third person (named), or to his order, or to the bearer.

> BILL OF EXCHANGE.—Two meanings:
> 1. A draft of which the drawer and the person drawn upon live in different countries.
> 2. Another term for a draft of any kind.

> CHECK.—A written order signed by one person, ordering a certain bank or banker, to whom it is directed, to pay a certain sum of money immediately to a third person (named), or to his order, or to the bearer.

> CERTIFICATE OF DEPOSIT.—A certificate issued by a bank or banker, showing that a certain sum of money has been deposited there, payable to a certain person, or to his order, or to the bearer.

Commission.—A percentage allowed to one in payment for certain services.

Commission Merchant.—One employed by others to sell for them merchandise which they send to him.

Common Carrier.—See under *Carrier.*

Common Law.—See under *Law.*

Company.—Two meanings:
1. A corporation. See *Corporation.*
2. A term often used in a firm name to designate the partners who are not otherwise named therein.

Compromise.—See under *Bankruptcy*.

Conditional Sale.—See under *Sale*.

Consideration (for a contract).—The thing given, done, or promised to be given or done by the person to whom the promise is made.

Consignee.—One to whom merchandise, given to a carrier by another person for transportation, is directed.

Consignor.—One who gives merchandise to a carrier for transportation to another.

Constitution.—See under *Law*.

Contract.—An agreement made between two or more parties; a promise assented to.

> EXPRESS CONTRACT.—An agreement definitely expressed in words. It may be *oral* or *written*.

> IMPLIED CONTRACT.—An agreement which is implied from all the circumstances of the transaction.

Copartnership.—Another word for *Partnership*.

Copyright.—The right granted by the government to an author, to prevent all others from printing or selling his work without his consent, within the country, for a certain number of years.

Corporation.—A number of persons associated together by law for a particular purpose, as a new and distinct individual.

> CAPITAL STOCK.—The fund or property, as a whole, contributed or supposed to have been contributed to a corporation at its organization, as its property.

> CAPITAL.—Another term for *Capital Stock*.

> STOCK.—Another term for *Capital Stock*. It is also used to denote the shares into which the capital stock is divided, as where one is said to own so much stock, meaning so many shares.

> CERTIFICATE OF STOCK.—A certificate given by the proper officers of a corporation showing that a certain person owns a certain number of shares of the capital stock.

> PAR VALUE.—A nominal value placed upon the stock of a corporation by its organizers at its organization.

> STOCKHOLDER.—The owner of one or more shares of the stock of a corporation.

> SHAREHOLDER.—Another term for *Stockholder*.

> ARTICLES OF ASSOCIATION, or }
> ARTICLES OF INCORPORATION. } A paper signed by the organizers of a corporation, preliminary to its organization, setting

forth its name, purposes and plan, and forming the basis of the corporation.

CHARTER.—A special act of a legislature creating a particular corporation.

RECEIVER.—A person appointed to take the property of a corporation on its dissolution, and to distribute it according to law.

Covenant (in a deed).—An agreement contained in a deed, additional to those parts which transfer the ownership.

Credit, Sale on.—A sale in which the payment is to be made at some future time.

Criminal Remedy.—See under *Remedy.*

Currency.—See under *Money.*

Damages.—See under *Remedy.*

Days of Grace.—Three days to be added to the time specified in a note or draft, at which it is to become due.

Deed (of real estate).—A written instrument transferring the ownership of real estate from one person to another.

Demand Note.—A note made payable by its terms on demand, or one in which no time of payment is specified.

Deposit (in banking).—To place money with the bank with the agreement that it or any part of it shall be repaid when called for.

Deviation.—See under *Insurance.*

Discount (of commercial paper).—To buy a note or draft before it is due, with the indorsement of the one from whom it is bought, paying its amount less a certain amount of interest.

Dishonor (of commercial paper).—A failure to pay it when due. Or, in a draft, a failure to accept it when presented for acceptance.

Distress for Rent.—The taking by a landlord of personal property found upon the land, for the payment of rent due.

Dower.—The right of a widow to a life interest in one-third of all the real estate owned by her husband at any time during their marriage.

Draft.—See under *Commercial Paper.*

Drawer (of check or draft).—See under *Parties to Commercial Paper.*

Earn (a premium).—See under *Insurance.*

Endorse.—Another word for *Indorse.*

Eviction (of a tenant).—Depriving him of the possession of the land.

Exchange. A collective term denoting drafts or bills of exchange upon parties in another State or country.

Execution.—See under *Remedy.*

Express Contract.—See under *Contract.*

Factor.—Another term for *Commission Merchant.*

Fail.—See under *Bankruptcy.*

Fee-simple.—The full absolute ownership of real estate.

Fire Insurance.—See under *Insurance.*

Firm.—See under *Partnership.*

Foreclosure.—A proceeding by which mortgaged property is taken or sold by the mortgagee in order to pay the debt. It very often consists of a suit at law.

Forgery.—The fraudulently making or altering of a written instrument

Fraud.—A statement of facts known to be false, or concealment of facts known to be true, made to induce a party to do something against his interest, when the case is not such that with reasonable caution and inquiry he could ascertain the truth for himself.

Freight.—Two meanings:

1. The compensation to be paid a carrier for the transportation of goods.
2. The goods themselves while being transported.

Full Indorsement.—See under *Indorsement.*

Full Insurance.—See under *Insurance.*

General Assignment.—See under *Bankruptcy.*

General Average.—A contribution to be paid by the different owners of a vessel and cargo to one of their number, when his property has been voluntarily and successfully sacrificed to save the rest. See also *Average* under *Insurance.*

General Partner.—See under *Partnership.*

Greenback.—See under *Money.*

Guarantee.—To agree to hold one's self responsible if another person does not do a certain thing he has agreed to do. It means the same as *Guaranty,* but is used both as a verb and as a noun, while the latter is only used commonly as a noun.

Guarantor.—One who agrees to hold himself responsible if another person does not do a certain thing he has agreed to do. Means nearly the same as *Surety.*

Guaranty.—Two meanings:

1. An agreement to hold one's self responsible if another person does not do a certain thing he has agreed to do. In this sense it means the same as *Guarantee.*

2. An agreement to hold one's self responsible if a certain thing does not turn out to be as represented. In this sense it means the same as *Warranty.*

Guaranty Commission.—The commission paid to a commission merchant who guarantees to his principal the payment of the money for which the goods may be sold

Highway.—A road which every one has the right to use.

    PRIVATE ROAD.—A road which only the owners of certain property have the right to use.

Hotel Keeper.—One whose business is to provide food and lodging for any one who may ask and pay for them.

House (in partnership).—See under *Partnership.*

Idiot.—See under *Lunatic.*

Implied Contract.—See under *Contract.*

Indemnity Bond.—See under *Bond.*

Indorsement (of commercial paper).—Two meanings:

1. A name, with or without other words, written on the back of the paper.

2. The agreement implied in one's writing his name on the back of commercial paper, to pay it if the principal debtor does not. A kind of guaranty.

    BLANK INDORSEMENT, or / INDORSEMENT IN BLANK. ∫ One in which no particular person is named as the one to whom payment is to be made. It ordinarily consists of the indorser's name alone.

    FULL INDORSEMENT, or / INDORSEMENT IN FULL. ∫ One in which payment is ordered to be made to a particular person named.

Indorser.—See under *Parties to Commercial Paper.*

Infringement (of a patent).—The making, using, or selling of a patented article without the permission of the owner of the patent.

Infringement (of a copyright).—The printing, publishing, or selling of a copyrighted article, without the permission of the owner of the copyright.

Infringement (of a trade-mark).—The using of another's trade-mark, or an imitation of it, without his permission.

Injunction.—See under *Remedy.*

Innkeeper.—Means the same as *Hotel Keeper.*

Insolvency.—Means the same as *Bankruptcy.*

Insurance.—A contract to secure one against certain risks.

> **FIRE INSURANCE.**—A contract to pay the owner of certain property all his loss (up to a certain amount), if it is damaged or destroyed by fire within a certain time.

> **MARINE INSURANCE.**—A contract to pay the owner of property a certain proportion of his loss if it is damaged or destroyed while on the sea within a certain time.

> **LIFE INSURANCE.**—A contract to pay a certain sum of money on the death of a certain person, or when he reaches a certain age.

> A. *Terms used in all kinds of insurance.*

INSURER.—The party (usually a company) agreeing to make the insurance.

INSURED.—The party agreeing to pay the premium.

POLICY.—The written contract of insurance.

PREMIUM.—The amount to be paid annually or otherwise for the insurance by the insured.

PREMIUM NOTE.—A note given in payment of a premium or a part of it.

EARN (a premium).—To become entitled to the premium because the risk has been assumed and incurred.

> B. *Terms used in fire and marine insurance.*

UNDERWRITER.—Another word for *Insurer.*

FULL INSURANCE.—Insurance, the total amount of which, whether by one or by several policies, equals the value of the property insured.

> C. *Terms used in marine insurance alone.*

OPEN POLICY.—Two meanings:

1. One which does not fix the value of the property insured.
2. One intended to cover all goods shipped within a certain time by a certain party, the particular goods and amounts of insurance to be indorsed upon the policy from time to time.

VALUED POLICY.—One which fixes the value of the property insured.

AVERAGE.—Loss or damage to property at sea, for which an insurer is responsible.

GENERAL AVERAGE.—A loss to be paid by an insurer who has insured particular goods, on account of a contribution paid by their owner to another owner of property upon that voyage whose property was voluntarily and successfully sacrificed to save the rest.

PARTICULAR AVERAGE.—Two meanings:

1. A loss to be borne by the particular owner or his insurer; any average not general.

2. A partial loss of the property insured; any loss or damage not a total loss.

DEVIATION.—A voluntary departure, not absolutely necessary, from the ordinary course taken in a particular voyage.

ABANDONMENT.—The giving up to an insurer by the insured of what remains, after a loss or injury amounting to one-half the property in value, and claiming the full amount of insurance.

Insurance Broker.—See under *Broker.*

Insured.—See under *Insurance.*

Insurer.—See under *Insurance.*

Interest.—See under *Principal and Interest.*

Judgment.—See under *Remedy.*

Landlord and Tenant:

LANDLORD.—One who has granted to another for a period the sole use of certain real estate.

TENANT.—One to whom another has granted for a period the sole use of certain real estate.

SUBTENANT.—The tenant of a tenant.

UNDERTENANT.—Another word for *Subtenant.*

Law.—A direction from the governing power of a country to its inhabitants, telling them what they must or must not do, and regulating the effect of their acts.

CONSTITUTION (in the U. S).—A written instrument adopted by the people of a State, or of the Nation, regulating certain fundamental matters of government.

LEGISLATURE.—A body created by a constitution, and given power by it to enact laws upon certain subjects.

STATUTES.—Laws enacted separately by a legislature.

COMMON LAW.—The great body of rules of law, established long ago in England, and adopted in each State as a body of law.

Lease.—A contract by which one grants to another for a period the sole use of certain real estate.

ASSIGNMENT OF A LEASE.—The transfer by a tenant to another person of all his rights to the real estate mentioned in the lease, for the whole unexpired period.

SUBLEASE.—A lease from a tenant to another person of the whole or a part of the land, for a part of the time.

UNDERLEASE.—Another word for *Sublease.*

Legal Holidays.—Certain days appointed by law upon which it is recommended that people refrain from their ordinary business.

Legal Rate (of interest).—See under *Principal and Interest.*

Legal Tender.—See under *Money.*

Legislature.—See under *Law.*

Letters Patent.—See under *Patent.*

Liability.—The state of being bound by law to take the legal consequences of a certain thing's being or not being done; responsibility.

Lien (on personal property).—The right of a creditor to keep certain property belonging to the debtor until the debt is paid.

Lien (on real estate).—The right of a creditor to have certain property, which at the time the lien was created did belong to the debtor, sold in order to pay the debt.

Life Insurance.—See under *Insurance.*

Limited Partnership.—See under *Partnership.*

Lunatic.—One who has once possessed reasoning power, but has lost it.

IDIOT.—One who never had reasoning power.

Maker (of a note).—See under *Parties to Commercial Paper.*

Marine Insurance.—See under *Insurance.*

Maturity (of commercial paper).—The time at which it is legally to become due.

Merchandise Broker.—See under *Broker.*

Minor.—A person under twenty-one years of age.

Money.—Anything accepted and used by the people of a country generally, as representing so much value.

LEGAL TENDER.—That kind of money which by law can be offered in payment of a debt.

CURRENCY.—Two meanings:

1. The same as *Money.*

2. Paper money.

BANK BILL.—A written promise to pay to the bearer on demand a certain sum of money, issued by a bank and used as money.

UNITED STATES NOTE.—A written promise to pay to the bearer on demand a certain sum of money, issued by the United States Government, and used as money.

COIN.—Pieces of metal stamped and intended to be used as money.

GREENBACKS.—The United States Notes.

Mortgage (of real estate):

1. *As to form:* A conditional deed; a transfer of ownership, to become void if a certain thing is done, usually if certain money is paid.

2. *As to effect:* A right given by a debtor to a creditor to have certain property sold (if necessary) in order to pay a certain debt.

MORTGAGOR.—One who gives a mortgage upon his property.

MORTGAGEE.—One to whom a mortgage is given.

Necessaries (for which a minor may bind himself by contract).—All things necessary or appropriate for the sustenance or convenience of the minor in his way of life.

Negotiability.—Two meanings:

1. The quality in commercial paper of being enforceable by one person who receives it under certain circumstances, even though not enforceable by the one from whom he receives it.

2. The quality of being salable in the market without difficulty; salableness.

Negotiable Note.—A promise to pay, at a certain time, to a certain person or his order, or to the bearer, a certain sum of money unconditionally.

Negotiable Securities.—All kinds of evidences of indebtedness, besides commercial paper, negotiable in form.

Non-acceptance (of a draft).—The neglect or refusal of the person drawn upon to accept it. See *Acceptance.*

Note.—See under *Commercial Paper.*

Notice to Quit.—A notice from a landlord to his tenant to deliver up possession of the premises to him at a certain time.

Open Policy.—See under *Insurance.*

Outlawed (spoken of a debt).—To have existed for the certain length of time, after which the law on that ground alone prevents its being enforced.

Par.—Means the same as *Par value.*

Particular Average.—See under *Insurance.*

Parties to Commercial Paper :

MAKER (of a note).—The person making the original promise, the signer.

DRAWER (of a draft or check).—The person making the original order (i.e., drawing the paper), the signer.

PERSON DRAWN UPON (in a draft or check).—The person to whom the order is addressed. In a check this is the bank.

PAYEE (of any kind of commercial paper).—The person named in the body of the instrument as the one to whom payment is to be made.

ACCEPTOR (of a draft) —The person drawn upon, after he has accepted it (i.e., agreed to pay it).

INDORSER (of any kind of commercial paper).—Any one who writes his name upon the back of it.

Partner.—See under *Partnership.*

Partnership.—Two meanings:

1. The relation established between two or more persons by an agreement to combine their money, property, labor, or skill in some lawful business, and to share its profits.

2. Another word for *Firm.*

PARTNER.—Any one of the parties agreeing as above to form a partnership.

SECRET PARTNER.—One who really is a partner, though not advertised as such to outsiders.

FIRM.—All the partners taken collectively.

HOUSE.—Another word for *Firm.*

ARTICLES OF COPARTNERSHIP.—A written agreement between partners, forming a partnership.

CAPITAL.—The money or property contributed by the partners to be used in the business.

LIMITED PARTNERSHIP.—One formed under a special law, and in which there are one or more partners whose property cannot be taken to pay the debts of the firm, beyond the money they have contributed to it.

SPECIAL PARTNER.—A partner in a limited partnership whose property cannot be taken to pay the debts of the firm, beyond the money he has contributed to it.

GENERAL PARTNER.—A partner in a limited partnership who is responsible for the debts to the same extent as in an ordinary partnership.

Party-Wall.—A wall owned and used jointly by the owners of two pieces of real estate.

Par Value.—See under *Corporation.*

Patent.—Two meanings:

1. The right granted by the Government to an inventor, to prevent all others from making, using, or selling his invention

without his consent, within the country, for a certain number of years. In this sense it is equivalent to *patent-right*.

2. The written instrument by which the Government grants the right. In this sense it is equivalent to *letters-patent*.

Pawn.—Means the same as *Pledge*, but is commonly used only in connection with a pawnbroker's business.

Pawnbroker.—One who makes it a business to loan money in small sums on pledges of articles of personal property.

Payee.—See under *Parties to Commercial Paper*.

Perils of the Sea.—Extraordinary risks attendant upon a sea-voyage which cannot reasonably be foreseen and provided against.

Personal Property.—See under *Real Estate*.

Pledge.—Two meanings:

1. A delivery by a debtor to his creditor of certain personal property with the agreement that it may be held as security for the debt. See also *Chattel Mortgage* and *Pawn*.

2. The property pledged.

COLLATERAL.—Personal property pledged.

Policy.—See under *Insurance*.

Power of Attorney.—See under *Agency*.

Preference (in general assignment).—See under *Bankruptcy*.

Premium.—See under *Insurance*.

Premium Note.—See under *Insurance*.

Price.—See under *Sale*.

Principal and Agent.—See *Agency*.

Principal and Interest:

PRINCIPAL.—The sum of money upon which interest is to be reckoned.

INTEREST.—A certain percentage to be paid by a debtor to his creditor, in addition to the principal, as compensation for its use.

USURY.—That part of the interest agreed to be paid for a loan of money, which exceeds the highest rate that the parties are allowed by law to make.

LEGAL RATE.—That rate established by law to apply to all cases where interest is allowed, but in which the parties have not specified any rate.

Principal and Surety:

PRINCIPAL.—A person for whose debt, default, or misconduct, another person has agreed with a third party to make himself responsible.

SURETY.—A person who has agreed with another to make himself responsible for the debt, default, or misconduct of a third party

Private Carrier.—See under *Carrier.*

Private Road.—See under *Highway.*

Promissory Note.—The same as *Note.*

Protest (of commercial paper).—Two meanings:

1. The presenting of the instrument to the principal debtor for payment or acceptance, and sending notice of its non-payment or non-acceptance to those secondarily responsible.

2. A written paper sometimes drawn up by a notary public, to be attached to dishonored commercial paper.

Public Agent.—An officer of the National, State, City, Town, or other Government; an agent of the people.

Ratification (in agency).—An adoption by the principal, either by words or acts, of some unauthorized act after it has been performed by some one as his agent.

Ratification (of minor's act).—A consent by the minor, after he becomes of age, to be bound by the act.

Real Estate.—Land and everything affixed or appurtenant to it.

PERSONAL PROPERTY.—All property not real estate.

Real Estate Broker.—See under *Broker.*

Real Property.—Another term for *Real Estate.*

Receipt.—A written acknowledgment by one receiving money or other property, that it has been received.

Receiver.—See under *Corporation.*

Recording (of deeds, etc.).—Handing the paper to the proper officer to be recorded.

Redeem (a pledge).—To pay the debt for which it is held.

Remedy.—A method provided by law of redressing a wrong, or of punishing a wrong-doer.

CIVIL REMEDY.—The method of redressing an injury inflicted by one person upon another.

CRIMINAL REMEDY.—The method of punishing a wrong-doer for some wrong committed by him against society.

DAMAGES.—Compensation in money to be paid by one person to another for an injury inflicted by the former upon the latter.

JUDGMENT.—The decree of a court.

INJUNCTION.—The decree of a court forbidding a certain person to do a certain act.

EXECUTION.—A written command issued to a sheriff, after a judgment, directing him to enforce it.

Rent.—Money paid by a tenant to his landlord for the use of the property.

Responsibility.—Two meanings:

1. The same as *Liability.*
2. The having of sufficient property to pay all ordinary obligations.

Revenue Law.—A law imposing a tax or duty.

Right of Way.—The right of the owner of one piece of real estate to pass over another's property at a certain place.

Sale.—An agreement between two parties that certain property, belonging to one, shall immediately belong to the other, and that he shall pay for it in money.

> AGREEMENT TO SELL.—An agreement between two parties that they will at some future time make an agreement of sale with regard to particular property.

> CONDITIONAL SALE.—An agreement between two parties that certain property belonging to one shall at some future time belong to the other, provided a certain thing does or does not happen.

> BARTER.—An agreement between two parties, when carried out, that certain property belonging to one shall immediately belong to the other, and that certain other property belonging to the latter shall immediately belong to the former.

> PRICE.—The amount of money for which the owner of property is willing to sell it; the money agreed to be paid in a sale.

> VALUE.—The amount of money people in general would pay for the property.

Salvage.—Two meanings:

1. The compensation allowed to one who voluntarily saves property abandoned or in great peril at sea.
2. The property saved after a disaster.

Searching a Title (to real estate).—Examining the successive deeds and records relating to the property.

Seaworthy (spoken of a vessel).—Able to withstand the ordinary dangers of the sea, and fully equipped with all the things usually needed on such a voyage as she is intended to take.

Secret Partner.—See under *Partnership.*

Security (for a debt).—Some right which the creditor has to rely upon, besides the mere promise of the debtor. Guaranty, lien, pledge and mortgage are instances of security.

Set-off.—A claim which one party has against another who has a claim against him; a counter-debt.

Shareholder.—See under *Corporation.*

Ship Broker.—See under *Broker.*

Shipper.—One who gives merchandise to another for transportation.

Sight Draft.—A draft made payable at sight.

> **Time Draft.**—A draft made payable at a certain time, or a certain number of days or months after sight.

Special Partner.—See under *Partnership.*

Statute.—See under *Law.*

Stock.—See under *Corporation.*

Stock Broker.—See under *Broker.*

Stockholder.—See under *Corporation.*

Stop Payment (of a check).—To notify the bank, before the check has been presented, not to pay it.

Sub-Agent.—See under *Agency.*

Sublease.—See under *Lease.*

Subtenant.—See under *Landlord and Tenant.*

Surety.—See under *Principal and Surety.*

Suretyship.—The state of being a surety.

Tenant.—See under *Landlord and Tenant.*

Third Party.—See under *Agency.* In general, this is a term used in connection with any transaction between two parties to denote any other person whom the transaction may affect at the time or afterwards.

Time Draft.—See under *Sight Draft.*

Title (to property).—The right to own it; the ownership.

Trade-Mark.—A peculiar device or name attached by a merchant or manufacturer to his own goods, as a mark by which they may be known.

Trust.—The holding of property by one for the benefit of another.

Trustee.—One who holds property for the benefit of another.

Underlease.—See under *Lease.*

Undertenant.—See under *Landlord and Tenant.*

Underwriter.—See under *Insurance.*

United States Note.—See under *Money.*

Usury.—See under *Principal and Interest.*

Value.—See under *Sale.*

Valued Policy.—See under *Insurance.*

Warranty.—An agreement to hold one's self responsible if a certain thing does not turn out to be as represented.

FORMS.

INDEX TO FORMS.

FORMS

OF ORDINARY BUSINESS PAPERS.

NOTES.
FORM 1. (a)

$200.   New York, Dec. 3, 1881.

Two months after date we promise to pay to the order of James S. Foy, Two hundred_____dollars. Value received.

Archibald Brothers.

FORM 2. (b)

$200.   New York, Dec. 3, 1881.

For value received we promise to pay sixty days after date to our own order, Two hundred dollars_____with interest at six per cent.

Archibald Brothers.

FORM 3. *(c)*

$354.72.

New York, Dec. 3d, 1881.

Eighteen months from date we promise to pay to James S. Fay, or bearer, Three hundred fifty-four and $^{72}/_{100}$ dollars at the Ninth National Bank.

Value received.

Archibald Brothers.

FORM 4. *(d)*

$300. New York, Jan. 5th, 1880.

On July 8, 1881, we promise to pay to Bearer the sum of Three hundred $^{\times}/_{100}$ dollars with interest.

Value received.

Archibald Brothers.

FORM 5. (a)

$47.75.

New York, Dec. 3d, 1881.

We promise to pay on demand to James S. Fay, or order, Forty-seven dollars and seventy-five cents.

Value received.

Archibald Brothers.

FORM 6.

NOTE NON-NEGOTIABLE IN FORM.

$200.   New York, Dec. 3, 1881.

Fourteen days after date we promise to pay J. S. Fay Two hundred dollars.

Value received.

Archibald Brothers.

DRAFTS.

FORM 7. (a)

$1000.

New York, Sept. 28, 1881.

At sight pay to A. B. Runyon & Co., or order, One thousand dollars, value received, and charge the same to account of   A. Y. Jones.

To William T. Barber, New Orleans, La.

FORM 8. (b)

$524 15/100

New York, Sept. 28, 1881.

To William T. Barber, Phila.

Ten days after sight pay to my order Five hundred twenty-four and 15/100 dollars, and charge to

A. Y. Jones.

FORM 9.   (*a*)

FOREIGN BILL OF EXCHANGE.

£50.   *New York, Dec. 3, 1881.*

Two months after sight of this first of exchange (second and third unpaid) pay to A. B. Runyon & Co. or order, Fifty pounds sterling, with exchange on New York, and charge to my account.

A. Y. Jones.

To William T. Barber, Liverpool.

FORM 10.   (*d*)

ACCEPTED DRAFT.

$24 ×/100

New York, Sept. 13, 1881.

September 17, 1881, pay to Bearer Twenty-four dollars, and charge to

A. Y. Jones.

To William T. Barber, Poughkeepsie, N. Y.

(Written across the face, *Accepted, W. T. Barber.*)

CHECKS.

FORM 11. *(a)*

$245 ¹⁴/₁₀₀

New York, Sept. 22, 1881.

Ninth National Bank.

Pay to the order of J. S. Fay

Two hundred forty-five ¹⁴/₁₀₀ dollars.

No. 37.   A. Y. Jones.

FORM 12. *(d)*

CERTIFIED CHECK.

$500.   New York, Dec. 3, 1881.

Ninth National Bank.

Pay to Bearer Five hundred dollars.

No. 342.   A. Y. Jones.

Written across the face,

Good, Alfred Bleecker, Cashier.

FORM 13. (a)

CERTIFICATE OF DEPOSIT.

Ninth National Bank.

$500. New York, Dec. 3, 1881.

This certifies that A. Y. Jones has deposited with the Ninth National Bank Five hundred dollars payable to the order of A. B. Runyon & Co., on return of this certificate properly indorsed.

Alfred Bleecker,
Cashier.

INDORSEMENTS.

FORM 14.

Pay to S B. Mapes

or order

James. S. Fay.

Pay to order of

James. S. Brown,

S. B. Mapes.

James Brown.

[The above is an example of the indorsements that would appear on the back of either Forms 1, 5, or 11, if Fay made a full indorsement to Mapes, Mapes a full indorsement to Brown, and Brown a blank indorsement to some one else.]

FORM 15.

Pay to J. S. Fay

or order

Archibald Brothers.

Pay to S. B. Mapes

or order

James S. Fay.

[The above is an example of how Form 2 might be indorsed.]

FORM 16.

Pay to order of S. B. Mapes,

A. B. Runyon & Co.

Pay to James Brown,

S. B. Mapes.

James Brown.

[Forms 7 or 9 might be indorsed thus.]

FORM 17.

INDORSEMENTS WITHOUT RECOURSE.

Pay to S. B. Mapes

or order

[in full]   *without recourse to me.*

James S. Fay

———

[blank]   *Without recourse*

S. B. Mapes.

FORM 18.

NOTICE OF NON-PAYMENT.

To Messrs. James S. Fay, S. B. Mapes, and James Brown, and each of them:

Gentlemen: You will please take notice that a note for $200, signed by Archibald Brothers, dated December 3, 1881, due February 6th, 1882, and indorsed by you, was duly presented by me, the holder, to the makers for payment and was not paid, and that I shall look to you for payment thereof.

Respectfully,

EUGENE H. LEWIS.

[The above would be appropriate to the case of non-payment of the note in form 1 indorsed as in form 14.]

FORM 19.

ARTICLES OF COPARTNERSHIP.

Articles of agreement made December 3d, 1881, between Charles S. Mead and Gregory Ross:

I. The said parties hereby agree to become co-partners, under the firm name of Mead and Ross, and as such partners to carry on together the business of buying and selling all sorts of dry goods, at No. 547 Fulton Street in the city of Brooklyn;

II. The said Charles S. Mead agrees to contribute two thousand dollars ($2000), to the capital of said firm; and the said Gregory Ross agrees to contribute one thousand dollars ($1000) to the same; the sum of $2500 of said capital to be expended in the purchase of a stock in trade;

III. The said Mead shall have exclusive charge of all the buying for the firm;

IV. All the net profits arising out of the business shall be divided in the following proportions, two-thirds to the said Mead, and one-third to the said Ross;

V. Each partner will devote all his time to the said business, and will use his best efforts to make the business successful, and promote the interests of the firm in every way;

VI. If on the closing out of said business there shall have been a net loss it shall be borne equally. CHARLES S. MEAD.

GREGORY ROSS.

[NOTE.—There are a great many other clauses which might be added, providing for different contingencies which might arise. Of course, the parties may make any sort of an agreement they choose. Unless they were fully acquainted with and could unreservedly trust each other, it would be unsafe to trust to so meagre a contract as the above.]

FORM 20.

CERTIFICATE OF STOCK IN A CORPORATION.

THE RIVER SHORE RAILWAY COMPANY.

This is to certify, that Caroline O. Holmes is entitled to fifty-four (54) shares of the capital stock of the River Shore Railway Company, of one hundred dollars each, transferable only on the books of the said company, by the said Caroline O. Holmes or her attorney, upon the surrender of this certificate.

Dated, New York, December 3d, 1881.

HORACE QUEEN, CHARLES MARTIN,
Treasurer. *President.*

FORM 21.

BOND OF INDEMNITY.

Know all men by these presents, that I, John A. Sergeant, of Cleveland, Ohio, am held and firmly bound unto Abraham Bell of the same place, in the sum of ten thousand dollars, to be paid to the said Abraham Bell, his executors or administrators, for which payment, well and truly to be made, I do bind myself, my heirs, executors and administrators, firmly, by these presents.

Sealed with my seal. Dated this 5th day of December, 1881. Whereas, Abraham Bell is about to employ my nephew, William K. Reynolds, as cashier in his store, for the term of one year from January 1st, 1882;

Now the condition of this obligation is such that if the said William K. Reynolds shall fully perform all the duties of his said employment, and promptly and correctly account for and pay over all the money or property of the said Abraham Bell which may come into his hands during its course, then this obligation shall be void; otherwise to remain in full force.

JOHN A. SERGEANT.

[This bond means this: that if Reynolds does his duties as cashier, Sergeant's bond will be superfluous and void; but if Reynolds should run away with any of Bell's money, or fail to perform his duties in any other way, then Sergeant must pay Bell the loss, up to $10,000. The effect is the same as if it read, "I, John A. Sergeant, agree to pay Abraham Bell whatever loss he may suffer through the fault of William K. Reynolds, as his cashier for one year from January 1, 1882, up to the amount of $10,000."]

FORM 22.

MERCHANDISE BROKER'S CONTRACT.

I.

MEMORANDUM TO BE GIVEN TO THE SELLER.

NEW YORK, Dec. 5, 1881.

Messrs. White, Ludlow & Co., 41 Broadway:

We have sold to-day on your account to Joseph Armstrong, 13 South William Street, the following goods: 1000 ounces Sulphate of Quinine B. and G. at $2.75 per ounce.

Respectfully,

MERRIAM & CHAPIN,

Brokers.

II.

MEMORANDUM TO BE GIVEN TO THE BUYER.

NEW YORK, Dec. 5, 1881.

Mr. Joseph Armstrong, 13 South William Street:

We have to-day bought for your account, from White, Ludlow & Co., the following:

1000 ounces Sulphate of Quinine B. and G. at $2.75 per ounce.

Respectfully,

MERRIAM & CHAPIN,

Brokers.

Form 23.

CHARTER-PARTY.

These articles of agreement made December 5th, 1881, between S. T. Riley, party of the first part, and Albert T. Mellon, party of the second part, witnesseth:

The said party of the first part has this day chartered and hired unto the party of the second part the ship The Nile, of New London, Conn., of the burden of 1000 tons or thereabouts, with all the appurtenances, cables, anchors, chains, etc., which belong to her, for the term of one year, from January 1st next, to be delivered at pier 30, East River, in the harbor of New York.

For the use of said vessel the party of the second part agrees to pay the sum of $2000, payments to be made as follows: one half thereof to be paid at the end of six months, and the other half at the end of the year.

The party of the second part shall be at all the expense of manning and furnishing said vessel, and shall return the same to the said Riley at the port of New London, in as good condition as she now is, excepting ordinary wear and tear.

In witness whereof the parties have hereunto set their hands and seals.   S. T. RILEY,   [Seal.]
                                                        A. T. MELLON.   [Seal.]

Form 24.

BILL OF LADING.

NEW YORK, December 6, 1881.

Shipped, in good order, and well conditioned, by *John C. Goddard* . . . . on board the ship *Nile* . . . .
whereof *Sylvanus Bond* . . . . is
Marked as follows:
Anthony Willoughby, master, now lying in the port of *New York* . . .
Rio Janeiro.   . . . . and bound for the port of *Rio Janeiro*. . . . . 1000 *barrels flour*, being marked and numbered as in the margin, and are to be delivered in the like order and condition at the port of *Rio Janeiro* . . . . (the dangers of the seas only excepted) unto *Anthony Willoughby* . . . .

or his assigns, he or they paying freight for the said cases, with ten cents primage and average accustomed.

In witness whereof I have affirmed to three bills of lading, all of this tenor and date; one of which being accomplished the others to stand void.   ALBERT T. MELLON.

[In above form Goddard is the shipper or consignor, Willoughby the consignee, and Mellon the carrier. It might be signed by the master (Bond) instead of by Mellon. Very often three bills are made out: one the master keeps and two are given to the consignor, of which he keeps one and sends one to the consignee.]

FORM 25.

FIRE INSURANCE POLICY.

I. THE MAIN CLAUSE.

No. 567,754. $5000.

THE FRANKLIN FIRE INSURANCE COMPANY, OF PHILADELPHIA,

In consideration of forty-five dollars, Do insure Edward A. Bradford against loss or damage by fire to the amount of five thousand dollars as follows:

On certain books, bound and unbound, engravings, steel and copper plates, and other merchandise now contained in the brick building No. 5 Barclay Street, New York City.

And the said company hereby agree to make good unto the assured, his executors, administrators, and assigns, all such immediate loss or damage (not exceeding in amounts the sum insured) as shall happen by fire to the property above specified, from the 17th day of October, 1874, at noon, to the 17th day of October, 1875, at noon, the amount of such loss and damage to be proven and paid, or made good according to the following terms and conditions:

[Here follow ordinarily a large number of additional clauses. *See below.*]

In witness whereof we have caused this policy to be attested by the president and secretary of the company the 15th day of October, 1874.

THEO. M. ROGER,   ALFRED G. BAKER,
       Secretary.   *President.*

II. EXAMPLES OF SOME OF THE ADDITIONAL CLAUSES.

(1.) No assignment of this policy shall be valid until indorsed hereon and approved by the company.

(2.) This company shall not be liable for loss in case of fire caused by rioting, or by explosion, or in case the assured shall keep on the premises gunpowder, fireworks, phosphorus, naphtha, etc.

(3.) This policy shall not be binding upon the company until the premium be actually paid.

(4.) In case there should be any other insurance on the property hereby insured, whether prior or subsequent, the assured shall be entitled to recover on this policy no greater proportion of the loss sustained than the sum herein insured bears to the whole amount insured thereon.

FORM 26.

RENEWAL OF FIRE INSURANCE.

NEW YORK, Oct. 17, 1875.

THE FRANKLIN INSURANCE COMPANY, OF PHILADELPHIA.

Do insure Edward A. Bradford, in consideration of forty-five dollars, being the premium on five thousand dollars: this being a renewal of policy No. 567,754, which is hereby continued in force for one year, to wit, from Oct. 17, 1875, to Oct. 17, 1876, at noon.

THEO. M. ROGER,   ALFRED G. BAKER,
    Secretary.   *Pres.*

FORM 27.

MARINE INSURANCE POLICY.

No. 56,721.

BY THE INTERNATIONAL INSURANCE COMPANY, OF LIVERPOOL.

John C. Goddard, on account of whom it may concern, in case of loss to be paid in New York in funds current to him, does make insurance and cause . . . . to be insured, lost or not lost, at and from New York to Rio Janeiro . . . . on 1000 bbls. flour . . . . laden, or to be laden on board the good ship called the Nile. . .

Aggregate insured, $5000.

Premium . . . . $62.50. The said goods and merchandises hereby assured are valued (premium included) at $5000.

Touching the adventures and perils which the said assurer is contented to bear and take upon itself in this voyage, they are of seas, men-of-war, fires, enemies, pirates, rovers, thieves, jettisons, letters of mart and countermart, reprisals, takings at sea, arrests, restraints, and detainments of all kings, princes, or people of what nation, condition, or quality soever, barratry of the master and mariners . . . . having been paid the consideration for this insurance, by the assured at and after the rate of one and a quarter per cent . . . .

Provided always, and it is hereby further agreed, that if the said assured shall have made any other assurance upon the premises aforesaid, prior in day of date to this policy, then the said assurer shall be answerable only for so much as the amount of such prior assurance may be deficient towards fully covering the premises hereby assured. . . . . And in case of any insurance upon the said premises subsequent in day of date to this policy the said assurer shall nevertheless be answerable for the full extent of the sum by it subscribed hereto. . . . . Other insurance upon the premises aforesaid of date the same day as this policy shall be deemed simultaneous herewith; and the said assurer shall not be liable for more than a ratable contribution in the proportion of the sum by it insured to the aggregate amount of such simultaneous insurance. . . . .

[There are usually other clauses in the policy.]

In witness whereof the attorneys of the International Insurance Company have subscribed their names and the sum insured, at New York, this 6th day of December, 1881.

($5000.)   Five thousand dollars. -   — ---

MACY & CARTER,
Attorneys.

[In above form Goddard is the shipper, the consignor, the owner of the goods, and the company insures him fully against loss. Usually there are other clauses in the policy, such as one giving the vessel the right to touch at other ports, or one making the company responsible for no loss unless it amounts to ten per cent of the value. There are also other and different forms used, as where a vessel is to be insured, or where a vessel or cargo is to be insured during a trip on a canal.]

FORM 28.

CERTIFICATE OF INSURANCE.

THE INTERNATIONAL INSURANCE COMPANY.

NEW YORK, December 8, 1881.

This is to certify that on the 6th day of December, 1881, this company insured, under policy No. 56,721, made for John C. Goddard, the amount of five thousand dollars on 1000 barrels of flour, valued at $5000, shipped on board of the ship Nile, at and from New York to Rio Janeiro, and it is hereby understood and agreed that in case of loss such loss is payable to the order of John C. Goddard on surrender of the certificate.

This certificate represents and takes the place of the policy, and conveys all the rights of the original policy-holder, so far as the goods above specified are concerned.

MACY & CARTER,
Attorneys.

[By transferring this certificate the rights under the policy may be transferred by Goddard to any one else, e.g., to one to whom he sells the flour before it arrives at Rio Janeiro.]

FORM 29.

LIFE INSURANCE POLICY.

No. 68,056. $1000.

THE OCCIDENT LIFE INSURANCE COMPANY,

In consideration of the representations made to them in the application for this policy, and of the sum of thirty-four dollars, and the further sums of thirty-four dollars to be paid on the 27th day of January and July of each year during the continuance of this policy, do insure the life of Jasper N. Cary, of Fort Leavenworth, in the county of Leavenworth, State of Kansas, in the amount of one thousand dollars for the term of his natural life. And the said company does promise and agree to pay the amount of the said insurance at its office in St. Louis to Jasper N. Cary's legal representatives, in sixty days, after due notice and satisfactory proof of his death during the continuance of this policy.

In witness whereof the said Occident Life Insurance Company has by its president and actuary signed and delivered this contract this 27th day of July, 1881.

ABIEL WRIGHT,   JONATHAN S. WILLS,
   Actuary.   *President.*

Premium $34, payable semi-annually.

FORM 30.

GENERAL ASSIGNMENT.

Know all men by these presents, that whereas I, James S. Fay, am indebted to divers persons in considerable sums of money, which I am at present unable to pay in full, and am desirous of conveying all my property for the benefit of my creditors :

Now, therefore, I, in consideration of the premises, and of one dollar to me paid by Samuel Coe, the receipt whereof is hereby acknowledged, have granted, bargained, sold, assigned, transferred, and set over, and by these presents do grant, bargain, sell, assign, transfer, and set over, unto the said Samuel Coe, all my property of every kind and description, except property exempt by law from execution; to have and to hold the same unto the said Samuel Coe in trust, to convert the same into money, and apply the proceeds as follows:

1. To pay the expenses of executing this trust;

2. To pay all debts which I may be owing, provided that if there be not sufficient to pay all my creditors in full, then the amount is to be distributed among them ratably in proportion to the amounts of their several debts;

3. The residue, if there be any, to be repaid to me, or my executors, administrators or assigns.

In witness whereof, I have hereunto set my hand and seal this 7th day of December, 1881.

JAMES S. FAY.   [Seal.]

FORM 31.

POWER OF ATTORNEY.

Know all men by these presents, that we, Archibald Archibald and Henry S. Archibald, doing business as Archibald Brothers, of New York City, do hereby make, constitute, and appoint William J. Kelly of Boston, Mass., our true, sufficient, and lawful attorney for us and in our name, to conduct and carry on the wholesale grocery business at 55 Washington Street, Boston, Mass., now established as a branch of our New York store, and to buy and sell and receive on commission all such goods appertaining to the grocery business as he may deem proper, and to do and perform all necessary acts in the execution and prosecution of the aforesaid business in as full and ample a manner as we might do were we personally present.

A. ARCHIBALD,
HENRY S. ARCHIBALD.

[This form grants broad powers to the agent. More often a power of attorney will limit the agent's powers, by specifying the different things which he shall or shall not have power to do. Of course, the parties may make as full or as limited a power as they choose. Between the principal and agent a power is a contract.]

FORM 32.

RECEIPT IN FULL.

ALBANY, January 9, 1882.

Received of Whitman, Lawrence & Co. twenty-five and $\frac{14}{100}$ dollars in full of account to date.
$25.14.

LONGMAN & GREEN.

[The above receipt is an acknowledgment by Longman & Green that Whitman, Lawrence & Co. owe them nothing. If something still remained due, if $25.14 was only a partial payment, the receipt would read "on account," instead of "in full of account." A receipt is not a contract; it is only evidence. Thus, if a receipt should happen to be given when there was no payment really made it would have no effect. The debt would still remain. One is always at liberty to prove the truth in spite of a receipt.]

FORM 33.

BILL OF SALE.

Know all men by these presents that we, Charles S. Mead and Gregory Ross, of the city of Brooklyn, New York, in consider-ation of the sum of five thousand dollars to us paid and to be paid by James S. Fay, of the same place, as follows, viz.: Two thousand dollars on the ensealing and delivery of this bill of sale, and the remainder in equal payments of one thousand dollars each on the first days of April, June, and September, 1882, respectively, (the said Fay giving herewith his three notes of one thousand dollars each, dated respectively on those days), have bargained, sold, granted, and conveyed, and by these presents do bargain, sell, grant, and convey unto the said James S. Fay, his executors, administrators and assigns, all the goods, wares and merchandise, furniture and fixtures, now in the dry goods store No. 547 Fulton Street, Brooklyn, and scheduled in the inventory hereto annexed: to have and to hold the same unto the said James S. Fay, his executors, administrators, and assigns forever. And we do for ourselves, our heirs, executors, administrators, and assigns, covenant and agree, to warrant and defend the said described goods hereby sold unto the said James S. Fay, his executors, administrators, and assigns, against all and every person and persons whatsoever.

In witness whereof, we have hereunto set our hands this 1st day of February, 1883.

CHARLES S. MEAD,
GREGORY ROSS.

[A bill of sale is not a document necessary to a sale. We have considered when a writing is necessary to a sale (pp. 36, 37). But a bill of sale is used when it is thought best to have some formal instrument showing the transfer, as where one sells his business and his stock in trade to another. The inventory would be on another sheet, would enumerate all the articles intended to be transferred, and should be signed.]

FORM 34.

CHATTEL MORTGAGE.

Know all men by these presents, that I, Oliver Ascham, of the city of New York, do hereby sell and assign to James Ellsworth, Jr., of the same place, all the tools and machinery now in my machine shop on West Street, enumerated in the schedule hereto attached, and made a part hereof; but if I shall on or before the expiration of six months from the date hereof pay unto the said James Ellsworth, Jr., the sum of five hundred dollars with interest at six per cent per annum, then this conveyance to be wholly void, it being intended merely as a security for the said payment.

NEW YORK, January 10th, 1882.

OLIVER ASCHAM.

[The above is a short form. Longer ones are often used. Notice that it is the same as a bill of sale, with the added clause showing that the sale is not a complete one, but only conditional. The property does not become Ellsworth's unless Ascham fails to pay the money before July 11th.]

FORM 35.

LETTER OF CREDIT.

Office of O. B. S. LONG & Co.,

No. 4562
Bankers.

    for £3000.

NEW YORK, January 25th, 1882.

TO OUR CORRESPONDENTS:

Gentlemen:—We beg leave to introduce to you Mr. John A. Sergeant in whose favor we have opened a credit for three thousand pounds sterling, say £3000.

We have to request you that you will furnish him with whatever funds he may require to the available extent of this credit against his drafts at 3 days sight on ourselves.

All drafts so negotiated should be indorsed on this credit, which will continue in force until July 1st, 1882.

Requesting for Mr. Sergeant your best attention, we have the honor to be, Gentlemen,

Your obedient servants,

O. B. S. LONG & Co.

Signature of the holder,

    JOHN A. SERGEANT.

[This is sometimes called a circular letter. The "correspondents" are different persons or firms situated at different places, who have agreed with O. B. S. Long & Co. to advance money in that way. The operation is as follows:

Suppose that Mr. Sergeant wishes to travel in Europe and to use money there; he will go to some firm (Long & Co.) issuing European letters of credit, and on depositing his money with them, obtain from them this letter. These correspondents we will suppose are situated one at London, one at Paris, one at Vienna, etc., etc. If in any one of those places he will draw his own draft for the amount needed upon O. B. S. Long & Co. in favor of the correspondent at that place, and that correspondent will pay him the money. The amount of each draft when drawn is indorsed upon the letter, and when he has drawn £3000 altogether he can draw no more. Thus, a letter of credit is a convenient way to carry money.]

FORM 36.

AFFIDAVIT.

STATE OF MICHIGAN, } *ss.:*
COUNTY OF KENT. }

James P. Longford, being duly sworn, deposes and says, that the account hereto annexed is in every respect a just, full and true statement of the account existing between deponent and the late Caroline Smith at the time of her death, and that the sum of $45.26 appearing thereby to be due to him from the estate of the said Caroline Smith, is justly and fairly due to him from the said estate over and above all set-offs, counter-claims, or payments.

JAMES P. LONGFORD.

Sworn to before me, this 10th }
day of February, 1882. }

O. P. BARNES,
Notary Public for the County of Kent.

[An affidavit is the written evidence of an oath. Occasions sometimes arise in business life when affidavits are required. Thus, if Longford had sold to Mrs. Smith during her lifetime books to the amount stated in the form, the executor of her estate might require a sworn statement from him before paying the bill. He signs the affidavit and swears before the notary (Barnes) that it is true, and the notary appends his signature.]

FORM 37.

GUARANTY OF NOTE.

·For one dollar to me paid I hereby guarantee the payment of this note.

JOHN B. ALLAN.

[Such a guaranty would be written on the guaranteed note itself.]

FORM 38.

DEED OF REAL ESTATE WITH FULL COVENANTS.

[*a*] THIS INDENTURE, made the 15th day of July in the year one thousand eight hundred and eighty-two, between James K. Robertson, of the City, County, and State of New York, and Alice B., his wife, parties of the first part, and Elias B. Clarkson, of the same place, party of the second part, WITNESSETH: That the parties of the first part, in consideration of the sum of fifteen thousand dollars lawful money of the United States, to them in hand paid by the party of the second part, at or before the ensealing and delivery of these presents, the receipt whereof is hereby acknowledged, and the said party of the second part, his heirs, executors, and administrators, forever released and discharged from the same,

[*b*] HAVE granted, bargained, sold, aliened, remised, released, conveyed, and confirmed, and by these presents do grant, bargain, sell, alien, remise, release, convey, and confirm unto the said party of the second part and his heirs and assigns forever,

[*c*] ALL that certain lot, piece, or parcel of land situated in the Eighth Ward of the City of New York, and bounded and described as follows: Beginning on the northerly side of Maynard Street at a point forty (40) feet easterly from the northeasterly corner of Maynard and Alcove Streets, running thence northerly on a line parallel with Alcove Street, and part of the way through the center of a party-wall eighty-eight (88) feet, thence easterly parallel with Maynard Street twenty (20) feet, thence southerly parallel with Alcove Street, and part of the way through a party-wall, eighty-eight (88) feet to Maynard Street, and thence westerly along Maynard Street twenty (20) feet to the place of beginning, being the premises known as No. 148 Maynard Street,

[*d*] Together with all and singular the tenements, hereditaments and appurtenances thereunto belonging or in any wise appertaining, and the reversion and reversions, remainder and remainders, rents, issues and profits thereof; and also all the estate, right, title, interest, dower, right of dower, property, possession, claim and demand whatsoever, both in law and in equity, of the said parties of the first part, of, in and to the above-granted premises, and every part and parcel thereof, with the appurtenances,

[*e*] To have and to hold all and singular the above-granted prem-

ises, together with the appurtenances and every part thereof, unto the said party of the second part, his heirs and assigns forever;

[*f*] And the said James K. Robertson, for himself, his heirs, executors, and administrators, does covenant, promise and agree to and with the said party of the second part, his heirs and assigns, that the said James K. Robertson at the time of the sealing and delivery of these presents, is lawfully seized in his own right, of a good, absolute and indefeasible estate of inheritance in fee-simple, of and in all and singular the above-granted and described premises, with the appurtenances,

[*g*] And has good right, full power and lawful authority to grant, bargain, sell and convey the same in manner aforesaid;

[*h*] And that the said party of the second part, his heirs and assigns, shall and may at all times hereafter, peaceably and quietly have, hold, use, occupy, possess and enjoy the above-granted premises, and every part and parcel thereof with the appurtenances, without any let, suit, trouble, molestation, eviction, or disturbance of said parties of the first part, their heirs or assigns, or of any other person or persons lawfully claiming or to claim the same;

[*i*] And that the same now are free, clear, discharged and unincumbered of and from all former and other grants, titles, charges, estates, judgments, taxes, assessments, and incumbrances of what nature or kind soever;

[*j*] And also that the said parties of the first part, and their heirs, and all and every other person or persons whosoever, lawfully or equitably deriving any estate, right, title, or interest of, in or to the above-granted premises by, from, under or in trust for them, shall and will at any time or times hereafter, upon the reasonable request, and at the proper costs and charges in the law, of the said party of the second part, his heirs and assigns, make, do and execute, or cause or procure to be made, done and executed, all and every such further and other lawful and reasonable acts, conveyances and assurances in the law, for the better and more effectually vesting and confirming the premises hereby granted or intended so to be in and to the said party of the second part, his heirs or assigns, forever, as by the said party of the second part, his heirs or assigns, or his or their counsel learned in the law, shall be reasonably devised, advised or required;

[*k*] And the said James K. Robertson, and his heirs, the above-described and hereby granted and released premises, and every part

and parcel thereof, with the appurtenances, unto the said party of the second part, his heirs and assigns, against the said parties of the first part, and their heirs, and against all and every person and persons whomsoever, lawfully claiming or to claim the same, shall and will warrant, and by these presents forever defend.

In witness whereof the said parties of the first part have hereunto set their hands and seals, the day and year first above written.

JAMES K. ROBERTSON, [Seal.]

ALICE B. ROBERTSON. [Seal.]

Signed, sealed and delivered)
  in presence of   )

     ALFRED B. ROBERTSON,
     JESSE PRICE.

FORM 39.

COVENANT AGAINST NUISANCES.

And the said Elias B. Clarkson, for himself, his heirs and assigns, does hereby covenant to and with the said James K. Robertson, his heirs, executors and administrators, that neither the said Clarkson, nor his heirs or assigns shall or will at any time hereafter erect or permit upon any part of the said lot any slaughter-house, smith-shop, forge, furnace, steam-engine, brass-foundry, nail or other iron factory, or any manufactory of gunpowder, glue, varnish, vitriol, ink, or turpentine, or for the tanning, dressing or preparing skins, hides, or leather, or any brewery, distillery, or any other noxious or dangerous trade or business.

[The above might be inserted in the deed in form 38 as a part of it. In such case Clarkson ought to sign the deed.]

FORM 40.

BOND.

Know all men by these presents, that I, Elias B. Clarkson, of the city of New York, am held and firmly bound unto Alfred Cornwell, of Chicago, Ill., in the sum of twenty thousand dollars ($20,000) good and lawful money of the United States, to be paid the said Alfred Cornwell, his executors, administrators, or assigns, for which payment well and truly to be made I do bind myself, my heirs, executors, and administrators, firmly by these presents.

Sealed with my seal and dated the first day of August, 1882.

The condition of this obligation is such that if the above-bounden Elias B. Clarkson, his heirs, executors, and administrators, or any of them, shall well and truly pay, or cause to be paid unto the above-named Alfred Cornwell, his executors, administrators, or assigns, the just and full sum of ten thousand dollars, on the 1st day of August, which will be in the year one thousand eight hundred and eighty-seven, and interest thereon at the rate of six per cent per annum, payable semi-annually on the first days of August and February in each year, then this obligation is to be void, otherwise to remain in full force and effect.

And it is hereby expressly agreed that should any default be made in the payment of the said interest or of any part thereof, on any day whereon the same is made payable as above expressed, and should the same remain unpaid and in arrear for the space of thirty days, then and from thenceforth, that is to say, after the lapse of the said thirty days, the aforesaid principal sum of ten thousand dollars with all arrearage of interest thereon, shall, at the option of the said Alfred Cornwell, become and be due and payable immediately thereafter, although the period above limited for the payment thereof may not then have expired, anything herein before contained to the contrary thereof in any wise notwithstanding.

Elias B. Clarkson.

Form 41.

MORTGAGE OF REAL ESTATE.

[a] This Indenture made the 1st day of August in the year one thousand eight hundred and eighty-two, between Elias B. Clarkson, of the City, County, and State of New York, and Charlotte, his wife, parties of the first part, and Alfred Cornwell, of the City of Chicago, County of Cook, and State of Illinois, party of the second part,

Whereas the said Elias B. Clarkson is justly indebted to the said party of the second part in the sum of ten thousand (10,000) dollars, lawful money of the United States, secured to be paid by his certain bond or obligation bearing even date with these pres-

ents, in the penal sum of twenty thousand dollars lawful money as
aforesaid, conditioned for the payment of the said first mentioned
sum of ten thousand dollars lawful money as aforesaid, to
the said party of the second part, his executors, administrators
or assigns, on the 1st day of August, which will be in the
year one thousand eight hundred and eighty-seven, and interest
thereon to be computed from August 1, 1882, at and after the rate
of six per cent per annum, to be paid semi-annually on the first
days of February and August in each year; and it is thereby
expressly agreed that should any default be made in the payment
of the said interest, or of any part thereof, on any day whereon
the same is made payable as above expressed, and should the said
interest remain unpaid and in arrear for the space of thirty days,
then and from thenceforth, that is to say, after the lapse of the said
thirty days, the aforesaid principal sum, with all arrearage of interest
thereon, shall, at the option of the said party of the second part, his
administrators or assigns, become and be due and payable immediately thereafter, although the period above limited for the payment thereof may not then have expired, anything thereinbefore
contained to the contrary thereof in any wise notwithstanding; As
by the said bond or obligation, and the conditions thereof, reference being thereunto had, may more fully appear,

Now this indenture WITNESSETH that the said parties of the first
part for the better securing the payment of the said sum of money
mentioned in the condition of the said bond or obligation, with interest
thereon, according to the true intent and meaning thereof, and also for
and in consideration of the sum of one dollar to them in hand paid
by the said party of the second part, at or before the ensealing and delivery of these presents, the receipt whereof is hereby acknowledged,

[b] HAVE granted, bargained, sold, aliened, remised, released,
conveyed and confirmed, and by these presents do grant, bargain,
sell, alien, remise, release, convey and confirm unto the said party
of the second part, and to his heirs and assigns forever,

[c] ALL that certain lot, piece or parcel of land situated in the
Eighth Ward of the City of New York, and bounded and described
as follows: Beginning on the northerly side of Maynard Street at a
point forty (40) feet easterly from the northeasterly corner of Maynard and Alcove Streets, running thence northerly on a line parallel
with Alcove Street, and part of the way through the center of a party-wall eighty-eight (88) feet, thence easterly, parallel with Maynard

Street twenty (20) feet, thence southerly parallel with Alcove Street and part of the way through a party-wall, eighty-eight (88) feet to Maynard Street, and thence westerly along Maynard Street twenty (20) feet to the place of beginning, being the premises known as No. 148 Maynard Street,

[d] Together with all and singular the tenements, hereditaments and appurtenances thereunto belonging, or in any wise appertaining, and the reversion, and reversions, remainder and remainders, rents, issues and profits thereof; and also all the estate, right, title, interest, dower, right of dower, property, possession, claim and demand whatsoever, as well in law as in equity, of the said parties of the first part, of, in and to the same, and every part and parcel thereof with the appurtenances;

[e] To have and to hold the above-granted, bargained and described premises, with the appurtenances, unto the said party of the second part, his heirs and assigns, to his or their own proper use, benefit and behoof forever;

[f] Provided always, and these presents are upon this express condition, that if the said parties of the first part, their heirs, executors, administrators, shall well and truly pay unto the said party of the second part, his executors, administrators or assigns, the said sum of money mentioned in the condition of the said bond or obligation, and the interest thereon, at the times and in the manner mentioned in the said condition, according to the true intent and meaning thereof, that then these presents, and the estate hereby granted, shall cease, determine and be void

[g] And the said Elias B. Clarkson, for himself, his heirs, executors and administrators, does covenant and agree to pay unto the said party of the second part, his executors, administrators or assigns, the said sum of money and interest as mentioned above, and expressed in the condition of the said bond. And if default shall be made in the payment of the said sum of money above-mentioned, or the interest that may grow due thereon, or of any part thereof, that then and from thenceforth it shall be lawful for the said party of the second part, his executors, administrators and assigns, to enter into and upon all and singular the premises hereby granted or intended so to be; and to sell and dispose of the same, and all benefit and equity of redemption of the said parties of the first part, their heirs, executors, administrators or assigns, therein, at public auction according to the act in such case made and provided.

[*h*] And as the attorney of the said parties of the first part for that purpose by these presents duly authorized, constituted and appointed, to make and deliver to the purchaser or purchasers thereof, a good and sufficient deed or deeds of conveyance in the law for the same, in fee-simple, and out of the money arising from such sale, to retain the principal and interest which shall then be due on the said bond or obligation, together with the costs and charges of advertisement and sale of the said premises, rendering the overplus of the purchase money (if any there shall be) unto the said Elias B. Clarkson, of the first part, his heirs, executors, administrators or assigns, which sale so to be made shall forever be a perpetual bar, both in law and equity, against the said parties of the first part, their heirs and assigns, and all other persons claiming or to claim the premises or any part thereof, by, from, or under them, or either of them.

[*i*] And it is expressly agreed by and between the parties to these presents, that the said parties of the first part shall and will keep the buildings erected and to be erected upon the lands above conveyed insured against loss and damage by fire, by insurers, and in an amount, approved by the said party of the second part, and assign the policy and certificates thereof to the said party of the second part; and in default thereof, it shall be lawful for the said party of the second part to effect such insurance, and the premium and premiums paid for effecting the same shall be a lien on the said mortgaged premises, added to the amount of the said bond or obligation, and secured by these presents and payable on demand with interest at the rate of six per cent per annum.

In witness whereof the said parties of the first part have hereunto set their hands and seals the day and year first above written.

E. B. CLARKSON, [Seal.]

CHARLOTTE CLARKSON. [Seal.]

Sealed and delivered in the }
  presence of   }

    REUBEN CHAPIN,

    S. T. JOLLY.

FORM 42.

CERTIFICATE OF ACKNOWLEDGMENT.

State of New York, City and County of New York, ss:

On this 1st day of August, 1882, before me personally came Elias B. Clarkson and Charlotte Clarkson, his wife, to me known to be the individuals described in, and who executed the within conveyance, and severally acknowledged that they executed the same for the purposes therein mentioned. And the said Charlotte Clarkson on a private examination by me made, apart from her husband, acknowledged that she executed the same freely, and without any fear or compulsion of her said husband.

ALOYSIUS MANWARING,
Notary Public,
for the City and County of New York.

FORM 43.

CERTIFICATE OF PROOF BY SUBSCRIBING WITNESS.

City and County of New York, ss.:

On this 2d day of August, in the year 1882, before me personally came S. T. Jolly, a subscribing witness to the within instrument, with whom I am personally acquainted, who being by me duly sworn, said that he resided in the city of Newark, in the State of New Jersey; that he was acquainted with Elias B. and Charlotte Clarkson, and knew them to be the persons described in, and who executed the said instrument; and that he saw them execute and deliver the same, and that they acknowledged to him (the said Jolly), that they executed and delivered the same, and that he (the said Jolly), thereupon subscribed his name as a witness thereto at their request

ALOYSIUS MANWARING,
Notary Public,
for the City and County of New York.

FORM 44.

LEASE.

This Indenture, made the 21st day of April, in the year one thousand eight hundred and eighty-three, between Elias B. Clarkson, of New York, of the first part, and Homer B. Abner, of the same place, of the second part, witnesseth: That the party of the first part has hereby let and rented to the party of the second part, and the party of the second part has hereby hired and taken from the party of the first part, the ground floor, cellar, and second story of the premises known as 148 Maynard Street, in the City of New York, with the appurtenances, for the term of three years, to commence the 1st day of May, 1883, at the yearly rent of eleven hundred dollars ($1100), payable in equal quarterly payments on the usual quarter days in each year.

And it is agreed that if any rent shall be due and unpaid, or if default shall be made in any of the covenants herein contained, then it shall be lawful for the said party of the first part to re-enter the said premises, and to remove all persons therefrom.

And the said party of second part covenants to pay to the said party of the first part the said rent, as herein specified, and that at the expiration of the said term, or other determination of this lease, the said party of the second part will quit and surrender the premises hereby demised in as good state and condition as reasonable use and wear thereof will permit, damages by the elements excepted; and the said party of the first part covenants that the said party of the second part, on paying the said yearly rent, and performing the covenants aforesaid, shall and may peaceably and quietly have, hold and enjoy the said demised premises for the term aforesaid.

In witness whereof, the parties hereto have hereunto interchangeably set their hands.

E. B. CLARKSON,
H. B. ABNER.

INDEX.